MORALITY AND THE LANGUAGE OF CONDUCT

MORALITY AND THE

LANGUAGE OF CONDUCT

edited by

Hector-Neri Castañeda and George Nakhnikian

WAYNE STATE UNIVERSITY

Detroit   Wayne State University Press   1965

Published simultaneously in Canada by Ambassador Books, Limited

Toronto, Ontario, Canada

Library of Congress Catalog Card Number 62-17557

Waynebook number 11

Paperback reprint, 1965

CONTENTS

Errata

page 2	line 7	read "equipments" for "equipment"
page 11	line 11	read "only if" for "if and only if"
page 12	line 7	insert comma for period after "judgment"
page 35	line 25	read "virtues" for "virtue"
page 58	line 7 from bottom	after "reasons." insert reference: 3) For the concept of a reason compare my "Action-guiding Reasons," *The Journal of Philosophy,* LX (1963), 702-718.
page 96	line 3 from bottom	read "with which" for "which which"
page 120	line 25	read "rules" for "rule"
page 126	last line	read "the having of the belief that" for "the learning and belief that"
page 232	line 4	read "latter" for "former"
	line 5	read "former" for "latter"
page 233	line 17 from bottom	read "components" for "component"
page 234	last line	read "this" for "his"
page 254	line 7 from bottom	read " (e)" for " (a)"
	line 10 from bottom	read "(e) and (f)" for " (a) and (b)"
page 256	line 17 from bottom	"however" for "on the contrary"

PREFACE

Here are nine essays in moral philosophy written independently of one another. Except for the one by Sellars, which is an extensively revised version of a paper published in *Methodos*, VIII (1956), all of the essays (including the essay by Aiken) were written for this volume. The first four explore the nature of morality. The rest deal with the nature and function of the language of conduct, although Sellars' paper, which discusses both the logic of obligation and the nature of morality, comes under both topics.

The first of the four essays on the nature of morality is Frankena's searching evaluation of the most important contemporary views of what morality is. Frankena favors a material (social) conception of morality. Falk and Aiken, whose papers follow Frankena's, agree that neither formal nor material conditions (in Frankena's usage of the terms) are either necessary or sufficient for explaining the meaning of the adjective "moral" as it applies to judgments, principles, reasons, obligations, rights, and the like. Brandt's attempt to work out a viable version of rule-utilitarianism—which, if true, would imply a material conception of morality—completes this symposium of sorts on the nature of morality.

Nakhnikian's paper introduces the group of essays dealing with the nature and function of the language of conduct. He argues that although Moore's attack on naturalism does not show that naturalism is in principle impossible, it does, either directly or by implication, point to six errors which ought to be avoided by anyone who tries to give a correct account of the nature and function of evaluative and moral discourse. Roughly the first halves of both Sellars' and Castañeda's papers discuss the logical interrelations among the principal subdivisions of the language of conduct, and both place obligation statements at the center of the discussion. They disagree on the role of imperatives and statements of decision in the elucidation of obligation statements, as well as on the logic of imperatives. Ladd's partial analysis of obligation statements emerges from his examination of the sense of duty and of the ways in which obligation is related to desires and motives. Raab's discussion of the ways in which moral considerations are involved in ascriptions of responsibility is an attempt to give a partial elucidation of the concept of responsibility without, however, any particular assumption concerning the nature of morality.

We wish to thank our colleagues, W. D. Falk and Alvin Plantinga, for their generous advice while we were preparing this volume.

H. N. C.
G. N.

1

RECENT CONCEPTIONS OF MORALITY

William K. Frankena *University of Michigan*

There has been an interesting shift of attention in recent moral philosophy. For a long time the primary concern was with the analysis, definition, translation, or elucidation of first-order ethical terms and sentences. Then the main debates were between intuitionist, naturalist, and emotivist or other anti-descriptivist analyses of such terms as "right" and "good." Lately, however, the concern has been more with the definition or elucidation of such second-order terms as "moral" and "non-moral" when these are applied, not to acts or kinds of acts, but to judgments, obligations, principles, reasons, and the like. This shift has, of course, not been complete—the later interest was present previously and the earlier one still persists—but it has been and is taking place. Contemporary moral philosophy may, therefore, be represented as primarily an attempt to understand what morality is, meaning by "morality" not the quality of conduct which is opposed to immorality but what Butler so nicely refers to as "the moral institution of life." The current endeavor is not to promote certain moral goals or principles, or to clarify only such words as "right" and "ought," but rather to grasp the nature of morality itself, as compared with law, religion, or science. In this endeavor both Continental and English-speaking philosophers are engaged, though to different degrees, in different ways, and with different equipment.

Recent moral philosophy has, however, not been entirely self-conscious in making this shift. Thus its readers and even its writers have not been fully aware of what is going on. While everyone was familiar with the issues, weapons, and opposing camps in the earlier strife of moral systems, nothing of the sort is true of the present one. There is indeed a sense of obtaining strife, but it is not generally clear that alternative conceptions of morality are being offered us, what these rival conceptions are, or on what grounds they are put forward.

The present paper is an attempt to make this clear. I shall try to describe the main conceptions of morality which are more or less explicitly present in recent articles and books; to lay bare the issues and oppositions involved; and to study some of the considerations which are or may be advanced in resolving them.[1] I shall not seek to come to a definite conclusion; my sympathies will be made clear, but also my doubts.

I

Among the older schools, intuitionism and naturalism did offer, at least implicitly, not only accounts of the meanings of "right" and "good," but conceptions of morality as a whole. But today, on both sides of the Channel, intuitionism and naturalism are very generally rejected. Except in Thomistic circles, the main effort toward understanding morality is based on the conviction that it is not a body of knowledge, natural or non-natural, empirical or a priori.[2] I shall, therefore, center my discussion on writers who share this conviction.

Three types of conceptions of morality may be found in these writers. The conception which we may call Position A is characterized by a certain individualism. Its most extreme form, perhaps, is the view of those existentialists who make morality a matter of authentic personal decision or commitment whose content is chosen not only freely but arbitrarily. This choice cannot be defended, they state, but neither can it be successfully attacked; in fact, if it is "existentially" made, it is self-justifying, whatever its content. Norms and values are in no sense valid in themselves; one creates one's own norms and values by one's act of espousal.

This Sartrian view transforms morality almost beyond recognition. Indeed, such existentialism is perhaps best understood as a proposal to replace what we call morality by an "ethos" of activism or heroism which is so different from morality that it can be called an ethic only because it takes the same room in our lives. A less extreme form of Position A accepts much of the Sartrian view, but mitigates it considerably by insisting that morality involves not just making an authentic choice but making a choice that one is willing to live with in the light of full knowledge. This position is expressed by R. M. Hare and P. H. Nowell-Smith. To quote Hare:

> . . . if pressed to justify a decision completely, we have to give a complete specification of the way of life of which it is a part. . . . If the inquirer still goes on asking "But why *should* I live like that?" then there is no further answer to give him. . . . We can only ask him to make up his own mind which way he ought to live; for in the end everything rests upon such a decision of principle. He has to decide whether to accept that way of life or not; if he accepts it, then we can proceed to justify the decisions that are based upon it; if he does not accept it, then let him accept some other, and try to live by it.

Such "ultimate decisions," Hare adds, cannot be described as arbitrary, as they are by the existentialists.

> Far from being arbitrary, such a decision would be the most well-founded of decisions, for it would be based upon a consideration of everything upon which it could possibly be founded.[3]

Hare's position is somewhat incompletely represented in these quotations. In addition to choosing a way of life for oneself in the light of adequate knowledge, morality for Hare entails universalizing: deciding on principles, not only for one's own conduct, but for that of everyone. One's thinking and deciding are moral only if they rest on principles which one is willing to act on and see universally acted on, that is, willing to have others act on in similar situations even if one is oneself the recipient of the results.[4]

This requirement to universalize our rules is widely regarded as essential to morality, both by those who hold Position A and those who do not, though some would say that moral rules need only be "general" and not "universal" in their intended application.[5] Even Sartre may be accepting it in the enigmatic passage in which he replies to the charge of excessive individualism by arguing that in fact one never chooses for oneself alone but always for all men.[6] Generally, however, existentialists reject the universalization requirement on the grounds that man's freedom is complete and every situation unique.[7]

Another formal condition which is often regarded as necessary for morality is that one's principles are moral only if one takes them to be supreme or overriding. This condition is suggested by J. A. Brunton, John Ladd, and Bernard Mayo,[8] and seems to be implicitly accepted by Hare and Nowell-Smith, as it was by Joseph Butler. In its fullest form, then, Position A holds that one has a morality if and only if one has principles which, in the light of full knowledge, one takes as supreme and is ready to see anyone else take as supreme; and that such principles are moral simply because they meet these formal conditions, regardless of their content and acceptability to others.[9] Moral reasoning is present and complete if and only if it rests on principles adopted under these conditions. In this form Position A does give to morality a certain social aspect, for here morality entails legislating for others; but it retains its basic individualism, since the content and the justification of such legislating remains entirely relative to what the individual is ready to live with and see lived with, given adequate relevant knowledge. It denies that any social concern is intrinsic to morality and that moral judgments are susceptible of any trans-individual justification or validity.

It is, of course, possible for a proponent of Position A to adopt benevolence or social utility as his moral principle.[10] But he must hold that anyone who adopts the opposite principle, as Nietzsche appears to do, may equally well have a morality, and he must allow, or even insist, that metaethically speaking, he cannot claim any validity for his principle which his opponent cannot also claim. Of course, he may, on the normative level, condemn his opponent's conduct as immoral, and his opponent may return the compliment. But the validity of his condemnation will be relative to *his* commitment, as that of his opponent's will be relative to *his*. Neither of the two, on this view, will even be *claiming* anything more.

2

Many, including myself, find it hard to believe that morality is not intrinsically social or trans-individual in nature. As H. L. A. Hart has recently said in a comment on Hare's book,

> To characterize morality . . . as *primarily* a matter of the application to conduct of those ultimate principles which the individual accepts or to which he commits himself for the conduct of his life seems to me an excessively Protestant approach. Important as this aspect or kind of moral judgment is, we need to understand it as a development from the primary phenomenon of the morality of a social group.[11]

Accordingly, Position B represents a way of building into morality a definite, if sometimes minimal, element of trans-individuality. Position B has two parts. According to Part I, when one makes a moral judgment, one is not merely expressing one's own attitude, emotion, or decision, plus, perhaps, trying to arouse a similar one in others (as the emotive theory has it); nor is one judging solely on the basis of principles which one adopts as supreme and wills to be universal laws; nor is one just claiming that everyone should do likewise, which is still a purely private claim as this is interpreted by Position A. One is claiming in addition that others who take the moral approach will themselves agree that they should do likewise if they share the same factual beliefs (including, perhaps, theological ones). That is, one is claiming that one's judgment is valid for others and is not merely a commitment of one's own (which one may be trying to sell to others).

This notion of morality may be found in Hume. It was reintroduced into contemporary discussions by Margaret Macdonald and H. D. Aiken.[12] Its most recent exponents are Mayo and Hart. To quote Mayo:

> . . . Mr. Hare's analysis does not bring out the point that in saying "You ought to do x," I am also appealing to a principle which I assume my hearer to adopt too. . . . I am appealing to something presupposed by the speaker-hearer community. . . . A moral judgment must be universalizable, firstly, in the sense that it applies not to a particular action, but to a class of actions; this is involved in the meaning of "principle" or rule. Secondly, it must be universalizable, in the sense that it applies not only to me but to you; not only to you but to me; not only to us but to everybody; this is involved in speaking of *moral* principles as opposed to maxims or private policies. And now thirdly: a moral judgment must be universalizable in the sense that others besides the speaker are assumed to share it.[13]

This view that a consensus of others is claimed or presupposed in moral judgments may be held in several forms, depending on the scope of the consensus in question and on its being actual or hypothetical. It may be held, for example, that if I am making a moral judgment I am claiming that everyone actually agrees, that members of my society generally agree, that everyone would agree if they knew the facts, or that they would agree if they knew the facts and were taking the moral point of view. Whatever view is taken in this respect, however, Position B, Part I, may still be held in either a weaker or a stronger form. In the weaker form it says simply that one's judgment, whatever words one uses, is not a *moral* one unless one claims some such consensus or intersubjective validity. In the stronger form it adds that the status of one's judgment is affected if the consensus claimed does not obtain. That is, it holds that my judgment is in some sense corrigible by reference to those of others; it must be revised or at least held only tentatively if others do not agree even when they take the moral point of view and have the necessary factual knowledge.

It will be clear that one who holds Position B, Part I, only in its weaker form has not moved far from Position A. Yet it is not easy to find clear cases of writers who assert (as I am inclined to) Position B, Part I, in its stronger form. Mandelbaum and Ladd both shy away from asserting it in this form. So does Mayo, for he reduces the claim to a consensus with others to an invitation for them to agree, in cases in which the speaker knows or finds that a consensus does not obtain.[14] Indeed, the position of these three writers remains virtually that of A. But B, Part I, in its stronger form, does seem to be accepted, implicitly at least, by Hart, John Rawls, and Roderick Firth.[15] It appears explicitly, but not fully, in some of Aiken's articles. For example, he writes:

> Morality . . . is social or it is nothing; and this, not merely in the sense that our obligations are in fact directed toward others, but also in the sense that they are sanctioned by an impersonal social authority which transcends our personal inclinations or preferences,[16]

and again:

> . . . it is not so much the individual conscience that determines the application of ethical terms, as it is the standard application of the terms which determines the conscience of the individual . . . And when, for whatever reason, the individual misuses or misapplies the terms of moral discourse, he is automatically subject to the same forms of verbal rebuke which, in other domains, are directed against those who will not "talk sense" or "listen to reason." [17]

Position B has another part, however. Part I, which distinguishes it from Position A, may be accepted by those, like Aiken, who hold what I shall call Position C. What distinguishes B from C is a point which B has in common with A. This second part of B is the assertion that a judgment, principle, or piece of reasoning is moral if and only if it passes certain formal conditions, regardless of its content. In other words, Position B, like A, regards morality as characterizable in purely formal or structural terms; it merely adds one more formal feature to the characterization, namely, the presence of an interpersonal claim. It denies just as emphatically as A that any social concern or content is intrinsic to morality.

In effect, then, Position B maintains that there is something which may be called the moral point of view. This point of view can be described in purely formal terms—readiness to think and to make practical decisions by reference to principles which one is willing to take as supreme and to see everyone else take as supreme, even in the light of the best available knowledge, etc. A judgment, however it is worded, is moral only if it is made from this point of view, only if it is supported by reasons involving principles chosen in this spirit, whatever the content of these reasons may be, and even if they make no reference to the welfare of society. All that must be added to make it fully moral is a claim that it is or will be sustained by others (including oneself on other occasions) when they review the facts from said point of view.

But according to Position B, that point of view has, *qua* moral, no content. Nothing is stipulated about what interests may govern the decision to be willing to take a certain principle as supreme and to see it universalized. There always will be interests controlling this decision, but, so far as Position B goes, having a morality does not require that this be one interest rather than another. The interest that controls my choice of principles to live by and to see others live by may be pure self-love or sheer aestheticism—or, for that matter, a combination of sadism and masochism. Provided only that a choice governed by this interest can fulfill the formal conditions indicated, and can claim the consensus of others, my principles may be called moral, and constitute a morality, as much as if their selection had been inspired by a love of mankind.

3

This consequence of Position B is also entailed by A, of course, for both positions deny that any material content or interest belongs to the definition of morality. It is on this point that these positions differ from Position C. This again is a family of positions, but they all hold that our judging and deciding is moral if and only if it is done from a certain point of view which is not definable in purely formal terms; its definition may include purely formal features but it must also include a material one. This material condition, moreover, must reflect a concern for others or a consideration of social cohesiveness and the common good; even if morality be limited to "justice," as distinct from "benevolence," it still must involve something of this sort.

What Position C asserts, then, is that some reference to the welfare of others, the security of social life, etc., is part of the meaning of words like "moral" and "morality" when used as second-order terms. Durkheim maintained this view in 1906: ". . . if there is a morality," he wrote, "it can only have as its objective the group formed by a number of associated individuals, that is to say, society." [18] But he added that society must be considered "as a personality qualitatively different from the individual personalities which compose it." This addition, however, is no part of Position C; in fact, most of its proponents would emphatically disown the notion of Society with a capital S. Without this notion, it was, perhaps, first formulated by Hume.[19] More recently it appears in an essay by W. Kneale:

> When we say that the moral law is the legislation of the reasonable man, we seem therefore to mean that it is, as Adam Smith suggested, a set of commands such as would be given by an impartial spectator who was endowed with sympathy and intelligence and possessed all relevant information.[20]

Aiken also seems to be taking Position C in some of his essays.[21] Thus he writes in one place that in moral judgment

> . . . a type of attitude is aroused which regards the object reflected upon from a certain point of view which we call "disinterested" or "social." We are induced, so to speak, to impersonate the role of a person imbued only with the fundamental social presses of the community.

And in another he says,

> The authority of the moral judgment helps to solidify, but it also in turn depends upon a sense of community with others. When

> it ceases to be thought of as a symbol of a larger common interest with which in part oneself is in sympathy, it loses its distinctive moral status as something which can oppose the inclinations of the individual as an impersonal or public "ought." . . . ethical terms . . . have conditions of sentential intersignificance which limit the range of their application. These conditions, I submit, are of basic social importance.

Morality is here conceived, not just as a mode of human guidance which has certain formal or structural features, but as one which by definition has a certain general social concern, content, direction, or goal.

This conception appears most fully in S. E. Toulmin's first book. In morality, according to Toulmin, "good reasoning is distinguished from bad . . . by applying to individual judgments the test of principle, and to principles the test of general fecundity." That is, I give a moral reason or justification for my claim that you should do a certain act, A, by showing that it makes for "the harmony of society" or promotes "general fecundity." If you still ask why you should do A after admitting all this, I can give no further *moral* reason, for we have come to the limit of morality. Any further reasons I may give must be "personal"; they can consist only in showing that A is necessary for your own happiness or for the kind of community in which you would personally prefer to live. Beyond that A "cannot be reasoned about at all." But why should we regard reasoning as moral (and as good moral reasoning) if and only if it directly or indirectly appeals to "the harmony of society"? Because by definition the function of morality is

> to correlate our feelings and behavior in such a way as to make the fulfillment of everyone's aims and desires as far as possible compatible. . . . What makes us call a judgment "ethical" is the fact that it is used to harmonize people's actions . . . The notions of "duty," of "obligation," of "morality," are derived from situations in which the conduct of one member of a community prejudices the interest of another, and are to be understood as parts of the procedure for minimizing the effects of such conflicts.[22]

A similar position is expressed in an article by J. Kemp:

> Cooperation with others . . . is part of the meaning of "morality"

> . . . the word "moral" excludes . . . action on a principle of pure selfishness.[23]

In a like vein K. Baier writes as follows in his recent book:

> The conditions so far mentioned are merely formal. They exclude certain sorts of rule as not coming up to the formal requirements. But moral rules should also have a certain sort of content. Observation of these rules should be *for the good of everyone alike*.[24]

Here, as in Toulmin, a certain material principle or goal is regarded as built into the definition of terms like "moral" and "morality" if these are used in anything like their normal sense. On such views, *moral* reasoning is present (and complete) if and only if this social goal or principle is appealed to, if not for the justification of a particular act, then at least for that of any rule used to justify the act. If a man rejects this appeal, "we can produce no reasons why he should [accept it], in the ethical sense of 'should'—we can, of course, argue . . . that he would be happier if he did, but this is [morally] irrelevant." [25] The man has simply put himself outside of morality altogether, and can be reasoned with only in non-moral terms, or not at all.

4

These seem to me to be the three main conceptions of morality in recent philosophy. Position A characterizes morality and the moral point of view in formal and individualistic terms, B in formal and social terms, and C in material and social terms. A fourth conception, a Position D, is obviously possible, namely, one which characterizes morality in material and individualistic terms. It would hold that an individual is judging and reasoning morally only if his judging and reasoning, perhaps in addition to satisfying certain formal conditions, appeals finally to a consideration of what promotes his good on the whole, his happiness, or his self-realization. Although A. C. Garnett seems to subscribe to this view when he says that "utilitarianism (in its non-hedonistic form) has correctly pointed to the *end* at which ethically right conduct must aim" but that "the self-realization theory has correctly stated the *ground* or *reason* why conduct aiming at that end is ethically required," [26] it has not found many takers in contemporary moral philosophy. We shall, therefore, continue to confine our discussion to Positions A, B, and C.

It is clear that the issues between these three positions center around two points: (1) whether or not a claim to intersubjective validity is to be taken as essential to moral judgment. (2) whether or not a more material social concern is to be regarded as intrinsic to morality. The considerations involved are most complex and perplexing. In the hope of bringing about a fuller discussion, I shall now review some of them.[27] Since I have already described those which favor Position B (Part I) as against A and those which favor Position C as against both A and B (Part II), we may limit ourselves to a review of the arguments which proponents of A may use against B, Part I, and against C, for they will include any arguments which proponents of B, Part II, may use against C.

Before we go on, however, it should be noticed that each of the three positions may be stated in two rather different ways. Each may be stated as a descriptive claim about the manner in which morality is or has been conceived, or as a normative claim about the manner in which it ought to be conceived. In other words, it may be offered as simply an elucidation of the way in which we actually use words like "moral" and "morality," or as a prescription or proposal telling us how we should use them, a use which may or may not coincide with the way in which we have been using them. One might, of course, maintain one position as a description of actual use and another as a recommendation for future use.

It is clear that the character of any debate between our positions depends on the way in which they are to be taken. In the literature these two ways of stating a position are usually not explicitly distinguished, leaving the reader uncertain about the way in which he is to understand his author. I doubt that any of the positions stated in recent writings are to be taken simply as descriptions or elucidations of the prevailing rules for using "moral," even though their authors usually talk as if they are merely describing or elucidating. Every writer seems, at least implicitly, to be accepting the rules which he discovers as a guide to future use.[28] Still, it seems possible that he should present a rule simply as one we actually do obey. Hence, while I shall stress considerations calculated to support recommendations about the use of "moral," I shall also give some attention to descriptive claims. In any case, the fact that a certain use of a term is in effect is, other things being equal, a reasonable argument for continuing to use it in that way.

It may be objected that, whichever position he takes, the moral philosopher should not take or propose it normatively, as embodying a rule for future use. If this means that a philosopher must simply elucidate present uses, without even accepting the rules he finds in the process or prescribing their continued adherence, perhaps on the very ground that they are the prevailing ones, as well as without proposing any revisions, then we may well ask why we should agree. What point has the analysis of present concepts other than to clarify future ones? And, if this is the point of such analysis, why must the analyst refrain from making recommendations? But the objection may be only to normative proposals about the use of "moral" and "morality," on the ground that such a normative proposal is itself a *moral* judgment. Here let us waive the question whether it is philosophically wicked to say, "We ought to use 'moral' in way x," if "ought" is used in a moral sense. We may still ask, however, if "ought" is necessarily used here in a moral sense. There are other uses of ought, for example, the prudential and the technical uses. Whether a normative proposal is a moral one depends on the kind of reasoning with which it is supported, and there is no reason why a proposal about the use of "moral" should be supported by moral considerations. Indeed, to call such a proposal and the reasons behind it "moral" out of hand is to prejudge precisely the question to which they are intended to give an answer.[29]

5

With these preliminaries out of the way, we may proceed. Let us consider first some actual or possible arguments for Position A against B, Part I.

(1) It might be argued that in our moral judgments we do not in fact claim them to have any validity beyond ourselves—that at most we use them to evoke or invite similar responses on the part of others. But this seems palpably false.[30] I may not claim the agreement of all others, but I do at least claim the agreement of a certain class of them, namely, those who belong to my society, or those who take the moral point of view, etc. A. J. Ayer contends that in an ethical dispute, if our opponent agrees with us about all questions of fact, then "we abandon the attempt to convince him by argument." [31] Perhaps. But do we also abandon the claim that our position is valid beyond ourselves, while at the same time maintaining it without question as a moral position? This I doubt. Ayer himself allows that we still say our opponent "has a distorted or undeveloped moral sense." He adds that this "signifies merely that he employs a different set of values from our own." It does not, however, signify this in the sense that this is what we mean, but only in the sense that it is all we can maintain (and we need admit this only if we already accept Ayer's metaethical theory). If we did consciously accept the fact that our disagreement is simply a *de gustibus* one, we might still keep our preference intact, but I doubt that we should insist with our initial confidence that it has a moral status (unless we think our opponent is not taking a moral point of view). I question, in other words, that we can at once admit that we are a party to an ultimate disagreement and still assert that both parties are taking the moral point of view.

(2) Holders of Position A may reply that, while a claim to a trans-individual validity is made in ordinary moral judgments, it is an illusory claim and should be dropped. But surely the claim to a consensus on the part of certain others, actual or hypothetical, is sometimes correct. It may also sometimes be

incorrect, but this would mean at most that the speaker must retract his moral judgment, not that he must give up making such a claim. It may be an illusion ever to claim that everyone actually does agree with one's judgment, but it has not yet been established that we will continue to disagree even if we take the moral point of view more and more devotedly, include more and more of mankind in our consideration, and obtain the utmost possible factual enlightenment. That those who share the moral point of view will agree in the end, as Peirce thought those will who share the scientific point of view, is thus a faith which we may still keep. Perhaps it is even a part of the moral point of view itself to keep this faith.

(3) It may also be argued against B, Part I (in its stronger form), that those who subscribe to it misunderstand the nature of morality. It may be held, for example, that to say one's judgment must somehow be readjusted if one finds that others who are morally qualified tend to disagree involves making a mistake about the logic of moral terms, since it is part of the meaning of "moral" as applied to a judgment that it is autonomous.[32] Now, we may admit that morality is a system of guidance in which the individual is meant to be autonomous or self-governing and that his moral judgments cannot simply be dictated by others or taken on authority. It does not follow, however, that his judgments are in no way corrigible in the light of a recurrent review of the facts by oneself and others from the moral point of view. In science, too, he is meant to be autonomous, yet he cannot maintain his findings unshaken if they are not confirmed by others who take the scientific point of view. So in morality he must judge for himself from the moral point of view in the light of available knowledge, but he claims that others who do so will, eventually at least, come to agree with him; and if they do not, he must ask himself if his judgment is really made from the moral point of view. As long as others who are qualified in the ways indicated come to different conclusions, he holds his position at a kind of risk to his status as a moral judge, just as he risks his status as a scientist if he propounds a deviant result or theory in science.

Of course, the situation in science and morality are not wholly analogous: claims to consensus seem to be more speculative in morality than in science. But the case of science does show that autonomy is compatible with corrigibility in view of the judgments of others, which is the point at issue in the present objection.

(4) At this point the objection may be made that Position B has the consequence that we can determine what is morally right by looking to see what is or rather will eventually be approved by fully enlightened people who take the moral point of view, or even that "x is right" means "x is or will eventually be approved by certain people." But such consequences, whether undesirable or not, do not follow from Position B any more than the parallel ones follow from Peirce's view that in scientific judgments we claim that what we say "is fated to be ultimately agreed to by all who investigate." [33] Even if we do make this claim when we assert, "Salt is soluble in water," it does not follow that we can verify this statement by looking at other investigators to see if they agree, or that "x is soluble" means something about the agreement of other investigators.

6

The objections to Position B, Part I, then, do not seem to be insuperable. Let us turn to objections to Position C. Its defenders hold that a material social concern is a *necessary* condition of morality, or both a *necessary* and a *sufficient* condition. We begin with objections to its being regarded as a necessary condition of morality.

(5) The first objection is that we do not in fact apply the term "moral" only to judgments and reasoning which appeal to such a social sentiment, principle, or goal. Some apply it also (and perhaps only) to judgments and reasoning which appeal to the will of God. Others say that a principle is moral, regardless of its content, if those who accept it have certain attitudes toward it and toward violations of it.[34] One recent popular writer finds it not unnatural to say, "Our prevailing ethics is 'enlightened self-interest.' " Earlier, Butler and many de-

ontological intuitionists found it plausible to deny that a social teleology is presupposed in all moral duties. Thus, Position C is mistaken if it is read as asserting that a material social concern is *in fact* taken to be a necessary condition of morality. It might still be contended that such a social concern does really reign over the moral institution of life in some recondite way. But unless we accept such a contention, we must admit that Position C can only be held either as a description of what is taken to be a *sufficient* condition of morality or as a proposal about our future use of "moral."

It is sometimes argued to a similar effect that a concern about social stability and welfare cannot be part of the definition of morality, because in the moralities of some cultures there is no such concern. Thus Ladd seems to take his conclusion that the Navaho morality is a prudentialist one as a ground for rejecting such views as I have put under Position C.[35] But he can do this only if he first assumes that every culture, including the Navaho, has a morality in our sense of the term, and this is precisely the question at issue.[36] One cannot say that the Navaho have a morality until after one has formed some conception of morality and found that the Navaho have such an institution. The fact that they have some kind of a code which partakes of certain formal properties proves that they have a morality only if these properties suffice to define morality. But this is our question. No doubt one wants some term for all such codes, but it may be that to call them all "moralities" is an undesirable departure from our traditional conception of such an institution. The fact that a certain code lacks a certain feature does not prove that this feature is and should be no part of our conception of morality; it may in fact be a reason for not calling that code a morality at all.

(6) A closely related objection has often been urged against Toulmin's view that a concern for the harmony of society is part of the meaning of "moral." It is argued that there are or might be people who deny that we ought to be concerned about the harmony of society, e.g. Nietzsche; that their opposing principles and the issue between them and Toulmin are, or may

properly be, or should be called "moral"; and that therefore Toulmin is wrong in thinking that a concern for the harmony of society is or should be a necessary condition of morality. For on his view his opponents cannot be said to have a morality at all, and the issue between himself and them is not an issue between two moral principles or moralities but between morality and something else. Toulmin is concealing the existence of radical ethical disagreement, it is said; he begs the question against opposing moralists, he takes sides in a moral issue while claiming to do "logic." [37]

This objection obviously can be generalized and directed against other forms of Position C. In reply we may remark, first, that the case of Nietzsche is not as clear as is here pretended. He does sometimes write as if he regards what he is advocating as a morality, but he also speaks of it on occasion as if it were something "beyond" or opposed to morality, as it would be on Toulmin's view. Second, whatever we think of Nietzsche, I see no reason in principle why the issue between Toulmin and his opponents should be regarded as an issue within morality and not as an issue between morality and some would-be successor of morality. Thought of in the latter way, it cannot be regarded as begged, concealed, or defined out of existence by such a procedure as Toulmin's.[38] We must remember, next, that his opponents' positions are not made moral merely by the fact that they are normative. And to say that they are moral simply because they fulfill certain formal conditions is to beg the question under discussion. But, it will be said, we do in fact sometimes call them moral, and we also sometimes label the issue between them and Toulmin a moral one. Both of these claims are true. The first shows again that Toulmin's material condition is not actually regarded as a *necessary* condition for applying the term "moral," but this is all it shows. One may still hold that it is actually accepted as a *sufficient* condition of morality or recommend that it be considered as a *necessary* one in the future. The second fact—that we call the issue between Nietzsche and Toulmin moral—need not be taken to show even this much. For we do sometimes label a conflict moral when we do not regard both parties to the conflict as moral. For example, we call a conflict between duty and interest a moral one. Why then should we not call a debate between Nietzsche and Toulmin moral, even if, like Toulmin, we consider Nietzsche as an anti-moralist?

Finally, we may note that an exactly parallel objection can be made to the view that the universalization requirement is a necessary condition of morality, a view which is held by many supporters of Positions A and B, as well as of C, and in particular by Hare. Thus MacIntyre contends that those who define morality in terms of universalizability are not neutral either, as they claim to be, that they too are begging questions, taking sides, for example, against the existentialists.[39] To this contention their replies must in principle be the same as those just indicated. Indeed, anyone who maintains that some particular requirement is essential to morality will have his Nietzsche, as Toulmin has his; and he must either give up his position or deny that his opponent's is a moral one, just as Toulmin must.

(7) We can take up only one kind of objection to the contention that a material social concern is a *sufficient* condition of morality. It might be objected here that this contention ignores such a necessary condition of morality as universalization, and is therefore false. A possible reply would be that this condition, even if necessary, is not independent—that it is derivative in one way or another from the fact that morality has the social concern in question. But we need not debate this point now, for the objection I wish to deal with in conclusion is one which, if it holds at all, holds also against the view that a social concern, when combined with universalization, suffices to define morality. The objection is that this view cannot be satisfactory, for one can still ask of a way of life which universalizes and is socially concerned, "But why should I live like that?" Morality, it is asserted, is something which carries its own sanction with it; any definition of it must be such that a youth cannot sensibly ask "Why?" even when morality whispers low. Morality must be so defined that an individual cannot sensibly ask for reasons for espousing it. Motivation for espousing it must be somehow built into its very nature; it must not only be morally self-

justifying, as Toulmin claims, it must also be personally self-motivating. Hence Position C is untenable.[40]

If this objection is meant to claim that we do not in fact apply the terms "moral" and "morality" to codes of which we can ask, "Why should I . . . ?" in this motivational sense, it is clearly mistaken. Even W. D. Falk recognizes that our moral terms do not always have this "internal" or motivational meaning. Nor can it be argued that the autonomy entailed by morality requires morality to be such that the individual must espouse it if he grasps its nature.

The objection must then be interpreted as a *proposal* that we henceforth use the words "moral" and "morality" only of systems for which it is not sensible to demand motivating reasons. But if it is a proposal to do this, then it must itself be supported by argument. It must be argued that it is more satisfactory to define the institution of morality so as to build in a sure-fire motivation for accepting it than to define it so as to build in a social concern or goal. But any such argument must involve a whole complex of considerations relating to our intentions in the development of a "moral institution of life," and, until our objectors produce such an elaborate argument, we may at least doubt that they are right. For, if Position C entails endangering motivation while ensuring social responsibility, Positions A and B entail risking social responsibility while ensuring motivation. Is it really clear that we should prefer to do the latter? [41]

As a matter of fact, I am inclined to think that we cannot plausibly define morality in such a way that the question "Why should I . . . ?" can never sensibly be raised. It must remain a system of guidance to which we do not automatically conform. Even if it is defined in egoistic terms, as the position we called D proposes, it will still be possible for us to ask why we should live by it. For, as Butler pointed out, our primary appetites may rebel even against the reflective policy of self-love. Hence a certain amount of gambling with human motivation is inherent in morality; the question is how much more gambling with it we are willing to introduce, and whether we are willing to gamble also with the responsibility of morality to society.

7

Such are the objections to a material and social definition of morality in favor of a more formal or individualistic one. We have seen that something may be said in reply to them. However, the questions involved are large and complex, especially since they cannot be answered simply by looking to see how we use the expressions "moral" and "morality." They need to be clarified further and to be discussed more fully. At least three sharply opposed conceptions of morality are in the field; fundamental and far-reaching questions are at issue between them; and the relevant considerations capable of influencing the mind one way or the other are varied and weighty.

NOTES

1. In somewhat different ways I have also done this in "Obligation and Motivation in Recent Moral Philosophy" in *Essays in Moral Philosophy*, ed. A. I. Melden (Seattle: University of Washington Press, 1958), and in "Ethics, 1949–1955" in *Philosophy in the Mid-Century*, ed. R. Klibansky (Firenze: La Nuova Italia Editrice, 1958). For an excellent review of recent ethical theory see H. D. Aiken, "Moral Philosophy and Education," *Harvard Educational Review*, XXV (1955), 44–53.
2. See, e.g., R. Mehl, *De l'autorité des valeurs* (Paris: Presses Universitaires de France, 1957), pp. 2–3; A. E. Duncan-Jones, *Butler's Moral Philosophy* (London: Penguin Books Ltd., 1952), p. 176.
3. R. M. Hare, *The Language of Morals* (Oxford: Clarendon Press, 1952), p. 69; see also P. H. Nowell-Smith, *Ethics* (London: Penguin Books Ltd., 1954), pp. 319–320; C. L. Stevenson, "The Emotive Conception of Ethics and Its Cognitive Implications," *Philosophical Review*, LIX (1950), 291–304.
4. See Hare, "Universalizability," *Proceedings of the Aristotelian Society*, Suppl. Vol. XXVIII (1954), pp. 295–312.
5. See Duncan-Jones, *op. cit.*, pp. 167–177; J. Ladd, *The Structure of a Moral Code* (Cambridge: Harvard University Press, 1957), pp. 79, 105; J. Harrison, "When Is a Principle a Moral Principle?" *Proceedings of the Aristotelian Society*, Suppl. Vol. XXVIII (1954), pp. 111–134; M. Mandelbaum, *The Phenomenology of Moral Experience* (Glencoe, Ill.: The Free Press, 1955), pp. 257ff.
6. J.-P. Sartre, *Existentialism* (New York: Philosophical Library, 1947), pp. 20–21.
7. See E. Gellner, "Ethics and Logic," *Proceedings of the Aristotelian Society*, Vol. LV (1954–55), pp. 157–178; G. Gusdorf, *Traité de l'existence morale* (Paris: Librairie Armand Colin, 1949); A. MacIntyre, "What Morality Is Not," *Philosophy*, XXXII (1957), 325–335.
8. J. A. Brunton, "Egoism and Morality," *Philosophical Quarterly*, VI (1956), 289–303; Ladd, *op. cit.*, pp. 101–104; B. Mayo, *Ethics and the Moral Life* (London: Macmillan & Co., 1958), Chaps. VIII, IX; Mandelbaum, *op. cit.*, pp. 277ff. Not all of these authors hold Position A, however.
9. See Harrison, *op. cit.*, pp. 121–122; Ladd, *op. cit.*, p. 315.

10. He may also hold that moral rules must be social in the sense of being rules about interpersonal relations. Like some existentialists he may even argue that human individuals require the society of others.
11. "Legal and Moral Obligation," in Melden (ed.), *op. cit.*, p. 100.
12. M. Macdonald, "Ethics and the Ceremonial Use of Language," in *Philosophical Analysis*, ed. Max Black (Ithaca: Cornell University Press, 1950), pp. 211–229; H. D. Aiken, "The Authority of Moral Judgments," *Philosophy and Phenomenological Research*, XII (1952), 513–525. See also Ladd, *op. cit.*, pp. 80, 84, 101–105; Mandelbaum, *op. cit.*, pp. 184–186, 257, 262–263.
13. *Op. cit.*, pp. 89, 91.
14. *Op. cit.*, pp. 89–90, 92. Later Mayo seems to reject B, Part 1, in its stronger form. See, e.g., pp. 169–170.
15. See Hart, *loc. cit.;* J. Rawls, "Justice as Fairness," *Journal of Philosophy*, LIV (1957), 653–662; R. Firth, "Ethical Absolutism and the Ideal Observer," *Philosophy and Phenomenological Research*, XII (1952), 317–345.
16. "A Pluralistic Analysis of the Ethical 'Ought,'" *Journal of Philosophy*, XLVIII (1951), 504.
17. "Moral Philosophy and Education," *Harvard Educational Review*, XXV (1955), 52–53.
18. E. Durkheim, *Sociologie et philosophie* (Paris: Presses Universitaires de France, 1951), pp. 52–53.
19. See the passages quoted by Mayo, *op. cit.*, pp. 83–88.
20. "Objectivity in Morals" (1950), in *Readings in Ethical Theory*, ed. W. S. Sellars and J. Hospers (New York: Appleton-Century-Crofts, 1952), p. 693.
21. For the following quotations see (respectively), "The Role of Conventions in Ethics," *Journal of Philosophy*, XLIX (1952), 175; "The Authority of Moral Judgments," *Philosophy and Phenomenological Research*, XII (1952), 523–524.
22. See *An Examination of the Place of Reason in Ethics* (Cambridge: Cambridge University Press, 1950). The quotations are (respectively) from pp. 160, 158, 202, 137, 145, 156–157. In the second article mentioned in note 1, I misinterpreted Toulmin's position.
23. "Foundations of Morality," *Philosophical Quarterly*, VII (1957), 316. Another passage (p. 312) seems to contradict this.
24. Baier, *The Moral Point of View* (Ithaca: Cornell University Press, 1958), p. 200; see also pp. 207–208. For another statement of Position C, see S. C. Pepper, *The Sources of Value* (Berkeley and Los Angeles: University of California Press, 1958), p. 519.
25. Kemp, *op. cit.*, p. 316.
26. *Can Ideals and Norms Be Justified?* (Stockton, Calif.: College of the Pacific Philosophy Institute, 1955), pp. 91–92; cf. p. 71.

27. K. Nielsen has good discussions of some of them. See "Justification and Moral Reasoning," *Methodos*, 1957, pp. 1–35; "Good Reasons in Ethics: An Examination of the Toulmin-Hare Controversy," *Theoria*, XXIV (1958), 9–28.
28. See M. B. Foster, "'We' in Modern Philosophy," in *Faith and Logic*, ed. B. Mitchell (London: Allen & Unwin, 1957), pp. 194–220.
29. With this and the previous paragraph cf. my "MacIntyre on Defining Morality," *Philosophy*, XXXIII (1958), 158–162.
30. See Mandelbaum, *op. cit.*, pp. 257–277.
31. *Language, Truth and Logic* (London: Victor Gollancz, 1936), p. 166.
32. Cf. Nowell-Smith, *loc. cit.;* Mayo, *op. cit.*, pp. 169–170.
33. C. S. Peirce, "How to Make Our Ideas Clear," Sec. IV, in any edition of *Collected Papers of C. S. Peirce*, ed. P. Weiss and C. Hartshorne, Vol. V (Cambridge: Harvard University Press).
34. See Harrison, *op. cit.;* Kemp, *op. cit.*, p. 312.
35. See *op. cit.*, pp. 76–77, 80, 313ff.
36. As Ladd seems to see on p. 314.
37. See the reviews of Toulmin's book by Hare, *Philosophical Quarterly*, I (1951), 372–375, and J. Mackie, *Australian Journal of Philosophy*, XXIX (1951), 114–124. See also Harrison, *op. cit.;* H. Feigl, "Validation and Vindication," in Sellars and Hospers (eds.), *op. cit.*, pp. 670–671.
38. However, Toulmin himself, quite unnecessarily, gives the impression that he is defining even this question out of existence.
39. *Op. cit.*
40. This objection is implicit in Nowell-Smith, *op. cit.*, *passim*, and explicit in W. D. Falk, "'Ought' and Motivation," *Proceedings of the Aristotelian Society*, Vol. XLVIII (1947–48), pp. 111–138.
41. For more on this point, see my "Obligation and Motivation in Recent Moral Philosophy," in Melden (ed.), *op. cit.*, pp. 40–81.

2
MORALITY, SELF, AND OTHERS

W. D. Falk *Wayne State University*

I

In: And how can you say that I never had a moral education? As a child, I was taught that one ought not to maltreat other children, ought to share one's sweets with them, ought to keep tidy and clean; as an adolescent, that one ought to keep one's word, to work, to save, to leave off drink, not to waste the best years of one's life, to let reason govern one's emotions and actions. Nor did I simply learn that one is *called upon* to act in these ways by paternal authority and social custom on pain of censure. I learned to appreciate that one *ought* to do these things *on their merits*, and that what one ought to do on its merits does not depend on the requests or enjoinders of anyone. The facts in the case themselves make one liable, as a reflective person, to act in these ways of one's own accord: they provide one with choice-supporting reasons sufficient to determine one if one knows them and takes diligent account of them.[1]

Out: I know you were taught all this. But why did your teacher say that you ought to act in these ways?
In: Why? For very cogent reasons. My tutor was a student of the Ancients. The moral man, "the man of practical wisdom," he kept quoting Aristotle, "is the man who knows how to deliberate well about what is good and useful for himself." And surely, he would say, you can see for yourself: if you don't act sociably, who will act sociably towards you? Uncleanliness breeds disease. Without work, how are you to live? Without savings, what about your future? Drink leaves one a wreck. Indulging one's sorrows makes them worse. The wasted years, one day you will regret them when it is too late. People who cannot govern themselves are helpless before fortune, without the aid and comfort of inner strength.
Out: And so you think that you had a moral education? Let me tell you, you never even made a start. For what were you taught? That there are things that you ought to do or to avoid on your own account. But one does not learn about morality that way. What one *morally* ought to do is what one ought to do on account of others, or for the sake of some good state of things in general. Now had you been taught to appreciate that you ought to keep clean so as to be pleasing to others, and that you ought to do what moral custom requires for the sake of the general good, then, and then only, would you have learned the rudiments of moral duty.
In: Very well, my upbringing was too narrow. One would hardly be a human being if the good of others, or of society at large, could not weigh with one as a cogent reason for doing what will promote it. So one has not fully learned about living like a rational and moral being unless one has learned to appreciate that one ought to do things out of regard for others, and not only out of regard for oneself.
Out: No, you have still not got my point. I am saying that only insofar as you ought to do things—no matter whether for yourself or for others—for the sake of others, is the reason a moral reason and the ought a moral ought. Reasons of self-

regard are not moral reasons at all, and you can forget about them in the reckoning of your *moral* obligations.

In: But this seems artificial. A moral education surely should teach one all about the principles of orderly living and the reasons which tell in their favor. And if there are also perfectly good personal reasons which tell in their favor, why suppress them? To be sure, in talking to people in ordinary life, we do no such thing. If they say "Why ought I to act sociably?" we say "For the general good as well as your own." If they say "Why ought I to be provident?" we say "For your own good as well as that of others." In short, we offer mixed reasons, and none of these reasons can be spared. One ought not to lie because this is a good social rule, and equally because the habit of evasiveness is destructive of oneself as a person. And one ought not to take to drink or indulge one's sorrows, or waste the best years of one's life primarily out of proper regard for oneself, much as there may be other-regarding reasons as well. If morality were all social service, and one had no moral responsibilities towards oneself or towards others, the moral inconveniences of life would be far less than they are. So I don't see the point of saying "But one has no *moral* commitment to do anything except insofar as one ought to do it on account of others." To say this seems like encouraging people not to bother about doing things insofar as they ought to do them only for personal reasons, as after all this is not a moral ought.

Out: But one does not speak of a moral duty to do things for one's own sake. If one ought to save in order to provide for one's own future, one regards this as a precept not of morals but of prudence. It would be different if one ought to save in order to provide for one's dependents. Moral commitments are those which one has as a moral being, and what makes one a moral being is that one has commitments towards others and does not evade them.

In: Not everyone will agree that as a moral being one has only commitments towards others or that only such commitments are properly "moral." The Greeks, for example, took a wider view. For Plato the equivalent of a moral being was the just or right-living person, and of a moral commitment the right and just course—the one which the right-living person would be led to take. And this right-living person was one who would keep himself in good shape as a sane and self-possessed being, and who would do whatever good and sufficient reasons directed him to do. This is why for Plato and the Greeks temperance and prudence were no less among the just man's commitments than paying his debts and not willfully harming others, and why the one was not treated any less as a moral commitment than the other. The Greeks placed the essence of man as a moral being in his capacity to direct himself on rational grounds; and his commitments as a moral being were therefore all those which he seriously incurred as a properly self-directing being.

Out: Citing the Greeks only shows how distant their concept of morality is from ours. We will not call every rational commitment "moral" or equate the moral with the rational man.

In: This is broadly so, although not entirely. Our concept of morality vacillates between the Greek and the Christian tradition. We associate "moral" with "social" commitment, and the "morally good man" with the "selfless man." But we also speak of man as a "moral agent," of his "moral freedom" and "moral powers"; and here we refer to his whole capacity of self-direction by good and sufficient reasons. One may speak without strain of a personal and a social ethic, and refer to the negligent disregard of oneself as a vice, and a sign of moral defect. We call the improvident man "morally weak," and we call the man who can resist drink in company on account of his health or who sticks to his vocation in adversity a man of "moral strength and character." There is certainly little difference in the qualities needed to live up to a social or a personal ought. It takes self-denial to provide for one's future, moral courage to stick to one's vocation. One may show one's mettle as a moral agent here no less than in selfless care for others. There are contemporary moralists who call "moral" any "authentic" commitment of a self-governing person, whether its grounds are social or personal. What justifies them is the broader use of the term which is also part of our language and tradition.

Out: And how eccentric this use is. Our very concept of a moral being is inseparable from the notion of submission of self to a good other than one's own. It is not conceivable that a man should have moral duties on a desert island, devoid of man or beast. Would one say that he still had a moral duty to do what was good for him? You may as well go on and say that if a shipwrecked fellow arrived to share his vegetables, it might be his moral duty to let him starve rather than starve himself.

In: The good of others need not always have the overriding claim on one, if this is what you mean. One could say to a good-hearted and weak-willed person, "For your own sake, you ought to stop neglecting your future, even if this hurts others." This would not be a typically "moral" ought, but one may be giving sound moral advice.

Out: And so, if beneficence had the better of this person, you should call him morally irresponsible and blameworthy. On your showing, he has evaded a moral commitment, and for such evasions one is held morally responsible and liable to censure. But surely, even if I granted your case, one would not call him blameworthy and a morally bad man; as indeed in any case where a person fails to do what his own good requires we do not call him morally bad, but only imprudent, unwise, rash. It is quite a different offense to be slack about brushing one's teeth, than to be negligent about providing dentures for others. And this is so precisely because the second is a moral offense and the first is not and because one is blameworthy for the one and not for the other.

In: I agree that there is a difference. One is only called morally bad and is held answerable to *others* for neglecting what one ought to do out of regard for them. And this is understandable enough. After all, insofar as one fails to do only what one's own good requires, the failing is no one's concern but one's own. But then I should not say that such self-neglect was in no sense morally irresponsible and blameworthy. If it does not call for blame by others, it still calls for self-reproach. A rational person is responsible to himself for not being evasive about anything that he is convinced that he really ought to do. And the lack of moral strength and courage in personal matters, although commonly viewed as an amicable vice, is an amicable vice only in the estimation of others since it is not directly a threat to them.

However, we are not making headway. You find it repugnant to call a commitment "moral" unless its grounds are social and unless its non-observance makes one liable not only to social censure but also to self-reproach; and so be it. Perhaps our disagreement is only verbal, and despite some misgivings, I am ready to settle for your usage. Let us only speak of a moral ought where one ought to do things on account of others. But let us not be misled. For it still does not follow that if one ought to do things on one's own account, this ought may not still be otherwise functioning *like* a moral ought.

Out: How could it be like a moral ought if it is not a moral ought?

In: Because when one thinks of a moral ought, one thinks not only that its grounds are social but also that it has a special force and cogency. A moral ought commits one in all seriousness and in every way, without leaving any reasonable option to act otherwise. Your view comes to saying that if an ought is to be moral it must satisfy two conditions: it must seriously bind one in every way, and it must do so for other-regarding reasons. On your showing, a personal ought cannot be moral, as it cannot satisfy one of these conditions simply by having personal grounds. But it may still satisfy the other condition, and be as cogently binding and action-guiding in its force and function as a moral ought. This is why I can only accept your usage with one proviso: that one may also say that there are other than strictly moral commitments which a right-living person may have to reckon with no less than his strictly moral ones.

Out: Surely you don't expect me to fall for this. When I say "Don't count the purely personal ought as moral" I am not saying "Count it as well, but call it by another name." My point is precisely that it does not function like a moral ought at all. Personal reasons do not commit one to do anything with the same cogency as social reasons. In fact, in calling them reasons of prudence or expediency, we deprecate them. We regard them as inferior, and often disreputable, guides to action. So I won't let you reduce my position to triviality. That only the social commitments are essentially moral must be taken as implying that only they have the characteristic moral force.

In: I thought that this was at the back of our discussion all along. It usually is so with people who are so insistent on your usage, although part of the trouble is that one can never be sure. First one is told that a moral ought is one that commits one on other-regarding grounds and that a personal ought is not a moral ought *for this reason.* But then comes the further suggestion that it is not only different from a moral ought in this way, but is also otherwise inferior. It gives directives, but directives of a somehow shady kind. One way or other, the idea is that a commitment that has personal grounds is either not properly a commitment at all, or, if one in any way, then one that belongs in some limbo of disrepute. But your argument so far has done nothing to prove this point. From your language rule, it only follows that the personal ought must be unlike a moral ought in one essential respect, but not, except by way of confusion, that it must be therefore also unlike a moral ought in other respects too. You might as well say "Surely a lay-analyst is not a doctor," as one is not a doctor without a medical degree, and take this to be proof that a lay-analyst cannot otherwise cure like a doctor either. "No lay-analyst is a doctor" is strictly and trivially true in one way, and may be misleading and tendentiously false in another. And the same with "No personal ought is a *moral* ought." Your language rule makes this strictly and trivially true; but it does not go to show that a personal ought cannot otherwise be *like* a moral ought by being seriously committing or by taking precedence in a conscientious calculus of action-guiding considerations. My point is that, even if this were so, your appeal to usage cannot settle this matter. Logical grammar can decree that only social reasons are properly called "moral." But it cannot decide what reasons can, or cannot, be seriously committing for human beings.

Out: But what I am saying seems substantially true. What one ought to do on account of others is the prototype of the categorically binding ought. Personal reasons have not got the binding cogency of other-regarding reasons, and one deprecates them as inferior and disreputable.

In: And there is some truth in this. Personal and social reasons are not on the same footing in the economy of action-guiding considerations. Personal reasons are very commonly less thoroughly committing, they are often inferior reasons, and not rarely discreditable. But why this is so is a different matter and has not yet been touched on in any way. What is more, personal reasons need not always be in this inferior position. They are often not intrinsically discreditable, and become inferior guides to action only where there are other reasons in the case deserving of prior consideration. Take someone concerned for his health, or future, or self-respect. Surely these are respectable aspirations and there may be things which he ought to do on account of them without violating other claims. His health requires that he be temperate, his self-respect that he live without evasion. Would it not then be positively remiss of him not to act in these ways? If he did not, one would say that he had failed to do what a man in his position really ought to have done, and precisely for the reason which he had. And, if one can say this, what remains of the blemish?

This is why it remains perplexing to me why commitments on personal grounds should be excluded from the orbit of moral teaching, and why modern moralists, unlike the Ancients, should disdain to mention them as an integral part of the moral life. For they may also be cogent and sometimes overridingly cogent commitments to action. And if they are not the whole of morals, why not count them as part of them? For it also seems natural to say that to teach someone all about morality is to teach him about all the valid directives for action; about all those things which he might not otherwise do readily but which, for good and compelling reasons in the nature in the case, he ought to do and would have to break himself into doing whether for the sake of others or his own.

There is, I agree, one tendency to say that the moral man acts in accordance with precepts of selflessness. But there is also another tendency to say that he is the man to organize his life in accordance with all valid precepts. Our disagreement has exhibited the kind of shuttle-service between rival considerations better known as the dialectic of a problem. It may be that this shuttle-service is maintained by a cleft in the very concept of morality. This concept may have grown from conflicting or only partially overlapping observations, which are not fully reconciled in ordinary thinking.

Out: If this is so, I would have to be shown, for common sense still seems to me right in its disparagement of personal reasons.

In: Very well, then we shall have to consider why personal reasons should function as a less cogent guide to action than social ones. I shall admit that in more ways than one the personal ought presents a special case, but not that it presents a case for disparagement except in special contexts. After this, the question of whether the personal ought is properly called moral or not will appear less important, partly because it will have become plainer why there is a question. Nor shall I try to offer a ruling on this point. With a background of discourse as intricate and full of nuance as in this case, discretion is the better part of valor, and clarification is a safer bet than decision.

2

Whenever one remarks that clearly there are things which one ought to avoid or do if only for one's own sake, someone is sure to say, "No doubt; but any such ought is only a precept of prudence or expediency." It is a textbook cliché against Hobbes that his account of morality comes to just this. And this is said as if it were an obvious truth and enough to discredit all such precepts in one go. This assumes a great deal and settles nothing.

What it assumes is this: that everything that one ever does for one's own sake, one does as a matter of prudence *or* expediency; that there is no difference between these two; that morality always differs from prudence as a scent differs from a bad smell; and that everyone knows how so and why.

None of this will do.

In the first place, not everything done for oneself is done for reasons of prudence. That one ought to insure one's house, save for one's old age, not put all one's money into one venture, are precepts of prudence. But it is not a precept of prudence, though it may be a good precept, that someone ought to undergo a dangerous operation as a long shot to restoring his health rather than linger under a disability forever after.

The point is that prudence is only one way of looking after oneself. To act prudently is to play safe, for near-certain gains at small risks. But some good things one cannot get in this way. To get them at all one has to gamble, taking the risk of not getting them even so, or of coming to harm in the process. If one values them enough, one will do better by oneself to throw prudence to the winds, to play for high stakes, knowing full well the risk and the price of failure. Explorers, artists, scientists, mountaineers are types who may serve themselves better by this course. So will most people at some juncture. Thus, if someone values security, then that he ought to save in order to be secure is a precept of prudence. But that someone ought to stick to his vocation when his heart is in it enough to make it worth risking security or health or life itself is not a precept of *prudence*, but of *courage*.

One says sometimes, "I ought to save, as I *want* to be prudent," but sometimes "as I *ought* to be prudent." One may also decide that in one's own best interests one ought to be prudent rather than daring, or daring rather than prudent, as the case may be. Now, that one ought to do something as it would be prudent is a dictate of prudence. But that one really ought to be prudent, in one's own best interests, would not be a dictate of prudence again. One then ought to play safe in order to serve oneself *best* and not in order to serve oneself *safely*.

A dictate of prudence where one wants to be prudent but ought to be courageous in one's own best interests is a dictate of timidity. A dictate of courage, where one feels reckless but ought to be prudent, is a dictate of foolhardiness. Both will then plainly be morally imperfect precepts. But there is nothing obviously imperfect about a dictate of prudence where one ought to be prudent, or a dictate of courage where one ought to be daring. Such precepts seem near-moral enough to allow one to call the habit of acting on them a virtue. The Ancients considered both prudence and courage as moral virtues. Oddly enough, in our time, one is more ready to view courage on one's own behalf as a moral virtue than prudence. It needs the reminder that precepts of self-protection may be precepts of courage as well as of prudence for one to see that any precept of self-protection may have a moral flavor. I think that the dim view which we take of prudence corresponds to a belief that to be daring is harder than to be level-headed, a belief most likely justified within our own insurance-minded culture. But such belief would have seemed strange to Bishop Butler and the fashionable eighteenth-century gentlemen to whom he addressed himself. Prudence in Butler's time, as throughout the ancient world, was not yet the cheap commodity which it is with us; and the price of virtue varies with the market.

There are other precepts of self-protection which are not "just a matter of prudence" either. That one ought not to take to drugs or drink, indulge oneself in one's sorrows, waste one's talents, commit suicide just in the despair of the moment, are precepts made of sterner stuff. One wants to say, "Surely, it is more than just a matter of prudence that one ought to avoid these things." And rightly so. The effect on oneself of taking to drugs or drink, or of any of the others, is not conjectural, but quite certain. To avoid them is therefore more than a matter of *taking no risks*. Sometimes, when one looks down a precipice, one feels drawn to jump. If one refrains, it will hardly be said of one, "How prudent he is, he takes no chances." The avoidance of excesses of all kinds in one's own best interests is in this class. The habit of avoiding them the Greeks called temperance, a virtue distinct from prudence.

Another error is to equate the prudent with the expedient, and, again, the expedient with everything that is for one's own good. To save may be prudent; but whether it is expedient or convenient to start now is another matter. With a lot of money to spare at the moment it will be expedient; otherwise it will not. But it may be prudent all the same. Again, one marries in the hope of finding happiness; but marriage in this hope is not a marriage of convenience. The point is that reasons of expediency are reasons of a special sort: reasons for doing something on the ground that it is incidentally at hand to serve one's purpose, or because it serves a purpose quite incidental to the purpose for which one would normally be doing this thing. One marries for reasons of expediency when one marries for money, but not when in hope of finding happiness. Hobbes said that "men never act except with a view to some good to themselves." This would be quite different from saying that "they never act except with a view to what is expedient."

There is also this difference between the prudent and the expedient: one can speak of "rules of prudence," but less well of "rules of expediency." The expedient is what happens to serve. It is not therefore easily bottled in rules.

The word "prudence" is used too freely in still one more context. When one wishes to justify the social virtues to people, a traditional and inviting move is to refer them, among other things at least, to their own good. "You ought to hold the peace, be honest, share with others." "Why?" "Because an order in which such practices were universal is of vital concern to you; and your one hope of helping to make such an order is in doing your share." The classical formulation of this standard move is Hooker's, quoted with approval by Locke: "If I cannot but wish to receive good . . . how should I look to have any part of my desire herein satisfied, unless I myself be careful to satisfy the like desire: my desire therefore to be loved of my equals in nature, as much as possible may be, imposes upon me a *natural duty* of bearing to themward fully the like affection."

Now, it is said again, "So defended, the social duties come to no more than precepts of prudence"; and this goes with the veiled suggestion that it is morally improper to use this defense. But, even if so defended, the social duties are not necessarily reduced purely to precepts of prudence. For they may be recommended in this way either as mere *rules* or as *principles* of self-protection; and as principles they would be misdescribed as mere precepts of prudence. The distinction is this: When one says, "People ought to practice the social virtues, if only for their own benefit," one may be saying, "They ought to practice them for this reason as a *rule*, i.e., normally, as much as each time this is likely to be for their own good." Or one may be saying, "They ought to practice them for this reason not merely as a rule but as a *matter of principle*, i.e., every time, whether at that time this is likely to be for their good or not." And one might defend the adoption of this *principle* by saying, "Because your best, even if slim, hope of contributing to a society fit for you to live in lies in adding to the number of principled people who will do their share each time, without special regard for their good at that time."

Now this seems to me a precept of courage rather than one of prudence. The game of attempting by one's actions to make society a place fit for one to live in is a gamble worth the risk only because of the known price of not attempting it. This gamble is a root condition of social living. One is sure to give hostages to fortune, but again, what other hope has one got? Hence, if a man practiced the social virtues, thinking that he ought to as a matter of principle, and on these grounds, one will praise him for his *wisdom*, his firm grasp of vital issues, his steadfastness, his courage. But one will not necessarily congratulate him on his prudence. For many times the prudent course might have been otherwise. It may be wise to persist in being honest with cheats, or forbearing with the aggressive, or helpful to those slow to requite helpfulness; but it might have been more prudent to persist for no longer than there was requital, or not even to start before requital was assured.

Now would it be a moral precept or not that, if only out of proper care for oneself, one ought to act on principles of wisdom and courage? That one ought to risk life in order to gain it? And, assuming a society of men acting fixedly on these principles but no others, would it or would it not contain men of moral virtue? One might as well ask, "Is a ski an article of footwear?" There is no more of a straight answer here than there. One may say, "Not quite"; and the point of saying this needs going into. But it would be more misleading to say, "Not at all." For it is part of the meaning of "moral precept" that it prescribes what a man would do in his wisdom—if he were to consider things widely, looking past the immediate concerns of self and giving essentials due weight before incidentals. As it is also part of what is meant by one's moral capacities that one can live by such considerations, it becomes fruitless after a time to press the point whether such precepts are properly called moral.

There are then varieties of the personal ought, differing in the considerations on which they are based and the qualities needed to follow them; and they all seem at least akin to a "moral" ought in their action-guiding force and function. But I grant that one does not want to speak of more than a kinship, and the point of this needs considering. One's hesitancy derives from various sources which have to be traced one by one.

Some of the hesitancy comes from contexts where one can say disparagingly, "He did this *only* for reasons of prudence, *only* for reasons of expediency, *only* for himself." This plainly applies sometimes, but it does not apply always. One would hardly say of someone without dependents, "He thought that he ought to save, but *only* for reasons of prudence"; or of someone, "He thought that he ought to have the carpenter in along with the plumber, but *only* for reasons of expediency or convenience"; or "He thought that he ought to become a doctor, but *only* because the career would suit him." "Only" has no point here. Why else should a man without dependents save, except to be prudent? Why else should anyone have the carpenter in along with the plumber, except for convenience? What better reason is there normally for choosing a career than that it will suit one? On the other hand, there is point in saying, "He held the peace only because it was prudent," "He saved only because it was convenient," "He practices the social virtues only for self-protection." It is plain why "only" applies here and is disparaging. One says "only" because something is done for the wrong or for not quite the right reason—done for *one* reason where there is *another* and nearer reason for doing it anyway. Personal reasons are often in this position, and then they are disparaged as inferior. One saves "only" because it is expedient, if one ought to have saved anyway for reasons of prudence. One holds the peace "only" because it was prudent when one ought to have done so anyway as a matter of principle and even if it had not been prudent. And one practices the social virtues "only" for self-protection when one does not *also* practice them for the general good.

The last case is different from the others. Plainly, one ought to practice the social virtues as principles of general good. But on none but perhaps pure Christian principles would it hold, or necessarily hold, that one ought to practice them on this ground unconditionally, however great the provocation to oneself. The case for the social virtues is weakened when the social environment becomes hostile and intractable by peaceable means; it is correspondingly strengthened where they can also be justified as wise principles of self-protection. That someone practices forbearance "only" as a wise principle of self-protection is not therefore to say that he practices it for a reason which is neither here nor there; but rather for a reason which falls short of all the reason there is. This was, in effect, the view of the old Natural Law moralists—Hooker, Grotius, Puffendorf: the social virtues derive joint support from our natural concern for our own good and for that of society. Hobbes streamlined this account by denying the second, which provoked subsequent moralists to deny the first. Both Hobbes's sophistical toughness and the well-bred innocence of the academic moralists since are distorted visions which are less convincing than the unsqueamish common sense of the philosophers and divines of earlier times.

3

So far we have met no reason for deprecating every personal ought. Men often have cause to be temperate, courageous, wise for their own good. This is often the only, or the nearest, reason why they should. It is then pointless to go on complaining, "But they still only act so for their own sakes." "Only" is a dangerous word.

Even so one feels that somehow a commitment that has only personal grounds is morally inferior. "One ought to risk one's life in order to gain it" seems near-moral enough. But compare it with "One ought to risk one's life in order to save others." This still seems different. And this is so not only because the one has a personal reason and the other has not, but also because where the reason is social rather than personal, the ought itself feels different—more binding, more relentless, and more properly called "moral" for this reason. The real inferiority of the personal ought seems here to lie in a lack of formal stringency.

There are such differences of stringency between "I ought to save, as I *want* to provide for my future" and "I ought to save, as I *ought* to provide for my children." The first prescribes saving as a means to an end which one *is* seeking; the second as a means to an end which in turn one *ought* to seek. The first therefore commits one formally less than the second. It leaves one at liberty to escape the commitment by renouncing the ultimate end, which the second does not. One may, as Kant did, call the first ought hypothetical and non-moral, and the second categorical and moral on account of this difference. The distinction is made to rest on a formal difference of the binding force and not at all on any material difference in the justifying grounds. The formally "moral" commitment is to an ultimate end or rule of life and to what one ought to do on account of it in any particular case.

Now the personal ought comes more typically as non-moral and the social ought as moral in form. One says, "You don't *want* to make your misery worse, so you ought not to dwell on it"; "You *want* to secure your future, so you ought to be prudent and save." One might also say "You *want* to provide for your children, so you ought to save"; and then formally this too would be a non-moral ought although its grounds are other-regarding. But this is the less typical case. One is often more grudging about the needs of others than one's own. So there is here less occasion for saying, "You ought to do this on account of an end which you *are* seeking"; and more for saying, "You ought to do it on account of an end which in turn you *ought* to seek."

This typical difference between the personal and the social ought raises two questions: one, whether it is an inherent feature of the personal ought to be never more than non-moral in form; the other, whether, even if this were so, it would be any the worse as a possibly serious commitment. Both of these positions have been taken. One's own good one always seeks. It is not therefore among the ends which one ever ought to seek in the absence of a sufficient inclination. But with the good of others, or the avoidance of harm to them, it is different. Here are ends which one does not always seek, but ought to seek all the same: ends which one may still have reason for seeking on their own account; which one would be led to seek on a diligently comprehending and imaginative review of them (of what doing good, or harm, inherently amount to). Only the social ought, therefore, may bind one to the choice of the final end as well as of the means, while the personal ought binds one only to the means on account of an end which one wants already. The personal ought is therefore only non-moral in form, and "only" once again signifies a defect. But all this is misleading. One does not always seek one's own good as much as one has reasonable ground for seeking it, and about this I shall say more later. But even supposing that one did, then all precepts of self-regard would prescribe what one ought to do consistently with an already desired end. But they would not therefore be negligible or improper all the time.

It is true that what one ought to do consistently with a

desired end need not be what one really ought to do at all. The end, or the means towards it, may prove undesirable on further scrutiny either by reason of what it is in itself or of the special circumstances of the case. I ought to save as I wish for security, and there is nothing inherently wrong with the end or the means, and so far so good. But I also ought to support my mother, and I cannot do both. Then maybe I ought not to do *all told* what otherwise I ought to have done. But in this case, the precept of prudence would have been less than "only" non-moral. It would have been invalid all told, and counter-moral altogether. But surely not every case is like this.

For often there is nothing wrong with the things which one cares for on one's own behalf, and one really does care for them. Even if one had the abstract option to give them up, one has no serious wish to do so. One often does care for one's life or health or career or the regard of others, and one often *may* without violating other claims. And one always *may* care, if one does, for one's peace of mind or self-respect. And so what one ought to do as far as these ends go one really ought to do. As one wants to live, one really ought to look after one's health. As one wants to be liked by others, one really ought to keep a civil tongue. As one wants to live after one's own fashion, one really ought to stick to one's vocation in adversity. As one wants to be able to respect oneself or, in Hume's phrase, "bear one's own survey," one really ought to conduct oneself as one thinks that one has good reasons for doing. All these precepts tell one what one ought to do consistently with a personal end which one actually has at heart; and where they hold after scrutiny, they hold no less validly and conclusively than any fully "moral" precept. The conscientious man would have to take notice of them no less than of the others. They deserve to be called "semi-moral" at least.

I keep allowing that a distinction remains. "I ought to work hard, as I *want* to succeed" is still a different kind of commitment from "I ought to work hard as I *ought* to provide for others." The difference is partly in the end, personal in the one case, impersonal in the other. But this quite apart, there is another reason for the difference. The second ought has a quality of sternness which is lacking from the first, and which is a product of its *form*, not of its *content*. For the second is an ought twice over. It says that one ought to take steps for an end which one ought to pursue ultimately. The first is an ought only once; it says that one ought to take steps for an end with regard to which one is at liberty as far as it goes. So the second ought subjects one to a regimen which is complete. It commits one *through and through*, whereas the semi-moral ought does not. And this through-and-throughness gives to the moral ought its notoriously stern flavor. It makes it more imposing and often more onerous. One is having one's socks pulled up all over. And additional qualities are required of one for appreciating it and acting on it: not only forethought and consistency, but also the ability to appreciate an end as committing by reason of its own nature, which, among other things, requires sympathetic understanding and imagination. No wonder that a moral ought inspires those confronted with it with awe. The semi-moral ought cannot compete with this, though when it comes to the precepts of wisdom and courage on one's own behalf they come near enough.

However, having given the formally moral ought its due, I want to add that respect for it should be no reason for slighting the other. For in the first place, and as a reassurance to those who regard lack of onerousness as a defect, though the semi-moral ought is not so bad, it may be bad enough. How hard it is to pull up one's socks does not necessarily depend on their number; two commodious socks may respond more readily than one shrunken one. One semi-moral and one moral case may serve as examples. If one really *wants* to do a thing and do it well, one ought to take trouble. And if one really *ought* to do good to the sick, one ought to telephone and inquire how they are getting on. The first requires a lot: putting oneself into harness, forgoing all sorts of things which one would rather do, particularly at that moment, coping with aches and pains and anxieties, playing the endless game of snakes and ladders with achievement, and yet going on, nursing one's purpose. The second, though in form a commitment through and through, requires nothing but getting up and dialing a number. It may need a great deal not to put things off, not to dwell on one's miseries, not to spend improvidently, all simply because one really ought not to in one's own best interest. The ought that lays down the law on these things may be little imposing in form. But such is the bulk of the stuff which compounds the "moral" inconveniences of ordinary life. And one also measures oneself and others by the show that is made on this front.

But then it is not the lack of onerousness as much as that of formal stringency that is felt to discredit the semi-moral ought. It still is not binding like the moral ought, simply as it is not committing through and through. Moreover, its very subservience to an end which is only desired seems something amiss, as if a man should rather act always for the sake of ends which he ultimately ought to seek, and not just of ends which he happens to be seeking even if nothing is wrong with them.

This sense of guilt about the non-obligatory rests partly on excessive zeal for original sin. What the natural man in one desires never can be quite as it should. It is always "Tell me what you want to do, and I shall tell you what you ought to do instead." But there is also a failure to see that not every semi-moral commitment is renounceable at will. Not every situation need confront one with a commitment through and through, and it is improper to demand that it should or to deplore that it does not.

When one ought to do a thing on account of some desired end, then one need not always be at liberty to escape the commitment by renouncing the end. It depends on whether one is free to give up the end itself, and this is not always so. One says of some ends, "If you want to seek it you may, and if you don't want to you need not." There is here no reason against seeking the end, nor reason enough to tell one to seek it in the absence of a desire for it. And one is free to escape a commitment on account of such an end simply by giving up the end. But in the case of other ends one will say, "If you want to seek it you may, but if you do not want to you still ought to all the same." Again there is no reason against seeking the end if one wants to, but here there would be still reason for seeking it even if one did not want to. A commitment on account of such an end one may not escape at will as one is not here free to give up the end. It is arguable whether commitments on personal grounds are not often in this position. One ought to be temperate as one wants to preserve one's health. And although this is a semi-moral ought as far as it goes, one need not be free to get out of it at will. For even if one ceased to care about the end, one might still here have reasonable ground for caring, and ought to care all the same.

An ought of this kind commits one on account of an end which one seeks as well as ought to seek. And this makes it like an ought through and through, but still not quite. There can be ends which one seeks and ought to seek. But insofar as one *is* seeking such an end, it is strained to say that one also *ought* to seek it at the same time. One would rather say that if one were not seeking it already, then one ought to be seeking it all the same. This is why, if someone is perfectly willing about an end, a commitment on account of this end would still not for him have the form of a commitment through and through; and this although it is potentially such a commitment and would turn into one as soon as he ceased to be readily inclined towards the end.

The point is that ought applies only where there is a case for pulling one's socks up. The same action may be viewed in otherwise the same circumstances either as one which one ought to do, or as one which one wants to and may do, according to the psychological starting point. One normally wants to have one's breakfast, and one would find it improper to have it put before one with the remark, "You ought to eat this morning." "Why ought I? Don't I eat every morning anyway?" But if one were convalescent, the remark would be in place. Nor would one say to a notoriously indulgent parent, "You ought not to be harsh with your children" (though one might wonder whether he *may* be so indulgent). The remark applies to a parent bad at controlling his temper. If I resolved to become an early riser and succeeded, I might report in retrospect, "For the first month it was a duty, but afterwards it ceased to be a duty and became a habit, if not a pleasure."

None of this should be surprising. Ought is an action-guiding concept. It expresses the notion that one is liable to direction by reasons in the case which would motivate one if one gave them due consideration. And one cannot be *liable* to direction by reasons except in a matter of doing what one is not fully motivated to do already. This is why it cannot be an obligation for one to do what one wants to do anyway, much as it might become an obligation for one to do it if one ceased to want to. This is also why, when one really wants to do something, the natural question to ask is not, "And *ought* I to do this thing?" but rather, "And *may* I do it?" or "Would there be anything wrong with it?" or "Ought I perhaps *not* to do it?" One looks for possible reasons against, not for possible reasons for. And what point would there be in doing anything more? When one really wants to do something, one already has, *for* doing it, all the reason one needs. And this is also why one only says "You ought to" to others when one takes it that there is a case for changing their present frame of mind. But to wonder whether one ought to (as distinct from wondering whether one may, or perhaps ought not to) where one already wants to would be like wondering whether to sit down when seated; and to say "You ought to" to someone quite ready to, would be like advising a sitting man to take a seat. *There is no ought for those blessed with wants which are not wrong.*

One may object: "But surely one can say that everyone ought to do good, and if there were benevolent people this would not make this false." And this is correct, but no refutation. What raises a problem are general statements like "People ought to do good," "One ought to be tolerant." But one may make a general statement without having to specify all the conditions when it shall or shall not hold. One says in general, "Butter will melt in the sun"; and if someone interjected, "But *not* when one has just melted it on the kitchen stove," this would be no rebuttal. "*This* butter will melt in the sun," when I am bringing it dripping from the kitchen, would be different. This particular butter is not *liable* to melt, even though it remains true that butter is. The same with "People ought to do good." This is a general statement, and one need not state the obvious: that it will not apply to someone whose heart needs no melting as it is soft already. Nor does one use "one ought to" directively to people, except for general purposes of propaganda. "I ought to" and "you ought to" are in a logically different class.

One makes general ought-statements about standard ends and practices towards which people commonly have no sufficient inclination. These ought-statements apply particularly to doing things for others, and less so to doing things for oneself. And this alone could explain why one normally does not say that people ought to care for their own good. For the question of whether they *ought* to does not here normally arise. They can be trusted with a modicum of well adjustment towards this end —they seek it, and, within limits, they may seek it. Hence, what one ought to do on account of one's own good is commonly a commitment on account of a desired end, much as it might also turn into a commitment through and through with a loss of immediate interest in the end. Nor could one reasonably hope that such commitments were more imposing in form than they are. On the contrary, one may say that the less imposing the ought, the better designed for living the man.

4

We are nearly out of the woods, but not quite. For the picture now before us still gives *Out* more than he can have. *Out* could say at this point: "By and large you have vindicated me. All your personal oughts are at best semi-moral. Only what one ought to do on account of others is in any way like what one morally ought to do. In fact, you have explained why this is so. Men are more immediately and unreflectively drawn towards their own good than towards that of others. So the pursuit of their own good as an end never comes to them as an obligation. But in the matter of considering others they need the full treatment. Here they must learn to care for the end as well as the means, and to care for the end even at cost to themselves. To do what serves social ends therefore comes as obligatory on one through and through. And this is the moral ought, the one that pulls one up without further question all along the line. However, you have convinced me on one point. Personal commitments need not always be negligible or discreditable. Sometimes one really ought to be prudent or courageous in one's own best interest, and the conscientious man ought to take notice of this and to conduct himself accordingly. So in a sense perhaps there is a personal as well as a social morality. But I still insist that the two are not on the same level, that only the social commitments are in every way properly 'moral,' and that only their neglect is a properly 'moral' failing."

This statement calls for two comments. The first is that *Out* is already loosening the hold on his position. He has to speak of morality in a strict and in a broader sense, and of the conscientious man as doing his share by both. And this rightly so. By a conscientious person one understands someone who will not be evasive about anything that he is convinced he really ought to do. He is the right-living man of the Greeks whose first commitment is to the principle of self-guidance by good and sufficient reasons. To observe his socially grounded commitments will be an imposing part of his job. But the whole job will be to conduct himself in line with all valid commitments, no matter whether they are imposing in form or not. One may say if one wishes that his properly "moral" commitments are only those which commit him through and through and out of regard for others. But then it must be granted that there is more to being a right-living person than only observing one's "moral" commitments; and that the neglect of a non-moral commitment, even if not strictly a "moral" failing, is nevertheless like one by being the evasion of a known commitment supported by valid reasons.

The second comment is that the case against *Out* needs pressing still further. It is also not the case that only the social commitments are ever fully moral in form. Commitments on personal grounds are less commonly so, because of the greater immediate regard which one has for oneself. One's own pain or unhappiness are closer to one than these same states in others. Unless they lie in the future it requires no effort of understanding and imagination to enable one to respond to them. But this immediate regard for oneself has its limits. Men may feel as unreasonably unconcerned for their own good as for that of others. Hume rightly spoke of "that narrowness of soul which makes us prefer the present to the remote"; and there are sick drives towards self-effacement and self-denial, so much so that it has been said that "man's inhumanity towards man is only equalled by his inhumanity towards himself." One meets the suggestion that everyone is at liberty to act as he will in the matter of his own life. But it would be odd if in this matter one were not liable to correction from a reflective appraisal of the nature of what one is doing. Men who are separated from their own good as an end may still have reasonable ground for seeking it in the absence of sufficient inclination. Their own good will then become something that they ought to seek and stand up for more than they are wont to or can readily bring themselves to; and to do the things which their own good requires will for them then become a commitment through and through.

It may also be that in a case like this someone ought to stand up for his own good even to the detriment of another. It could be sound advice to say to a woman in strife with herself and tied to a demanding parent, "You ought to consider yourself, and so break away now, hard as it may be on the parent." One is then saying more than simply, "If you wanted to you would have a right to." One is saying, "I know you are shrinking away from it, but this is what you ought to do, and above all else." In form this is an ought through and through, and an overriding one at that, but its ground is not other-regarding. And even true Christian charity might not here prescribe anything different. One cannot love one's neighbor as oneself if one has not also learned to accept one's own wishes as a proper object of respect and care, as one's own wishes are the paradigm of all wishes. There is a profound sense in which charity begins at home. For some this acceptance of themselves is hard, and it may confront them with a personal commitment as categorical and as onerous as any. Is this then a "moral" commitment or not? Here language fails one. For the usual conjunction between the categorical and the socially grounded commitment has come apart and turned into a clash. It is to strain the usual associations of language to the limit to speak of a moral commitment to put one's own good before that of another. But the unqualified refusal to call this a moral commitment is strained too and may be tendentiously misleading. For apart from not being grounded in regard for others, such a commitment may be precisely like the typical moral commitment in its cogency, its form and its action-guiding relevance.

There is still another type of case. One's own good comprises not only one's states but also the possession of one's self as a mind. One cannot earnestly wish to lose hold of oneself, to be reduced to a shaky mess when in trouble; one needs to be in control and to be able to cope with whatever may come. And this preservation of oneself as a capable ego is also something that one may find that one ought to care for when one is too driven or despondent to be inclined to care for it. Kant spoke of the duties of self-perfection, the commitments which subserve the protection of one's rational nature; and he did not hesitate to include them among one's moral duties along with the social ones. And this quite consistently so, as here is a type of concern for oneself for which one has reasonable ground though one is not always ready for it by inclination. Moreover, this type of personal commitment is morally relevant in a special way. For among the duties of self-perfection is the conscientious man's commitment to live without evading any issue—to seek out and weigh what cogent reasons would lead him to do, and to submit himself without self-deception or evasion to their determination. One cannot derive that one ought to live in this manner from one's special obligations towards others. For one may never duly confront any of one's special obligations unless one is already willing to live that way. All principled conduct which is reasoned practice and not just well-bred habit turns on this commitment as its pivot. It involves the acceptance of the principle of non-escapism as an over-all rule of life. And this commitment has the most intimately personal reason. It rests on an individual's inmost concern to preserve himself intact as a living and functioning self: mentally in possession of himself and of his world, able to look at himself and what he is doing without having to hide himself from himself. The penalty for slighting this need is his undoing as a person.

And now is one still to say that only what one ought to do with a view to the good of others can have the *cogency and force* of the "moral" commitment? The claim has been further reduced. Only most commitments which are committing through and through rest on other-regarding considerations. There can also be such commitments which rest on personal considerations, and they may on occasion take precedence over one's social commitments. And there is one commitment whose ground is intimately personal and which comes before any other personal or social commitment whatsoever: the commitment to the principled mode of life as such. One is tempted to call this the supreme moral commitment, but if no commitment may count as "moral" unless one has it on account of others, then the commitment to the practice of non-evasive living cannot properly count as a "moral" commitment at all.

That the social commitments make up the bulk of the formally imposing ones is, of course, a fact which one has no reason to deny. The good of others is the standard case of an end towards which men commonly find themselves less drawn by inclination than committed to on due reflection, through the exercise of understanding and imagination. But it illuminates the logic of the case that this is so as a matter of fact and of none else. Suppose that we were made the opposite of the way we are: that we were concerned about the good of others as immediately as we are now concerned about our own, and were concerned about our own good no more readily than we are now about that of others. Then the whole moral machine would be working busily in reverse. The bulk of the formerly imposing duties would be those which prescribe the subordination of our excessive regard for others to a proper regard for ourselves. Morality, in effect, would no longer serve primarily an order of mutual consideration, but the protection of the individual from being overwhelmed by his social sentiments. Nietzsche's transvaluation of all values was the claim that the hidden facts were such as to make this morality's real task. "Men are too weak-minded to be self-seeking." Their besetting vice is morbid pity, a guilty fear of their own wishes, self-hate, and resentment against others under the guise of concern. The moral machine needs putting into reverse.

I am not saying with Nietzsche that it does, though it may well with some. My point is rather to insist that a morality, if by this we mean a reasoned body of action-guiding principles and commitments, is always a morality for someone; and a morality for humans is one for humans. This is why in our morality, and in spite of Nietzsche, the socially grounded commitments have a special place. They are, even if not the only, the standard case of what reflective human beings meet as committing through and through. But this is so because men are what they are and their situation is what it is: because they do not live alone; because they can identify themselves with the concerns of others and of the communities of which they are members and can care about them; and because they can learn to care as much as they are able to by learning to comprehend. One commonly takes it that materially moral or social reasons are in some measure ought-implying for everyone. And this is fair enough if taken as a regulative principle, or presumption, with a massive, if incomplete, backing in experience. The presumption is that such reasons can be treated as standard reasons; that anyone can be taken to be accessible to them (although to an extent for which there is no standard measure) unless he is willfully uncomprehending, mentally disordered, or immature for reasons of age or cultural background. But there can be no demonstrative certainty of this being so. The case of an otherwise human being congenitally inaccessible to other-regarding considerations may be treated as *incredible*, but not as *inconceivable*.

There is also, however, the suggestion that one means by "moral" reasons more than this. "Moral" reasons are considerations of social good which are always binding, and in case of conflict with personal good, always *overridingly* binding on every reflective human being alike. But while one may *conceive* of moral reasons in these terms, there is nothing gained by doing so. For no conceptual gerrymandering can settle what will then be the crucial question, namely, whether what is here termed a "moral" reason is a concept applicable to human beings; and, if so to any extent, then by way of anything but a massively grounded presumption.

One may still say that the social commitments are the only "moral" ones properly so called. One is then making a *material* criterion a necessary condition for applying "moral" to a commitment. A "moral" commitment must not only be validly action-guiding and committing through and through; it must also be incurred on account of others. By this language rule, "moral" is used to mark off the species of social grounded commitments from the genus of validly action-guiding commitments in general. That there is this language rule is not disputed. The sole point at issue is that one should not be misled by it. The rule entails that none but the socially grounded commitments are properly "moral," but only for a reason which does not imply that they alone are seriously cogent, or committing through and through, or that they alone can take precedence in a proper calculus of action-guiding considerations. No answers to the questions, "How ought one to live?" and "What ought one to do?" must be taken as prejudged by the semantic taboo on calling a personally grounded commitment strictly "moral." No real-life possibility is excluded by the insistence that a Nietzschean "morality" would not properly be a "morality" at all. The question of what can or cannot be validly action-guiding principles and commitments for a reflective and human being is not settled by appeal to a linguistic convention.

5

I have argued that one may say that only the socially grounded ought is properly "moral"; but that, if the only reason for this is semantic, nothing substantial follows. Personal considerations, though not called "moral," could still be as seriously choice-supporting and binding on one as properly moral ones. But this conclusion may still seem unconvincing. One may object that we simply do not think that doing the right thing by oneself is ever *binding* on one in the same way as doing the right thing by others. In the matter of acting as we ought on our own account we consider ourselves free and not responsible to anyone. But in the matter of acting as we ought on account of others we consider ourselves obligated and responsible to them. This suggests that the personal and the social ought are not after all on the same footing; that the social ought carries with it an added authority which derives from the very fact that it is social, and that this is implied in calling it alone "moral."

It remains to be shown that here is another line of argument for the non-formalist, like *Out*, to follow; that this line of argument is indispensable to the understanding of the complex phenomenon that morality is; but that its ultimate relevance must not be overrated.

One may argue as follows. There is one plain difference between ought-abiding conduct in social and in personal matters. Other people have a stake in the first which they have not in the second. Their legitimate interests are involved in our social conduct; they hold us accountable for doing the right thing by them. This applies particularly to those rules and practices which, in a given society, are regarded as the backbone of the social order. Society credits its mature members with the ability to appreciate that they ought to respect these rules for their social merits. If they violate them without valid excuse they act counter to what others have a stake in their doing; and they are made responsible for their conduct. One may ask them to justify themselves, admonish and censure them. And this is why it may be said that the social ought alone is called moral; not only because it is social, but also because it has a special authority. When it comes to respect for social rules and the good of others, society obligates one to act as one ought on pain of moral sanctions. One is here, as it were, doubly bound; by the voice of reason and by the majesty of the law; by the knowledge that one ought to, and by one's accountability to others for doing it. None of this applies to one's conduct in the matter of acting as one ought on one's own account. One is not here socially obligated; one is a morally bad and socially guilty person for not acting as one ought.

Contemporary writers like Hart [2] are inclined to make this point more strongly. They suggest that the sense in which social ought-abidance is *obligatory*, and personal ought-abidance not, is the only proper sense of this term. Traditional philosophy, it is said, has ignored that "ought" and "obligation" are different concepts. Ought-language is "teleological"; only obligation-language is "deontological." That one ought to do something is to say that it is the "best" or "reasonable" thing to do, but not yet that one is obligated or bound to do it. Words like "obligation" or "duty" are at home in legal or quasi-legal contexts and apply only to social injunctions or prohibitions. Any other use of them is a philosopher's extension of language, a use which is as unwarranted as it is misleading. "Duties" are something assigned to one, "obligations" something imposed on one. Both are liabilities created by a public rule or requirement, or liabilities which one incurs by giving rise to claims against oneself as in giving a promise, or becoming a husband or father. It will then follow that a moral *obligation* can be only a liability created by a social rule or demand on one; and that what makes this liability "moral" is that its force derives from moral sanctions or from an internalized sense of moral propriety. The definitive authority which one associates with moral injunctions and prohibitions will then derive solely from this source. There may be things which one ought to do even on a desert island; but one is not bound, let alone morally bound, to do them outside a social context which alone can create an obligation.

Here, then, seems to be another way of diagnosing the formalist's error. He assumes correctly that moral judgments have a special authoritative role. And he argues from this that every authentic and definitive ought-judgment is a moral judgment. But it now turns out that no ought-judgment, whether its grounds are personal or social, has the characteristic force of a moral judgment. Moral judgments relate to obligations; ought-judgments only to what is "reasonable" or "best." Even what one ought to do on account of others is a *moral* ought only insofar as one is socially answerable for doing it. What falls within morality is only a segment of ought-abiding conduct. And what segment this is, what will count as *morally* obligatory or permissible, will be settled exclusively by our looking over our shoulders for the frowns and smiles of the social order. I doubt that those who press for a sharp distinction between "ought" and "obligation" would wish to go all the way with this conclusion. But this conclusion is implicit, and, given the premises, not easily avoided. If the conclusion seems extreme, the question is, Why?

There is rarely smoke without a fire: social ought-abidance plainly is of social concern, and blame and admonition have a place in it. Equally plainly, personal ought-abidance is treated differently. Our evasions here count as amicable vices, and not as moral turpitude. We may take the censure of others amiss, and require them to mind their own business. And the same with their admonitions. To say "you ought to" to another is always a kind of interference; and the propriety of *saying so* (as distinct from having a judgment about it) varies with the case. Ought-judgments and ought-speech, ought-judgments and judgments of blame or of praiseworthiness have different and variable functions. Again, the language of "ought" and "obligation" is infected with these distinctions. There is a sense in which obligations are social liabilities, and moral obligations such liabilities as are morally sanctioned. In this sense one has no obligation, moral or otherwise, to do the right thing by oneself. Nor has one, in this sense, a moral obligation to do everything that one's social conscience may tell one to do. Society only requires our conscientiousness in standard situations; it treats deeds which only an exceptionally sensitive regard for others would prescribe as acts of superarrogation. To devote one's life to the care of lepers is praiseworthy but "beyond the call of duty." But, true as this may be, this fashionable observation also shows the limitations of the view. We do not conceive of moral obligations as only dependent on social requirements and their external or built-in sanctions. Saints and heroes go beyond these in what they judge they must or ought to do. And it would be farfetched to say that, when they follow their judgment, they are not doing what they think is their duty. "Duty" and "obligation" are not words unequivocally tied to the socially obligatory.

Nor is the "morally permissible" tied only to the socially welcome. There may be occasions when someone may validly judge that he ought to put his own good before that of another. Here others may not readily welcome his ought-abidance. They may have a stake in discouraging it and be tempted to censure. But, granted that one accepts the authenticity of his judgment, one will here forbear censure, and consider him morally justified. The measure of moral justification is here his conviction that he ought to. But it is well to note how this case puts the social orientation of our moral thinking under stress. The upright deviant from social norms and interests is not judged "morally bad," but not "morally good" or "praiseworthy" either. We have to grant to others, as we must insist on for ourselves, that conscientious ought-abidance is the supreme moral rule for any agent in the situation of choice. But, socially, such conduct need not be an unmixed blessing. And if we may not condemn it on moral grounds, we need not bless it either. "Moral goodness" is a term of appraisal so geared to socially welcome conduct that not every morally *correct* choice makes one a morally *good* man.

There seems to be, then, a sense in which "ought" and "moral obligation" are not sharply separable; though there also is another in which they are distinct, and in which social ought-abidance has the added force of an obligation. How then do these two senses relate to one another? The question may be answered by considering the view that what gives to the social ought the force of a special *obligation* adds significantly to its action-guiding authority. For while this view is correct in one way, it is false in another. While social ought-abidance is required of us socially, we are surely not bound to it *only* on this account. The social ought differs in this respect from the obligations created only by law or custom. One has a legal obligation simply by being required by an appropriate public rule. But with the things which one ought to do on social grounds this is not so. What is here socially required of one is moral conduct: conduct in line with what one ought and can be reasonably expected to know that one ought to do. The very requirement presupposes that one has already an antecedent obligation to do it, insofar, namely, as one knows already that one ought to do it.

This would have seemed plain language in the past. What then is at issue in debarring us from using it? The traditional philosopher may have been guilty of an unidiomatic extension language in speaking here of an antecedent commitment or obligation. He may well have made light of the common or garden use of these terms for a liability created by an external rule. But sometimes an unidiomatic extension of language is less misleading than a narrow insistence on linguistic propriety; and if there is cause for complaint here the cure seems worse than the disease. The traditional philosopher wanted to bring out that if a deliberative person ought to do a thing he is to this extent also bound to do it *in some manner*. He is facing, if not a conventional, then a "natural" duty or obligation. And this extension of language has a warrant. Where one has an obligation or commitment to do something one is up against a characteristic constraint or limitation of one's freedom to act otherwise. And some language is needed to make the point that the demands or assignments of others are neither the only nor the most decisive form in which this constraint can be incurred.

A person who is obligated to do something is under a constraint which is not purely psychological or physical. He need not feel impelled to do it, he is not made to do it by main force, it is not causally impossible for him to act otherwise. The constraint is conceived as latent rather than actual, and as arising not from causes, but from reasons. The situation has features which *tell* for or against some action: they need not determine a person's choice, but they would if he knew them and took careful account of them. A deliberative person who can appreciate that he has such reasons will meet in them a latent limitation of his freedom to act otherwise. Obligations in the common or garden sense are a special case of this. One meets a constraining reason in a social rule or demand on one which one can ill afford to ignore. Such obligations are imposed on one from without. The rule or demand issues from others; their insistence is the feature in the situation which supplies as well as creates the reason which limits one's freedom of action. But not all liability to direction by known reasons is like this. There are choice-guiding considerations which are not first imported into the situation by others with a view to direct one: they exist and can be found in the nature, effects, and implications of actions and principles themselves. A deliberative person need not wait for others to bring them to his notice; nor in being guided by them is he doing their bidding. That he is up against such reasons for doing things is equivalent to saying that he ought to do them, of his own accord and prior to being asked. This is why one may speak of a "natural obligation": of an *obligation* because a person is up against a latent limitation of his freedom by reasons; of a *natural* obligation because the limitation is the work here not of *anyone*, but of reasons to be found antecedently in the nature of the case.

Where one *ought* to do things on account of others, one is therefore *socially obligated* to do only what one has an antecedent natural obligation to do already. One is answerable to others, as someone against whom they have legitimate claims, precisely because one ought, and can know that one ought, to give them consideration to begin with. And this is why one's answerability to them cannot here significantly add to the weight and authority of one's commitment. It may do so *de facto*. When a person hesitates to do what he has no doubt that he ought to do, the reminder that he is accountable to others is a potent consideration. The mere thought of incurring recrimination and blame evokes apprehension and guilt. But these are not considerations to increase the force of a moral commitment *de jure*. A reflective person has no need of coercive reasons for acting as he ought. He does not require the fear of blame as a reason for not evading his own better judgment. And this is also why the absence of coercive reasons, where one ought to do things on one's own account, or on account of others, but beyond the call of conventional duty, could not allow one seriously to breathe a sigh of relief. Whatever one judges that one seriously ought to do, whether the reasons for doing it are ultimately social or personal, whether one is socially blameworthy for the omission or not, one is sufficiently committed to do and responsible to oneself for doing unasked. It is inconsistent with the concepts of mature moral thinking to keep looking for the differentia of the authority of the moral commitments in one's social answerability for observing them.

6

I am saying "with the concepts of mature moral thinking" advisedly. For the complex fabric of moral thinking contains still another notion of the moral bond. And the view that moral commitments have a special authority which derives from the sanctioned demands of the social order keeps drawing support from it. In fact, here is the primary concept of the moral bond, the one from which it derives its name, and the one which comes first, not only in the history of the race, but also in that of the individual. For as one grows up this is what happens. Father says, "Don't lie, don't be slovenly." Mother says, "This is what father says." The world says, "Don't be promiscuous." Father says, "This is what everyone says, this is also what God says." Father also says, "Do what God says," and, he says, "God says, 'Do what father says.' " Here is a mixed barrage of requests made on one or reported to be made on one. They specify what one is to do or not to do. They come from "out there," though their precise imponent is obscure. They are addressed to one not without heat and are backed not by main force, like the law, but by moral suasion—smiles or frowns, approval or disapproval, the promise of bestowing or the threat of withdrawing love. And in these requests everyone first meets the demands of "morality." They are the first model for the notions of "moral law" and "moral duty," the first standard of "moral right" and "moral wrong." They create the moral obligations in their primary sense: as restrictions on one's freedom of action by the "mores" or "manners" of a social group. These obligations are like the legal obligations in being barriers against license maintained by social consensus for the protection of the social order. They only differ from them by the kind of sanctions employed, and by the absence of institutional procedures for their promulgation, codification, and administration.

Confusion keeps arising from the complex relations between the primary moral bond and the commitments of a reflective person by cogent considerations. As one's understanding develops one becomes acquainted and learns to live with both, yet without learning to keep them distinctly apart. One's moral commitments, in the mature sense, may oblige one to defer to the same rules on which the mores insist. In fact, this is how they come to be called "moral" commitments. The notion of the natural moral commitment arrives on the logical scene when it comes to be understood that a person who can use his own judgment does not need the insistence of the mores to defer to the rules which they prescribe. There are reasons why he ought to do so unasked, and, if not, then there are reasons why he ought to defer to other rules more adequate to the underlying social purposes of the moral code. This is how the word "moral" is transferred from the one level to the other. The commitments of a reflective person, by social considerations especially, are called "moral" because they incorporate and supersede the obligations by the mores in their role of protecting the social order. Social reasons become "moral" reasons, and the powers of mind and agency on which unforced self-direction by reasons depends, become "moral powers" on account of their continuity of function with the purposes of primary morality. But these new connotations are acquired at the loss of others. The new-style moral commitment is no longer a creation of the social order. To call it "moral" is no longer to imply that its *authority* depends on the apprehension of guilt for the violation of a public rule. It is "moral" as backed by considerations which, while prior to the demands of primal morality, are favorable to its purposes; and it has authority if and when these considerations prove cogent on a due appraisal of the case.

This is how the word "moral" acquires its multiple associations. Such notions as the "moral order," or "moral rule," may all be viewed in *two ways:* as a body of rules or a rule publicly maintained by moral force; and as a body of rules or a rule which the members of a group ought, and can be expected to know that they ought, to respect unasked. Each time, the moral commitment to defer to the rule may be said to arise from the "requirements of the social order." But the ambiguities of this expression easily pass unnoticed. In the one case, the commitment arises from what the *will* of society "requires," i.e., insists on. In the other, it arises from what the *needs* of society "require," i.e., causally presuppose for their satisfaction, and from what a due appraisal of these needs "requires" one to do, i.e., provides one with telling reasons for doing. Both notions are settled parts of ordinary thought, in which the mind moves hazily from viewing the morally right or wrong as being so by a rule whose violation makes him socially guilty to viewing it as being so by a rule to which he ought to conform anyway. Moreover, the primary associations of "moral" are so ingrained that it is hard to appreciate that there really is a level on which public demands and the apprehension of incurring social guilt are irrelevant to the authority of a commitment considered as "moral." There is a standing temptation for the philosopher no less than for the ordinary person to import the quasi-legal features of the primary model into the mature one and to expect them to persist where they no longer have a place.

What furthers confusion is that even in the mature perspective the action-guiding role of the mores is not entirely superseded. There is a presumption (of which one can make too much as well as too little) that a rule strongly insisted on by the mores will also have valid prior reasons in its favor. And there is ground for caution in pitting one's own judgment too readily against the presumptive wisdom of the moral code. A commitment to a rule of the mores on this ground is still, in a way, created for one by the moral code. But there is a difference. The existence of the moral code is here no longer the *ratio essendi* of a moral commitment viewed as primal. It is rather that the moral code has become the *ratio cognoscendi* of a moral commitment on the level of maturity. A moral education is commonly a training in the mores as a first guide to what one is to do or not to do. But it will be a moral education in quite different senses, depending on whether one is introduced to the moral code simply as a body of morally sanctioned demands, or as a first, though by no means the last, ground for the determinations of mature moral thinking.

I have argued that the mature moral commitments are incurred through the unforced appreciation of cogent reasons in the case. Their authority owes nothing to the coercive moral pressures. They are roughly called "moral" because they are commitments which supersede the primary moral law in its action-guiding role. But the question of why and when they strictly deserve this name cannot well be settled.

We are inclined to conceive of morality by the joint application of two criteria. "Moral" principles commit one in a special and cogently authoritative manner; and they commit one in this manner to conduct which is, or is held to be, socially desirable. This concept is applicable well enough to primary morality. The primary moral law (on its own level and by its own means) supplies an authoritative rule of life which obligates everyone alike, and in the social interest. The coincidence between rules with moral force and in the service of social ends can here be counted on: it is contrived, albeit unwittingly, and where it is wanting it can be mended. One can define morality, on the primary level, as authoritative action-guidance whose function is to regulate the social order. But morality, on the mature level, is less well-conceived in this way. There are difficulties in uniting the authoritative and the social associations of "moral" in one concept.

It is plainly not the principal function of mature morality to protect the social order, if by the "function" of a practice is meant the reason why it exists and is carried on. The commitments by cogent reasons in the case are not imposed on one from without for social ends. One incurs them, if through anyone's doing, through one's own: as someone willing to seek direction from the counsel of cogent reasons. The involvement of human beings in this practice is personal: it turns on their stake in the kind of self-preservation which requires that one should be able to bear before oneself the survey of one's own actions. Responsibly reason-guided and ought-abiding living exists, in the first place, for the sake of sane and ordered individual being, and not for the regulation of the social order. Nor is the coincidence between ought-abiding living and the social interest axiomatic.

The fact—which traditional moral philosophy seems almost to exist to dispute away—*is that primary morality has no unequivocal successor on the level of autonomous choice.* The "moral law" (whether the actual law of the tribe, or the ideal law that would best suit its needs) has no identical counterpart in a "law of our own nature." It is true that the commitments by non-coercive reasons (like the primary moral law) supply a *definitive* guide to conduct on their level; and that where they have other-regarding grounds, they are in the *social interest.* But the agreement between the definitive commitments on this level and those typically geared to the social interest is not here guaranteed. The agreement is not contrived; the social order cannot lay down what reflective choice shall bid a mature person do, or for what reasons. Nor is the agreement logically necessary. Valid ought-judgments rest on the backing of choice-supporting reasons: of facts in the case which can dispose those who know and review them in favor of or against the choice. There is therefore no logical limit to what may be a valid ought. The care of others may be a valid ought for one, and so may be the proper care of oneself. Either end may manifestly direct one to seek it on a diligently comprehending view of it. Either, or both, may be valid premises for a particular ought-judgment. One may be conscientiously ought-abiding in serving one's community, or in seeking personal salvation behind the walls of a Buddhist retreat. Considerations of prudence and wisdom may relevantly add to the reasons why one ought to practice the social virtues, along with reasons of humanity and compassion. What is judged a valid ought, on a due appraisal of the facts and their force for one as deciding reasons, may have all manner of grounds; it may protect individual as well as social needs; it need not be the same for everyone alike. Nor need every ought be an ought for one through and through in order to be a seriously cogent ought, and among one's responsibilities as a right-living, reason-guided person. The ought-judgments which are formally imposing and backed by materially moral considerations are the standard case for human beings of the formally imposing ones; but they are no more than a species of the broad genus "definitively action-guiding ought-judgments."

Is one to say then that the mature moral enterprise is the general practice of conscientiously ought-abiding living? Or that it is only the part of it which is socially beneficial and a matter of active social concern? Are the mature moral commitments those which *formally*, or only those which *formally and materially*, continue the job of the primary moral law? Usage here leans uneasily either way. That man is a "moral agent" with "moral freedom" is associated with his power for responsible self-direction. "Moral strength" or "moral weakness" are terms which relate to the exercise of this power. But the "morally good man" connects with the "selfless man." The "moral" commitments of a mature person are conceived as essentially self-incurred through the responsible exercise of his moral powers and also as grounded in regard for others. There are those who insist that mature morality is socially beneficial ought-abidance: that language prescribes a material as well as a formal criterion for the use of "moral." There are others who will call "moral" any definitive and "authentic" commitment of a self-directing person, whether its grounds are social or personal.

Here is a semantic issue which it is far more important to understand than to take sides on. For whatever one says—whether it is the more consonant with ordinary language or not—must be semantically disquieting. Usage (at any rate, current English usage) backs the non-formalist more than the formalist. The mature moral commitments are those to conduct which is of social concern: they are properly called "moral" *as they supersede the primary moral law in its social role*. This usage is unexceptionable as long as its implications are faced. The *moral* and the *definitive* commitments on the mature level need not then coincide. One must grant that "morality" on this level is demoted from its accustomed place of being the sole and final arbiter of right and wrong choice. This is why, much as the non-formalist has semantically a case, the formalist has one too. He is opting for the other horn of the dilemma. The moral commitments on the mature level are *those which supersede the primary moral law in its role of supplying an authoritative and supreme rule of life*. And this rule is in the definitive—but not necessarily only materially moral—commitments which a reflective person incurs on a non-evasive appreciation of all the reasons in the case; and, in the last analysis, in his first commitment to the "authentic" way of life itself.

If both alternatives are repugnant, it is because both fall short of expectations. The unequivocal successor to the primary moral law should be a commitment by non-coercive reasons, manifestly binding on everyone alike, to give precedence always to the claims of beneficence and the requirements of social living. But there is no warrant for assuming such a commitment on the level of autonomous choice. The rules of language cannot furnish it any more than pure reason, or intuition. The hard fact is that the rational and autonomous mode of life overlaps, but no longer necessarily coincides, with the moral mode of life as conceived from the point of view of the social interest. The autonomous agent can be a debatable social asset. It is vain to expect morality on all levels to do the same kind of job as the institution of the law. The concept of morality itself bears the accumulated scars of conceptual evolution. Its multiple associations are a bar to summing it up in any one way.

NOTES

1. For the use of "ought," compare my " 'Ought' and Motivation" (1947–48) in *Readings in Ethical Theory*, ed. W. S. Sellars and J. Hospers (New York: Appleton-Century-Crofts, 1952), pp. 492–510; "Goading and Guiding," *Mind*, n.s. LXII (1953), 145–171; and "Morality and Convention," *The Journal of Philosophy*, LVII (1960), 675–685. Parts of the last paper have been incorporated in the present essay.
2. H. L. A. Hart, "Legal and Moral Obligation," *Essays in Moral Philosophy*, ed. A. I. Melden (Seattle: University of Washington Press, 1958), p. 82.

3

THE CONCEPT OF MORAL OBJECTIVITY*

H. D. Aiken *Harvard University*

"That God is the creator of the world and its provident Ruler; that the eternal law commands the natural order to be maintained, and forbids that it be disturbed; that the last end of men is a destiny far above human things and beyond this sojourning upon earth; these are the sources and these the principles of all justice and morality."

Pope Leo XIII

"Morality . . . is mere symptomatology."

Friedrich Nietzsche

"Welcome O life! I go to encounter for the millionth time the reality of experience and to forge in the smithy of my soul the uncreated conscience of my race."

James Joyce

* Grateful acknowledgment is made to Alfred A. Knopf, Inc., for permission to reprint this essay, which appeared in *Reason and Conduct*, a collection of Professor Aiken's essays, published in October 1962.

INTRODUCTION

What are ordinary persons, including philosophers in their ordinary moments, doing when they raise doubts about the objectivity of particular moral judgments? And how, as moral agents and critics, do they go about resolving such doubts? These questions, one would think, must occur to anyone who in an idle moment bethought himself about the nature of moral objectivity. Yet in spite of the interminable debate between the ethical objectivists and their critics, or more likely for that very reason, its participants seem rarely, if ever, to come in sight of them. In the case of the subjectivists this is hardly surprising, since it would be fatal to their cause to admit that such questions may be seriously raised at all. But the objectivists make no use of this advantage; in fact they manage merely to create the impression that the notion of moral objectivity is question-begging. The reason for this is evident: no objectivist has examined the use of the concept of objectivity in moral contexts without preconceptions about its generic meaning derived from a continuing philosophical tradition for which formal logic and natural science have provided not only exemplary but paradigm cases of objective discourse. Suppose that we challenge these presuppositions: Why, for example, should it be assumed in advance of analysis that moral judgments cannot be objective unless such words as "right" and "good" are terms of "objective reference" or unless such judgments are true or false statements about something called "objective reality"? For that matter, why should we not take that reality to be whatever, in context, answers to our objective questions? Why should we assume that proper application of the concept of objectivity in all contexts involves the notion of a consensus of "competent," "rational," or "ideal" observers? And, if not, why must we assume that meaningful application of the concept involves definitive disciplinary procedures or rules to which anyone who sets up for a moralist is logically bound to submit?

When I first came within range of the ideas underlying the

preceding remarks, they at once appeared to me to open a path through a swamp of controversy to a firm and neutral ground where I could proceed without ado to a constructive analysis of the concept of moral objectivity. The questions raised at the beginning of this paper seemed completely irenic; they were calculated, so I thought, not to increase pre-existing philosophical doubts about the possibility of objective moral judgments, but rather to allay them. For if these questions can be asked at all, then such doubts, as well as the controversies to which they give rise, must surely be both gratuitous and perverse. The implication, plainly, is that instead of endlessly arguing whether, in principle, objective moral judgments are possible, philosophers would do better to ask themselves how a serious problem about the objectivity of morals could even arise. But there precisely is the rub. Whether or not my questions are neutral, they at any rate are not pointless. Why not? Let us consider an analogy. Why is it that since Plato there has been no philosophical interest or stake in the concept of mud? To be sure, lexicographers have asked (and to their satisfaction, have quickly found answers to the question), "What is the meaning of 'mud'?" But among philosophers only Plato has ever thought of asking that question, and he did so without staying for an answer, merely in order to illustrate a point. The philosophical interest in the concept of moral objectivity is of another sort. In this essay I am not trying to illustrate a point at all, but rather to resolve genuine philosophical doubts, not only about the meaning, but also about the meaningfulness of the concept of moral objectivity. The fact is that philosophers, unlike lexicographers, never inquire into the meaning of any concept in a purely speculative frame of mind. For them there are always two questions to be asked: (1) "What is the meaning of 'X'?" and (2) "Why ask such a question?" This means that within a philosophical context no question about the meaning of a word, or the use of an expression, is ever purely irenic, and no answer to it is significant until it is shown how it bears upon the perplexities, at once intellectual and practical, that dispose us to ask it. Indeed, it is only its power to resolve such perplexities that convinces us that the answer itself is substantially correct. The trouble is that the perplexities themselves prevent us from seeing where the answer lies.

These remarks apply directly to the case at hand. There would be no philosophical reason to undertake an analysis of the concept of moral objectivity were it not for the widespread, morally destructive doubts about the meaningfulness of such a concept. Such doubts may once have been gratuitous; they are so no longer. On the contrary, philosophical preconceptions about the nature and conditions of any objective discourse have, in one form or another, so conditioned our thinking that laymen, as well as philosophers, take it for granted that rejection of ethical objectivism automatically commits us to the thesis that, despite appearances, moral objectivity is an illusion and hence that the ordinary language of morals is systematically misleading. Thus, those who accept the responsibilities of objective judgment in morals have been impelled, as in the case of the authorities of the Roman Catholic Church, to pretend that their own principles are laws of nature or definitive principles of morals which cannot be challenged without declaring one's immorality or else one's incompetence as a moral being. On the other hand, those who regard all such positions as morally untenable on the ground that they profoundly jeopardize the principle of moral autonomy or freedom, seem thereby committed to some form of moral subjectivism which precludes us, on principle, from asking whether our judgments and principles are objective.

Meanwhile our ordinary moral practices are hobbled for want of a clear and morally suitable conception of their critique, and the whole institution of morality gradually acquires the appearance of a system of arbitrary dicta which have not yet attained the status of positive laws. The moralist is demoted to the rank of a busybody who has fortunately not yet discovered his vocation for politics, and the immoralist assumes the status of cultural hero whose bad conscience is treated as a red badge of courage. The rest of us—which, I suspect, includes practically everyone for whom neither immorality nor morality is a vocation—find ourselves, when we reflect, involved in a practical dilemma which forces us to vacillate perpetually between the bad conscience of objectivism and the equally bad conscience of subjectivism. Our unhappy situation is this: we wish to honor, indeed, we cannot escape, the obligation to be objective in our moral decisions; yet we seem unable to do so without at the same time committing ourselves to a conception of morality which, if taken seriously, destroys our autonomy as moral agents and critics. On the other hand, we find ourselves committed to a principle of moral freedom which apparently dooms us to acquiesce in a radical ethical subjectivism that renders meaningless the very effort to search for objective moral judgments.

This predicament, let me emphasize, is not merely theoretical but practical; or better, the problems with which it confronts us are not speculative problems about moral discourse, but theoretical problems that arise within it whenever we are obliged by moral necessity to go to the fundamental principles underlying our moral practices. Until they are solved—or resolved—judicious men who wish to view moral reflection as a part of the life of reason must continue to have grave, even paralyzing, doubts about the mutual consistency of the basic critical practices from which our familiar notions of the moral life are ultimately derived. Thus, although I still take seriously the questions posed at the beginning of this essay and presently hope to find answers to them, it would be philosophically pointless to proceed to a constructive analysis of the concept of moral objectivity without regard to the philosophical perplexities which provide the only reason for analyzing it. This delay, however, is not without its reward. For, as I have found, it is precisely by facing these perplexities that we come gradually in sight of a conception of moral objectivity to which, without illusion, practicing moralists, as well as moral philosophers, can give credence.

My first task, then, will be to spell out the ethical antinomy which gives rise to the question how objective moral judgments are possible. My second task will be to find a way out of this antinomy which, without compromising what seems essential to the principles of moral autonomy, nevertheless preserves intact the basic minimal claims embodied in the principles of moral objectivity. Such a solution, of course, is possible only at a price. In this case, fortunately, the price is not exorbitant; indeed, it can be readily paid without in the least compromising what remains of our common moral sense. The conclusion to which I am forced is that, at least so far as ethics is concerned, traditional philosophical notions concerning the meanings of the terms "objective" and "subjective" must be abandoned once and for all, and that neither empirical science nor formal logic can any longer serve philosophers as *the* models of objective discourse. I shall argue that it is precisely the uncritical application of such notions, and the noetic models from which they are derived, beyond the domains of science and logic, that is ultimately responsible for the widespread moral scepticism with which at present most of us are afflicted.

To anticipate, I shall attempt, in particular, to show how groundless is the supposition that there can be objective moral principles only if there is some universal standard or principle of moral right and wrong which is acknowledged as binding by all men of good will. Commitment to the ideal of moral objectivity does not entail the sceptical conclusion that no principle can be regarded as morally valid unless it can be viewed as binding upon every "competent" moral agent; nor does it commit us to the impossible thesis that the fundamental responsibilities and rights of all moral persons must be substantially the same. Quite the contrary. There is no such thing as a competent or incompetent moral agent; indeed, the supposition that there is is itself a sign of moral immaturity. The ideal of moral objectivity must be adjusted to the possibility of an essential diversity of moral codes and not merely to an accidental diversity of moral opinions. There can be no such thing as "the moral point of view," and if any supposed rule, whether linguistic, legal, or theological, were to serve as a moral principle, it is only we as individual moral agents who could make it do so. If the maxims or precepts that now serve many of us as moral principles should ever come to be understood as definitive principles of morals, then the whole notion of moral agency as it is now understood would simply disappear. But it is only when the implications of this fact have been fully appreciated that we can adjust ourselves to the ordinary notion of moral objectivity whose meaning it is my eventual purpose to explain.

I

THE ANTINOMY OF MORAL OBJECTIVITY AND FREEDOM

In principle, it is always proper to inquire of any moral judgment whether it can be objectively sustained. It is also proper to ask of most moral principles whether they are objectively valid. But no such judgment or principle can be regarded as objectively valid unless there are certain definitive principles of morals which are binding upon the judgment and conduct of every moral agent. It does not suffice, as Kant implies, that every moral agent must be ready to treat the maxim of his judgment as the principle of a universal legislation, for this plainly leaves open the possibility that conscientious men could consistently differ on all matters of moral principle. Objective moral principles are possible only if there is at least one universal principle of morals to which every moral judge and agent is beholden in justifying particular moral judgments and lower-order principles. Since one of its essential functions is to guide our conduct in our interpersonal dealings with one another, morality cannot be regarded as a positive science; so much may be conceded with impunity to those so-called non-cognitivists who mistakenly deny that moral judgments are true or false statements. However, this does not imply that in ethics anything goes or that there is no such thing as a *discipline* of morals by appeal to whose rules it can in principle always be decided whether any moral judgment is true or false. Like positive science, morality must be understood as a universal discipline to which every moralist must submit. And it is for this reason that we may speak in ethics, as in science, of "qualified observers."

For the sake of clarity, it is well to point out certain consequences of these principles which moral objectivists usually fail to acknowledge. Morality, as we have seen, must be regarded as a discipline. However, every featherless biped must decide for himself whether he should submit to this discipline. In this respect, morality may be likened to a game. That is to say, any man must act in accordance with the rules of the moral "game" if he is to "do" morals at all. But there can be no moral rule which makes it necessary for every human being to play the game of morals, or if there were, then it would be up to every individual to decide for himself whether he wishes to be regarded as a "human being." Most of us are forced by the circumstances of social life to submit to the discipline of morals or at least to give the appearance of doing so. But other ways of handling one's personal relations are clearly conceivable. And if an individual is willing to risk being unpopular with the moralists, he is free not to play or, having played for a term, to play no longer.

There are other consequences of the principles of moral objectivity which many will find more agreeable. For one thing, if there are certain universal and necessary principles of morals, then in principle every contingent moral disagreement can be rationally resolved. Accordingly, every such disagreement may be properly understood as merely a disagreement in opinion rather than a disagreement in principle. Owing to the intrusion of such subjective factors as self-interest, stupidity, and ignorance, such disagreements may be in practice extremely difficult to settle. Nevertheless, we must assume that there is at least a tendency toward agreement on the part of conscientious moralists as the facts come more fully into view and as they become more fully aware of the nature of their commitments as moral beings. In short, underlying every substantive moral disensus there is a basic consensus which ensures the possibility of a rational resolution of any moral disagreement that may arise.

When moralists pass beyond a certain point in their disagreements, the issue between them becomes a concealed verbal dispute over the meaning of the concept of morals itself. This fact helps to explain why, in certain instances, the controversialists tend to go round and round without being able to compose their differences. When such situations arise, an objective solution may still be reached, but only by appealing to the rules governing the common use and application of the concept of morals itself. Should doubts persist past this point, then the reply must be that they involve a scepticism about the language of conduct generally which can hardly be sustained apart from a scepticism about the rules of ordinary language as a whole. But in that case, the issue has already passed outside the domain of moral philosophy into a sphere where the very notion of an objective disagreement is largely meaningless.

According to the preceding conception of morals, the principles of morals, like the rules of a game, are only hypothetically binding upon the individual person: if anyone elects to do morals, then, as a moralist, he must conform to its disciplinary principles. On such a view, accordingly, the individual acquits himself morally so long as his actions accord with such principles, regardless of his personal reasons for conforming to them. In other words, as a moral being anyone is ultimately responsible only to the principles of morals, not to his own conscience. To be sure, a man may be excused from responsibility for wrong actions if he conscientiously performs them in the belief that they are right; but such an excuse makes sense only if (1) the moral agent has (mistakenly) judged that his action is, on the evidence, the objectively right thing to do, and (2) there is in the situation an objectively right thing to be done which others may know as well as, or better than, he.

This view of morals is incompatible with the principles of moral autonomy or freedom. According to these principles it is not enough that the moral agent should be capable of making mistakes, nor is it enough that he should be free to violate the moral law. As a moral being he must also, in principle, decide absolutely for himself what that law really is. As we sometimes loosely and misleadingly say, every genuine moral agent must be regarded as a law unto himself. That is to say, no man is morally responsible for actions unless they are performed for the sake of principles which he cannot in conscience disavow. Here we do not just excuse a man who acts on principles which, as we may think, are objectively wrong. On the contrary, if he sticks to his principles "though the heavens fall," he is entitled to our respect and perhaps even to our admiration. It is for this reason that morally sensitive men not only forgive those who conscientiously oppose them on the ground that the latter "know not what they do"; when the issue between them is a matter of principle, they generously, if also tragically, honor them for exhibiting a moral integrity as great as any to which they themselves may aspire. A more sensitive Antigone would understand that she cannot totally condemn Creon without at the same time condemning herself.

The fundamental point is that morality cannot properly be regarded either as a form of law, as a book of rules, or as a set of socially authoritative commands. It does not suffice, as the objectivists maintain, that a man may be excused or forgiven if he happens unintentionally to do what is objectively wrong. For who is entitled to excuse him and who is in a position to grant him forgiveness? In morals there is and can be nothing to do save to follow the principles to which, upon reflection, one finds oneself committed. Such principles present themselves in conscience as categorical imperatives, not as laws, rules, or commands which are binding upon us *if* we are pleased to do the moral thing. But just because of this it makes no sense, in the moral sphere, to speak of a discipline of morals or of *the* principles of morals; here, indeed, we can speak only of "my principles," "our principles," "his principles," or "their principles." And the ordinary language of morals must and does accommodate itself to this fact.

In the domain of science and logic where we can speak with a straight face about disciplinary principles or rules, situations often arise in which we properly defer to the authority of observers whom we recognize to be more competent or qualified than ourselves. And it is because of this that, without qualms, we accept certain statements as objectively true even though we ourselves do not fully see why they are so. But in morals such situations can hardly arise. For just as no one can live by another's principles, so no one can be expected to conform his judgment and his will to certain allegedly objective principles which he has not in conscience made absolutely his own. Nor is this situation altered by the fact that some men take their principles from some "authority." For that authority can make no moral claims upon anyone who does not adopt it as *his* authority. In short, while a man may adopt as his moral principle, "Always act in such a way as would meet with the approval of (say) the church," that principle is no less a personal precept than the principle of utility or the principle of veracity.

The principle of moral autonomy can now be restated in the following way: Every moral principle must be regarded as nothing more than a first-personal precept. To be sure, such precepts may be either singular or plural. But no matter how extensive may be the community which commits itself to a particular moral practice or principle, it is morally binding only upon the members of that community. The principle of moral autonomy is thus incompatible with the very notion of a universal discipline of morals to which the conscience of every moral person is objectively beholden. Hence, so far at least as the concept of objectivity depends in principle upon the idea of an underlying consensus of "competent" or "qualified" moral judges, it has no application within ethics. To that extent there can be no such thing as a principle of moral objectivity. Moral discipline is merely a personal regimen, or way of life, whose character is definable only in terms of those precepts to which the individual moral agent holds himself responsible.

By the same token there can be no paradigm cases of a moral principle which every person who understands the language of morals is bound to accept. For if there were such a principle then every moral agent would automatically have to regard it as binding upon his own judgment and conduct. But the principle of moral autonomy itself precludes such a possibility even in the case of the principle of compassion itself. In rejecting the principle of compassion, Nietzsche, for example, did not thereby declare himself to be going beyond moral good and evil but only to "transvalue" the principles of what he considered to be a "slave morality." Those who really go beyond moral good and evil do so for one reason only: because for them the whole idea of moral obligation—like the idea of God for some others—is simply dead.

It follows from the principle of moral autonomy that meaningful disagreement is possible only among the members of a particular moral community. "Cross-cultural" moral criticism can only be regarded as a kind of propaganda, the main function of which is to reassure those "at home" of their moral rectitude. At this level the distinction between "justifying" and "exciting" reasons has no application. And those who talk, philosophically or theologically, of an objective moral law, natural or otherwise, delude no one but themselves.

In the light of these remarks we begin to see the use to which the autonomist is likely to put Moore's "open question" argument. In conscience we are morally free to question any alleged principle of morals. In order to assert our autonomy as moral beings we may even be obliged, in certain circumstances, to defy it. This, so far as I can see, is the principal point concealed in Nietzsche's "transvaluation of values." Its significance lies not so much in the fact that it rejects the principle of compassion, but that it asserts the right of autonomous moral agents to reject any principle when it is presented authoritatively as the principle of morals. In short, from the standpoint of the principle of moral autonomy, ethical naturalism in any form and on any level, is *morally* subversive.

2

TOWARD A RESOLUTION OF THE FOREGOING ANTINOMY

Let us now examine, somewhat dialectically, certain internal weaknesses in each of the preceding views. For convenience I shall henceforth refer to them as "objectivism" and "autonomism." As we proceed we will also consider reformulations of them designed to remove such weaknesses. In so doing it is my aim to show how we are driven at last to a conception of moral objectivity radically different from that to which objectivism itself appears to commit us. This conception is entirely compatible with at least one form of the doctrine of moral autonomy. But first we must overhaul that doctrine itself.

Now a thoughtful objectivist may point out that autonomism, as it stands, is internally inconsistent and that in removing this inconsistency the autonomist must acknowledge the basic minimal claim of objectivism itself. But when this claim is admitted the case for autonomism is radically weakened, since there are other principles whose claim to be regarded as definitive of morality is prior to those of moral autonomy. This may be seen in the following way: the autonomist claims that there can be no definitive principles of morals since, if there were, no moral agent could be regarded, as he must be, as a law unto himself. But if every moral agent must be regarded as a law unto himself, then the principles of moral autonomy must be themselves viewed as disciplinary principles of morals. In that case the autonomist must admit on principle that there is at least one principle by appeal to which particular moral judgments and principles may be objectively verified (or falsified).

To this the autonomist may reply simply by taking the bull by the horns. He may agree that his position, as previously stated, is inconsistent, and that what he should have claimed is that since the principles of moral autonomy are definitive principles of morals there can, by the nature of the case, be no other such principles. The principles of moral autonomy are, so to say, principles to end all ideas of morality which dispose us to treat our moral precepts as objective laws or rules of conduct. These principles are not only a guarantee against moral presumption, but a charter of absolute moral freedom. Such a view—let us call it "essentialistic autonomism"—obviously commits its proponent to a definitive closing of the open question so far as the concept of *morals* is concerned. But this (so it may be said) is no cause for alarm since what it closes is only the question concerning the nature of *moral* judgment or of *moral* right and wrong. As such it does not in the least run afoul of Moore's naturalistic fallacy argument which holds—so far it does hold—only against descriptive definitions of such words as "good," "right," and "ought."

It may be questioned, however, whether, with respect to the concept of morals, the open question can be closed without violence, or whether, even if it can be, the autonomist himself is in a position to close it. For the sake of argument let us assume that in principle it can be closed. But definitive principles of morals should be able to meet the test of counter-instances. This, it may be argued, the principles of moral autonomy cannot do. It is very easy to imagine a serious person who would disallow any alleged obligation as a *moral* obligation if its fulfillment involved the performance of an unjust act, regardless of the fact that it was performed in accordance with precepts conscientiously avowed by the agent himself. Of course, a sufficiently resolute autonomist might deny that such an example provides a true counter-instance. His only mistake, in that case, would be to suppose that he thereby secures his own position. For in thus privileging the principles of moral autonomy he thereby automatically converts them into a statement of the conditions under which alone he himself is prepared to judge an act as morally obligatory. Such a statement may, in one sense, be regarded as a definition. But what it defines is merely a particular style of moral judgment. It leaves the concept of morals itself untouched.

Suppose, now, that the autonomist sees that his doctrine cannot plausibly be defended in its essentialistic form. That is to say he at last realizes that the principles of moral autonomy can be regarded as formal principles only in the sense that they define what he himself accepts as a standard of "good form" in matters of moral judgment. He also sensibly acknowledges that the only reason he can disallow his critic's supposed counter-instance is that it functions in effect only as an *exemplary* counter-principle. In a word, the autonomist now frankly regards the principles of moral autonomy themselves as first-personal precepts which serve to define only his own moral point of view. What they prescribe, so far as he is concerned, is that the conscientious judgment of every moral agent *ought* (not must) absolutely to be respected and that no action performed for the sake of the principles embodied in such judgments is morally censurable.

Such a position—let us call it "preceptive autonomism"—is perhaps not inconceivable, however hard it may be in practice consistently to maintain. There are, however, a great many prima-facie duties which ordinary men, including most autonomists, do not question in their dealings with their fellows. The principles of moral autonomy require the autonomist to respect such duties in others; within the limits of that respect they permit him to acknowledge such duties for himself. But they provide no standard for judging which duties are to take precedence when they conflict with one another. Nor do they provide the only principle for making the legitimate exceptions to which, in practice, virtually every moral principle is subject. In practice, I suppose, most men would hold that a promise may properly be broken if keeping it involved a great deal of suffering to innocent people. But the principle of moral autonomy entitles us to break a promise only when the keeping of it infringes on the moral freedom of others. Many men also, would probably agree that it is proper to tell a lie in order to give comfort to a person at the end of his tether. But the principle of moral autonomy provides no basis whatever for making such proper exceptions to the principle of veracity. In short, while the principles of moral autonomy provide a final restraint in judging the conduct of others and a minimal basis for making exceptions in the case of our own prima-facie duties, they otherwise leave individual conscience completely without guidance.

It is precisely at this point that the objectivist has another inning. For the autonomist, like anyone else, has the problem of deciding what he really ought to do when a conflict of duties occurs within the limits set by the principles of moral autonomy. How is such a conflict to be resolved? It is entirely possible, moreover, that a particular duty, such as compassion, may oblige him to press beyond those limits. What then? Since the principle of moral autonomy is itself merely a precept, on what basis is the autonomist to decide to adhere to the principle of autonomy rather than to follow the obligations of compassion? He may reply that he needs no basis for deciding since, for him, the question is already settled. But then he must admit that his decision is completely arbitrary and that, in good conscience, it might just as well have gone the other way. Next week he may find that it does go the other way; he will then have just as much or just as little reason for the line he takes.

But the situation is even worse than this. Suppose that the autonomist sticks to his principles absolutely and without exception. For him there is no moral conflict between the principles of moral autonomy and other principles since the latter simply give way whenever the limits imposed by the former have been reached. But what are those limits, and how are they to be found? It should be borne in mind, as Aristotle long ago reminded us, that ethical concepts have not the same exactitude as those employed in logic or science. Here *judgment* is required if they are sensibly to be applied. But what shall guide the autonomist's judgment when he has to decide whether a prima-facie duty has trespassed upon the moral autonomy of other persons? Indeed, it may be argued that the very admission of the necessity of judgment in applying the principles of moral autonomy involves another principle more absolute than autonomy itself. But even if the autonomist refuses this gambit, the problem of boundaries remains a source, not just of theoretical perplexity, but of constant practical moral doubt. For the frontiers of moral autonomy are nowhere clearly marked, and the petitions of supposedly lower-order principles for satisfaction of their claims are bound to be an every-day occurrence.

Beyond such commonplace harassments there also remain more general problems of application to which the principles of moral autonomy themselves provide no clue. For example, does the principle of autonomy entail respect for those individuals who profess no moral principles and whose lives are dedicated exclusively to their work or to their own pleasures? Does it entail respect for those whose only conscientious aim is to subvert the whole enterprise of morality? Do the principles of moral autonomy permit us to attempt the re-education of those who are not themselves autonomists, or does the respect we owe to moral persons require that we accept every such person once and for all just as we find him? Above all, who shall count as a "moral person," and when does he attain his majority? These problems are not external problems pressed upon the autonomist from a different moral point of view. They are wholly internal to autonomism itself, and pending the answers that are to be made to them, autonomism remains, morally, a merely abstract entity. From the depths of the autonomist's own conscience there comes the demand for some way of knowing what autonomism really is, what it really commits him to.

In another domain this is precisely the predicament of Descartes, whose invocation of the principle of intellectual autonomy at the same time forced him to look within his own consciousness for a way to distinguish subjective appearances from objective reality. "But surely," the objectivist will reply, "this is just what cannot be done. Nothing will come of nothing, and if Descartes claims absolute freedom to think for himself, then whatever rules of method he finally adopts can be nothing but subjective precepts. The 'reality' which he claims to discover by their application remains a merely subjective reality." It is here that the objectivist may hope to make his stand. But let us now have a look at the internal problems in which his own position is involved.

In the first place, as the autonomist will quickly point out, the very difficulties which we observed in the case of essentialistic autonomism also beset every objectivist at every turn. For no matter what principles of morals the objectivist comes up with, he must submit his theory to the test of counter-instances. If, when a counter-instance is seriously proposed he refuses to accept it as a counter-instance, then he shows by that very fact that his principles are definitive, not of morality as such, but only of his own style of moral judgment. But if he accepts it, his theory is overturned. Is there any such theory that remains beyond the reach of counter-instances? Or, how are we finally to determine just what the principles of morals really are? The question is exigent since unless actual principles of morals can be supplied objectivism is merely a vacuous possibility. In a word, objectivism can be shown to be possible only by confronting us with the unassailable fact of definitive principles of morals to which no one who understands what is being said can seriously make objection. This is a tall order.

There are only two alternatives. One way is for the objectivist himself simply to tell us, without ado, what really are the principles of morals. But this venture will not do unless every moralist, without exception, acknowledges that every action prescribed by the principles in question *must* be *morally* right. None of the traditional forms of objectivism has managed to meet so stringent a test. We have already observed the difficulties in which the objective autonomist finds himself. Counter-instances—if that is what they are—have been proposed to every known form of theological objectivism. The only theory known to me which seems to stand a chance of survival is that form of humanitarian ethics which claims that what we mean by a morally right act is one which by intention is compassionate, i.e., which seeks, so far as possible, to relieve suffering. The difficulties involved in such a view are notorious: for example, there are many conscientious moralists who would accept acts of compassion as morally right only if their performance does not violate the personal integrity of the individuals involved. At best, the compassionist may argue that no act is morally right which involves unnecessary or needless suffering. But, what is to count as "needless suffering," and who shall decide? There are also moral obligations which, as such, have nothing to do with questions of suffering at all: for example, the obligation to be fair in one's dealings with others, the obligation to tell the truth, or the obligation to keep promises sincerely made. Here the principle of compassion itself works primarily as a principle of exception which, by that very fact, presupposes that there are, in principle, non-compassionate forms of *moral* obligation.

It may be argued, however, that we have hitherto failed to distinguish sharply enough between material or substantive moral principles and formal or definitive principles of morals.

But where is the razor's edge which divides them? The principle of compassion, let us agree, is a substantive principle like the principles of autonomy. But then, if we are objectively to resolve disagreements about the commitments which these principles enjoin, there must be certain *other* principles which really do define what is meant by a "morally right action," and which, because of this, state what every moral agent or judge must consider in trying to decide whether adherence to such substantive principles is morally right. What *are* these purely formal principles?

It is at this point that the other alternative open to the objectivist appears most appealing. He may now suggest that our difficulties have been due precisely to the failure of the older objectivists to be sufficiently abstract. Suppose, however, that the very concept of objectivity itself is viewed as a formal standard of moral right and wrong. In short, what if it were argued simply that all and only those acts are morally right which would be approved by any one who views them objectively? What is wanted is a definitive statement of the characteristics of an objective observer.

3.

MORAL OBJECTIVITY AND THE "IDEAL OBSERVER"

Now it turns out that this alternative has already been carefully explored by Professor Roderick Firth in his essay, "Ethical Absolutism and the Ideal Observer." [1] Accordingly, by examining it in some detail, we may, I think, take the final measure of objectivism in its most rigoristic form.

As Firth is aware, his analysis is not without precedent. Read in one way it may indeed be viewed as an attempt to clarify the doctrine of a disinterested or impartial spectator which, in one form or another, is to be found in the writings of Hutcheson, Hume, Adam Smith, and Kant. Firth takes these writers to be arguing, in effect, that an ethical judgment is in essence a statement about how an "ideal observer" would react to a certain state of affairs or, variously, how any observer would react to a certain state of affairs under "ideal" conditions. This is an exceedingly plausible reading of them. And although I now take a somewhat different view of Hume's "intentions," I myself so construed him in the Introduction to my edition of *Hume's Moral and Political Philosophy*. In that work I described Hume's position, as it appears in the *Treatise*, in the following terms: "(a) . . . Moral judgments are not merely *expressions* of our approval or disapproval; they have descriptive meaning and are capable of truth and falsity; nevertheless, they are empirical and hence corrigible. (b) Moral distinctions have a certain objectivity and universality in the sense that they refer to what an impartial and benevolent spectator *would* approve, and not necessarily to what most of us in fact do approve. . . ." [2] What distinguishes Firth's analysis is the care with which he analyzes characteristics of omniscience, omnipercipience, disinterestedness, dispassionateness, and consistency which he takes to be the fundamental hallmarks of the ideal spectator whose reactions we allegedly have in mind in trying to decide what is morally right or wrong.

Whether this particular list of characteristics—which notably does not include Hume's "benevolence" or any term usually associated with a particular moral attitude—is really necessary and sufficient we may leave to the absolute objectivists to debate among themselves. But on any such list the concept of disinterestedness, no doubt, would doubtless be prominently displayed. Moreover, Firth's analysis of it is typical of his treatment of most of the others. For these reasons we may treat his definition of disinterestedness as a test case for the success or failure of his theory as a whole. If it can be shown that any such definition, whose whole point must be to eliminate all reference to sentiments or principles antecedently acknowledged as *moral*, fails to meet the test of plausible counter-instances, then by a kind of intuitive induction we may conclude that no supposedly formal principle of objectivity can serve as a definitive principle of moral right and wrong.

According to Firth's account, any observer is "disinterested" if and only if he is totally lacking in "particular interests" where the phrase "particular interests" is taken to refer to any interest whose object cannot be defined without the use of proper names and such egocentric particulars as "I," "here," "now," and "this."[3] Now it is no part of my purpose to deny that such a definition might do for certain senses of the term; the only question here is whether it suffices for what we have in mind when we use the term in moral contexts. Imagine, then, an observer who is devoid of "particular" interests, in Firth's sense, but so single-minded in his devotion to the pursuit of knowledge that he always reacts with pleasure to any proposal that would increase it, regardless of its consequences. Among such consequences, we may easily suppose, would be a certain amount of unavoidable mutilation of young children, at least some confessions obtained by torture, and a few instances of scientific eavesdropping on persons at religious confession. Or, again, imagine a great artist, also devoid of particular interests, who is so dedicated to the art of painting that he always ignores even the most elementary claims of veracity, kindness, or loyalty when they interfere with the demands of the art. Now I suppose that from a certain standpoint such individuals may be regarded as "disinterested," perhaps even admirably so. But, if so, it is a form of disinterestedness which, as such, has nothing to do with morals; on the contrary, it involves forms of behavior which most of us would regard as prime examples of moral obtuseness, if not flagrant immorality. More important, we would probably also agree that such individuals displayed a singular lack of the sort of disinterestedness required in moral situations.

But, for the sake of argument, let us assume that Firth's definition of disinterestedness can, in principle, be amended so as to rule out all such offending non-particular interests. Our formula, accordingly, will be that any person may be said to be morally disinterested if and only if (1) he is devoid of particular interests (in the sense defined above), and (2) he is devoid of any non-particular interest of type *G*. But how, pray, is this type to be defined? The suggestion which may occur to some moralists is that it should include all non-particular interests, professional, artistic, or institutional, which would dispose one to be indifferent to the suffering of other persons.[4] But aside from the difficulty that the concept of a person is itself by no means a neutral term in moral contexts, it seems evident that we are now attempting to write a particular moral principle into the very definition of moral disinterestedness. In that case, however, the concept of disinterestedness loses whatever virtue it may have had as a critical standard to which appeal could be made in trying to decide, among other things, whether that moral principle itself is objectively to be preferred to all others, or whether, in certain circumstances, it should be subject to exception.

The situation seems to be this: the concept of moral disinterestedness, and hence of moral objectivity, cannot be successfully defined wholly without reference to principles antecedently acknowledged as moral. But neither can it be defined in terms of any particular moral principle without at once losing its use as an independent standard of objective moral appraisal. Firth's analysis avoids the latter difficulty; its weakness is that it countenances forms of "interest" which many moralists would regard as obviously partial and which some would regard as immoral on the face of it, partial or otherwise. Nor does there seem to be any way of amending Firth's definition which would remove that weakness without at the same time destroying the very feature which originally appeared to recommend it.

For the moment, however, let us waive the difficulty that from a moral point of view many non-particular interests seem, ethically, as partial as any particular ones. What we have now to consider is the more delicate problem whether, so far as morality as such is concerned, anyone saliently affected by particular interests of any sort is to that extent lacking in moral disinterestedness and objectivity. In brief, *must* we suppose that a principled concern for "one's own" is always evidence of partiality and hence of a lack of objectivity? This does not appear to me at all obvious. Consider, for example, a highly conscientious mother who, upon careful reflection, always, and in good conscience, preferred the well-being of the members of her own family to that of any other group in which they happened to be included but which is definable in wholly non-particular terms. Here it is well to bear in mind that Firth's "particular interests" are by no means always self-interested, and that a person such as I have just described may be quite as selfless as any Saint Just who ever dedicated himself to the "universal" principles of liberty, equality, and fraternity. Is such a person, morally, any less disinterested than a Saint Just or, better, a Tom Paine who so appealingly avows that "wherever there is injustice, there is my country?" On what grounds that are not at the same time morally question-begging? She is indifferent to "non-particular" claims that, from the standpoint of her principles, appear impossibly general and abstract; he is indifferent to "particular" claims that, from her point of view, are always overriding. To him she seems insufferably parochial; to her he seems virtually inhuman, a monstrous justice-machine dedicated unfeelingly to mere *names* of virtue. Which, morally, is the more disinterested? Without enlarging our own point of view there is, so far as I can see, no way whatever to decide. One seems as interested-disinterested as the other; the only difference between them is one of moral perspective. Once again, compare a man who is exclusively dedicated to the welfare of the members of his own country with another who is similarly dedicated to the happiness of white Protestants, whatever their country. Is the former person, because of his particular interest, any less impartial than the other? Without regard to any other considerations already acknowledged to be morally relevant, I do not see how it could be denied that both parties are pretty much in the same boat. Within the range of his principle, each may be completely disinterested; with respect to his principle itself, one seems quite as partial as the other.

It may be replied, of course, that a person may prefer his own to any "outsider's" without being guilty of any partiality, but only on the condition that he is prepared to accept the possibility that everyone else does so as well. In that case his particular interest turns out, innocuously, to be merely an application to his own situation of a non-particular concern for a state of human affairs in which every individual gives the nod to his own when his interests happen to conflict with those of outsiders. This reply is unsatisfactory. It is not hard to imagine a person who would reply, upon reflection, that he simply does not know whether to prefer a world in which everyone gives the nod to his own, whoever they are, but that he, at any rate, knows that he ought to prefer "his own" whenever their interests conflict with those of any outside group which he can seriously envisage. Is his reaction lacking in *moral* impartiality? But, again, on what non-question-begging grounds? He has not refused the demand to reconsider; he has entertained and then been obliged to suspend judgment concerning the universalistic covering principle in question; and despite this, his original commitment has not been shaken. Once more, I contend, there is no way of convicting him of partiality without introducing other moral principles which he himself has temporarily forgotten, but which, upon further consideration, he is prepared to acknowledge. Apart from them he is no less (and no more) disinterested than a Crito whose dedicated love of Socrates, as it turns out, is merely a disguised interest in the wisest of all men.[5]

From a *morally* disinterested point of view, the question is not whether an interest is particular or otherwise, but only whether, all things considered, it still appears right to realize it. And among the things that saliently require to be considered in such a case are precisely those prima-facie duties to which one is already conditionally committed.[6]

Consider another problem which often presents itself to the practicing moralist. From his own point of view he may fail to be objective, not only because he is influenced by extra-moral interests, whether particular or general, but also because of an obsession with moral rights of a particular sort. Thus, for example, he may be overborne by a particular prima-facie duty to which he blindly refuses to acknowledge exceptions he knows to be legitimate. Or he may give the nod to a principle whose place in his moral scheme of things is entirely subordinate, ignoring superordinate principles of justice or humanity upon which the whole virtue of the principle in question entirely depends. I am inclined to think that failures of moral disinterestedness occur most frequently, not because we are overborne by extra-moral considerations, but because we are temporarily blinded by particular moral sentiments such as indignation, whose "rights" are extremely limited. The would-be objective moralist is thus always placed in double jeopardy; on the one side he is tempted by a host of non-moral inclinations, both particular and general, and on the other by "particular" (used here in its ordinary, non-technical sense) duties that, on second thought, have no such absolute claim to fulfillment as he permits himself for the moment to believe.

In this connection it may also be well to mention a type of moral problem which is frequently misconceived by moral philosophers. Now it is true that in attempting to reach an objective decision most moralists believe they have some obligation to listen to the considered opinions of other judges. But this obligation, like any other, may itself become obsessive so that the moralist, ignoring other exigent demands which his conscience makes upon him, loses objectivity through the very attempt to achieve it. An individual may well believe that he is morally obliged to suspend judgment, for the time being at least, when he finds that there is a strong consensus of moral opinion against him. But that obligation is one among many. And if he is overwhelmed by it he may be as much incapacitated for objective judgment as when he responds too promptly to his sense of indignation.

Contrary to the prevailing view in philosophy, there is, in general, no necessary connection between objectivity of judgment and intersubjective agreement. Nor do we automatically establish the objectivity of a judgment merely by multiplying subjective opinions or attitudes. Intersubjective agreement, however extensive, remains nothing more than that; it becomes a test of objective validity only when, as in science, the very form of the activity demands it. There are many forms of activity in which such agreement is not required and, where it exists, does nothing to increase the likelihood of objective certainty. In such cases, too much concern for the opinions of others may well be the greatest handicap to objective judgment. This is obviously true in the case of literary and art criticism; it is true in the domain of religious belief; it is true also in the sphere of moral judgment where the demands of conscience may require one to stand completely alone.

What has been said above about the concept of moral disinterestedness applies, by analogy, to such other "characteristics" of an ideally objective observer as dispassionateness. I shall, therefore, not pause to make detailed criticisms of Firth's treatment of them. It is time to make a more general point. Now the common notion of moral objectivity (of whose use I have already given some intimations) has no tendency to breed a general "philosophical" scepticism about the validity of moral judgments and principles. However, Firth's absolute objectivism, when pressed, gradually forces us back upon a principled moral agnosticism which, if taken seriously, would result in the destruction of our ordinary sense of right and wrong or, which comes to the same thing, the complete paralysis of our moral will. "Judge not!" now becomes not just an exemplary counsel of moral humility but, in effect, the defining principle of morals itself. In a word, if the traits of an "ideally" objective observer are taken as providing *the* definitive principle of morals, then moral right and wrong become vacuous conceptions, the use of which answers to no conscientious human concern.

This point can be shown in a variety of ways. As we have already seen, Firth's analysis of disinterestedness fails to meet the test of counter-instances. But the attempt to amend it in a way which at the same time avoids reference to principles antecedently acknowledged as moral leads us first into a blind search for a way to eliminate offending non-particular interests, next to the admission that particular interests are not necessarily less disinterested than any others, until finally we begin to wonder whether all "interests"—including even the obligation to respect the judgments of other persons—must not be eliminated before we can secure that pure and perfect disinterestedness which (by hypothesis) is involved in the very meaning of moral right and wrong. Disinterestedness thus becomes a kind of "hidden God" which, just to the extent that the concept of morals is made to depend upon it, forces us to question more and more grimly whether that concept has any intelligible meaning. In another way the search for an ideal observer whose attitudes and opinions are *merely* objective leads eventually to the conception of a being who has no favorable or unfavorable reactions at all. We are reminded at this point of Job, who, as he comes to realize that his notions of justice provide no measure of God's justice, is forced to admit that although he must be a sinner in God's eyes he can never know how or why. To this the reply must be that though moral understanding is a pearl of great price, it loses all value if we make the price so high that it cannot possibly be paid.

4

THE NATURE OF MORAL OBJECTIVITY

The merit of the ideal-spectator theory is that it enables us to see just what absolute ethical objectivism comes to when we try to formulate definitive principles of moral judgment or something called "*the* moral point of view" in total abstraction from any substantive principles and practices to which, in the ordinary course, moral agents find themselves committed. Is such a point of view consistent with the ideal of moral autonomy to which, within limits, most moralists are committed? It is impossible to say. Who knows, in practice, how an absolutely objective spectator, bereft of moral principles, would react to any situation? In effect, the spectator theory would replace all of the little perplexities that beset us when we worry about the objectivity of particular moral judgments with one big perplexity about the nature and reactions of the ideal spectator himself. Unhappily, the more we contemplate this big perplexity the more we wonder whether the idea of morality itself may not be a conceptual monster, a mere idea of reason, to which no definite meaning can be assigned.

These doubts can be removed, not by further logical analysis, but only by returning, conscientiously, to the world of workaday moral problems and judgments. In that world the problem of moral objectivity is mainly a problem of piecemeal mutual adjustment of acknowledged commitments within a loose framework of precepts and practices, none of which is ever permanently earmarked as an absolutely first principle and each of which is subject to a list of exceptions that can never be exhaustively stated. In practice, moral error is due not so much to our lack of omniscience about matters of fact as to philosophical misconceptions about the drift of the terms of our discourse and to our inveterate tendency to adhere inflexibly to particular principles in the face of other loyalties whose claims upon us are equally compelling.

What is wanted is not a better understanding of the hypothetical reactions of a perfectly objective somebody-else, but that conscientious second thought which enables us to take a more general view of our own existing responsibilities. Such a general view provides no definition of moral right and wrong; it does not require us to ignore "our own" when we find that their claims upon us cannot conscientiously be universalized; it does not demand that we treat "everybody," whoever they may be, as moral persons; nor does it commit us to some supposed consensus of moral opinion which all other "competent" moral agents must be presumed to share. In brief, there is and can be no absolute or universal vantage point from which conscientious moralists, regardless of their sentiments, may make an objective appraisal of their particular moral decision and principles. Morally, we are always in the middle of things, confronted with eternally exceptionable precepts which, until such exceptions have been made, still lay presumptive claims upon us that we cannot in conscience disavow. What provides the basis for such exceptions? Nothing save other particular principles which, in turn, we are forever driven to qualify in the light of still other principles. And when we come temporarily to the end of a line of qualifications what do we find? To our dismay, nothing but the very "first-level" duties which which we began.

The ordinary principle of moral objectivity thus prescribes, not that we look beyond the moral life itself for a ground of criticism, but only that we search within it for the soberest and steadiest judgment of which, in the light of all relevant obligations, we are capable. When a question arises concerning the objectivity of a particular moral judgment or principle, our task is always and only to look beyond *it* to the other relevant commitments which we ourselves acknowledge. And if this answer seems inadequate, then the reply must be that there is, in conscience, nothing else to go on. In the moral sphere it is always, finally, up to us; nor is there anyone to whose steadier shoulders our burden of moral judgment can be shifted. That is the agony of the moral life; it is also its peculiar glory.

The only principle of objectivity in morals is, then, essentially a principle of reconsideration. What it demands, when a question about the objectivity of a particular judgment or principle arises, is that we consider whether such a judgment or principle, as it stands, can be consistently upheld in the face of whatever other moral considerations might be thought, in conscience, to defeat it. What do such considerations include? It is beyond the scope of this essay to attempt a codification, even if such were possible, of all of the sorts of consideration that might, in principle, serve to defeat or falsify a moral proposition. It must suffice here to indicate in very general terms a few of the main factors involved, and for the rest to remove certain prevailing misconceptions.

In many situations the objectivity of a particular moral judgment is sufficiently established simply by bringing it under an appropriate covering principle which, in effect, simply classifies the action in question as an act of a certain sort, the performance of which, other things being equal, is a moral duty. As a rule we determine at once that feature of an action which enables us to classify it as an act of a certain sort, the performance or non-performance of which is at once required by a relevant covering principle. What creates a problem for us are other features of the situation not covered by the principle appealed to and which make of the action in question something more, or less, than merely an act of a certain sort. A certain line of action involves us, say, in the act of telling a lie, and the telling of lies, other things equal, is proscribed. But it may be that what is proposed, the action to be performed, is more than an act of lying; perhaps it may also be viewed as an act of kindness. In that case it falls under another principle which, other things being equal, provides the basis of a second obligation. In such a situation it is commonly supposed either that there is a clear order of precedence among such principles—that is, an obvious principle of hierarchy—or else that both principles are merely summary applications of some more fundamental principle, such as the principle of utility, by which both such "first-order" principles are justified and from which both are ultimately derived. It is also commonly supposed that such principles define certain distinct "practices" each of which can be criticized only as a whole in the light of some "second-order" principle, such as "justice" or "utility," which alone provides an objective standard of appraisal. Such facile descriptions of the ways out of our moral perplexities usually will not do.

In the first place, moral principles cannot be arranged in a flat hierarchical order. For example, we cannot say without qualification that the principle of kindness takes absolute precedence over the principle of veracity; we cannot say without qualification that promises may be broken when the consequences of keeping a promise are more unpleasant for the people involved than those of breaking it. It all depends upon how much unpleasantness is involved in keeping the promise or how much unkindness is involved in telling the truth; conversely, it also depends upon our considered views of the importance of telling the truth and of keeping promises. These practices, for most of us, are important commitments in their own right which are not to be evaluated simply by reckoning the amount of discomfort (or unkindness) keeping or breaking a promise, telling or not telling the truth would involve. They are, in short, independent sources of moral excellence which require no justification on merely utilitarian grounds.

Secondly, it is a mistake to suppose that what we call the practice of promising, for example, can be understood in complete abstraction from the principles of exception which, on occasion, justify the breaking of a promise. Part of what we understand by the practice of promising is the recognition that promises may, under certain conditions, be broken and that no promise is absolutely inviolate. Not only is every principle subject to exceptions, but the fact that such exceptions are allowable belongs to the very concept of a practice itself. There is, in short, no such thing as the practice of promising, the practice of veracity, or the practice of justice, independent of the principles of exception which qualify such practices. This means that the principles which form the parts of a moral code can be understood only in relation to a network of such principles, no one of which can be evaluated in isolation from the rest. Nor is there any unqualifiable "second-order" principle so absolute and so impervious to exceptions that it provides a unique and final basis for objective criticism of the rest. Objective criticism of moral principles is mainly a matter of piecemeal qualification of particular practices with a view to their greater coherence within a moral system. The only test of objectivity, so far as principles and practices are concerned, is thus their ability to survive without further qualification by the other principles or practices with which they may conflict. When qualification is required, nothing provides an objective basis for decisions save the other practices with which, by mutual adjustment, it must be reconciled.

But there is a feature of the moral predicament still more basic than any hitherto mentioned. Now most philosophers hold that what distinguishes moral from merely expedient action is the fact that moral actions are performed not only on, but also for the sake of, a principle. What is morally right in one case is right only if it is so in cases of a similar sort. Yet this approximate truth must accommodate itself to another, no less fundamental. No action is exhaustively definable simply as an act of a certain sort any more than an individual substance is exhaustively definable as a member of a certain species. It may exhibit morally significant aspects beyond any that have been covered by our prevailing system of moral acts. For this reason it is always possible to maintain of a particular line of action that *it* ought to be followed even though its performance goes against every principle in the book. In other terms, one may be more certain that a line of action ought to be carried out than of any principle that might be thought to justify or to condemn it. In that case, the action becomes, as it were, a principle unto itself and at the same time establishes the basis for the introduction of a new moral principle.

It is essential that I not be misunderstood on this point. It is theoretically possible to say of a particular moral judgment that it is objectively defensible even though it cannot be justified by appeal to any hitherto existing principles of justification or exception. But there is a world of difference between a judgment which is sustained after a full and impartial review of the whole moral situation, including the principles that appear to be applicable to it, and one for which certainty is claimed in advance of inquiry. I am making no defense of moral dogmatism; on the contrary, I maintain that the principle of objectivity may require reconsideration of any judgment. But this applies no less to principles themselves. It is quite as dogmatic and unobjective to maintain a moral principle regardless of the judgments which, upon second thought, may disallow it as to insist upon a particular judgment without regard to the principles which might be thought to invalidate it.

In summary, there is and can be no definitive criterion of moral objectivity and, hence, no definitive principle of moral right and wrong. When a serious question about the objectivity of a particular moral judgment or principle arises, there is simply the further *moral* obligation to re-examine it in the light of the other obligations and duties that have a bearing upon it. If it should be replied that objective reconsideration requires, also, an endless search for new facts which, if known, might alter our notions of our obligations and duties themselves, the answer must be that such a search would defeat the very purpose of moral reflection, which is *judgment*. The principle of objectivity requires only that we take account of any hitherto unconsidered facts to which we may reasonably be expected to have access. But in that case what is reasonable? There is no formula for answering such a question; our judgment can be formed only by weighing the obligation to look for relevant facts against other obligations. In a word, the principle of moral objectivity can neither supply the materials for moral judgment nor tell us where to go in search of them. If we have no time to search for further possibly relevant facts, the principle of objectivity will provide us with not one moment more; if we are otherwise lacking in moral sensibility, it will not make good our deficiency by so much as a single obligation. What it can do—and it can do no more—is to dispose us to review our decisions so that we may neglect no pertinent fact that, in the time we have, is available to us and that we may neglect no obligation which deserves to be considered. Primarily, therefore, it functions as a principle of falsification, and what consistently survives the general scrutiny which it demands may pass as objectively valid or true.

5

A NOTE ON MORAL TRUTH

This last remark provides, in essence, our final answer to objectivism. But so profound are prevailing misconceptions that a further word about moral truth is required before I bring this paper to a close. All contemporary moral philosophers, regardless of school, take it for granted that there is an intimate connection between the concepts of objectivity and truth. They may believe, as do the emotivists, that neither concept has a moral application; or they may hold, with the naturalists, that the conditions of moral objectivity and truth are no different from those of empirical science. But they all agree that the connection between the concepts is analytic. They all assume, moreover, that truth, which they tend to restrict to statements verifiable by the procedures of science or of formal logic, is logically the more fundamental concept. On these points a statement by Bernard Mayo is typical: "The deepest issue, and the most violent controversy, in contemporary moral philosophy is between those who assert, and those who deny, that moral judgments can be true or false. This difference can indeed be taken as the simplest way of defining the meaning of the pair of correlative terms 'objective' and 'subjective.' What is objective is capable of being true or false, of being a statement, a belief or opinion; what is subjective is not capable of a truth-value, but is an expression of some psychological state." [7] Mayo's own view is that moral assertions, although subject to "criteria of correctness" are not verifiable by procedures akin to those employed in science; he concludes, therefore, that they cannot be true or false and hence that they cannot be regarded as objective statements at all.[8] Kurt Baier, who takes virtually the same position as Mayo toward the relations of truth to objectivity, comes to precisely the opposite conclusion. Accordingly, although he, like Mayo, holds that moral judgments are essentially guides to conduct, he pulls and hauls in order to show that by his definitions moral appraisals are also empirically verifiable and, hence, that they may be regarded as objective statements.[9] It seems not to occur to either writer that verifiability (or falsifiability) is not a concept for which empirical science alone has a use, and that in certain domains questions of truth are settled entirely by the conclusions of objective judgment itself.

Such, at any rate, is the position of this essay: at least so far as morals are concerned, the concept of objectivity is logically more primitive than that of truth, and the verification of a moral proposition occurs when, and only when, we judge objectively that it survives re-scrutiny. The plausibility of such an analysis is very great. We have already seen that moral objectivity does not depend upon the possibility that moral judgments are statements of fact, verifiable by procedures analogous to those employed in empirical science. We have seen, indeed, that moral objectivity does not even presuppose that there are definitive principles of morals of any sort. This, however, does not in the least imply that moral propositions are not statements. In its familiar applications, the term "statement" is by no means limited to empirical descriptions and predictions. Thus, even if it were granted that only statements can be true or false, this leaves us with a very wide range of possibly true or false utterances. For in addition to statements of (empirical) fact, there are statements of intentions, statements of policy, statements of principle, bank statements, and a hundred and one other forms of statement, almost as various in their logical functions as discourse itself. I do not, of course, claim that all statements are objective and true or false. I claim only that the use of the concept of a statement is no more the exclusive prerogative of the empirical scientist and the logician than that of objectivity, and that from the premise that a statement is non-factual, in the empirical sense, nothing whatever can be inferred about the possibility of its being verifiable. The only fundamental question, so far as verifiability is concerned, is whether the statements in question are corrigible and whether, when we affirm them, we are, in any meaningful sense, subject to correction. In the case of morals, I contend that possibility is guaranteed by (and only by) the possibility of objective judgment itself.[10]

To say, then, that a moral statement is true is simply: (1) to reaffirm it and (2) to avow that it meets whatever tests of objectivity are deemed proper by the moral judge himself. He who affirms that a moral proposition is true when it will not abide such tests, speaks falsely. No moral judge, in affirming the truth of a particular judgment or principle, presupposes that anyone else must agree with him, regardless of his own moral obligations. For in morals there can be no guarantee that all objective judges will acknowledge the same principles of moral obligation.

This means that rational disagreements in morals cannot range beyond an implicit framework of common principles and practices shared, in conscience, by the disagreeing parties. Similarly, meaningful interpersonal discussions of the truth of a particular moral judgment presuppose the existence of a moral community to which, in conscience, both discussants are committed. This does not preclude the possibility that moral judges may contradict one another; it precludes only the possibility that contradiction can occur outside the limits of a particular moral community. To the extent that moral communities differ fundamentally in regard to their moral precepts and practices, it is pointless to speak of their judgments as logically contradictory. For in that case it is also pointless to talk of an objective settlement of their differences. At such a point, what is wanted is not argument, but education, not the appeal to nonexistent principles of morals, but companionship and love.

NOTES

1. Firth, *Philosophy and Phenomenological Research*, XIII (1952), 317–345.
2. H. D. Aiken (ed.), *Hume's Moral and Political Philosophy* (New York: Hafner Publishing Co., 1948), p. xxxvi.
3. Firth, *op. cit.*, pp. 338–339.
4. Firth, I assume, would have no part of such a suggestion.
5. Firth, *op. cit.*, p. 339.
6. At this point it becomes desirable to remark upon the distinction between lack of objectivity and mere subjectivity. Objectivity is a form of achievement one can miss for a multitude of reasons; such reasons have nothing necessarily to do with subjective preoccupations. On the other hand, subjectivity itself may serve as a kind of principle which, in certain contexts, functions as a test of one's powers of objective judgment. In short, what causes a man to be non-objective in his decisions and judgments is not simply a preoccupation with matters pertaining essentially to himself, but, rather, those beliefs, attitudes, and interests, whatever their objectives, that deflect him from the ends or prevent him from conforming to the principles characteristic of the activity in question. No doubt there are forms of activity with respect to which any subjective concern is evidence of a lack of objectivity. But there are others with respect to which lack of objectivity may be owing to persistent intrusion of completely selfless general concerns that confuse or corrupt one's sense of what is relevant to the form of activity in question. Thus, for example, a Ricardian "economic man" loses objectivity, not when he becomes completely preoccupied with his own greatest material good, but when he allows sentimental "moral" considerations to deflect him from the rational pursuit of that good itself.
7. Mayo, *Ethics and the Moral Life* (London: Macmillan & Co., 1958), p. 69.
8. Mayo's analysis is inconsistent on this point. Since he regards "objective" and "substantive" as correlative terms, it would seem to follow that he regards ethical assertions, even though subject to "criteria of correctness," as mere expressions of psychological states. However, at one point (*op. cit.*, p. 88) he goes so far as to say that "what we call objectivity in the former case [that is, the case of visual

perception] we call impartiality in the latter saying that morality too can be objective."

9. Cf. Baier, *The Moral Point of View* (Ithaca: Cornell University Press, 1958), pp. 77ff.
10. I believe that the situation is much the same in many other spheres of discourse. However, I am arguing here only the case of moral truth.

4

TOWARD A CREDIBLE FORM OF UTILITARIANISM

Richard B. Brandt *Swarthmore College*

INTRODUCTION

This paper is an attempt to formulate, in a tolerably precise way, a type of utilitarian ethical theory which is not open to obvious and catastrophic objections. It is not my aim especially to advocate the kind of view finally stated, although I do believe it is more acceptable than any other type of utilitarianism.

Utilitarianism is a topic discussed by contemporary moralists in either, or both, of two contexts. One of these contexts is that of traditional normative discussion of the correct answer to such questions as "What do all right actions have in common?" Many linguistically oriented philosophers do not believe such questions are a proper subject for philosophical discussion, but noncognitivists in metaethics can, as well as anyone else, consistently defend (or criticize) a utilitarian normative ethic, not claiming that such a theory is strictly true but nevertheless offering arguments of a kind.

Utilitarianism also plays a substantial part in contemporary metaethical discussions. If you ask some philosophers what can count as a good or valid reason for an ethical judgment, you may be told that some kind of utilitarian reason—inference from good consequences to rightness—is one kind, or even the only kind. This view may be supported by urging that this is the kind of reasoning people actually do use, or by saying that this is the kind of reasoning used in reflective moments by people whom we should count as reliable moral judges. Alternatively, it may be argued that this kind of reasoning is the kind that should be used—regardless of whether it is used—in view of the function of ethical reasoning and conscience in society, or in view of what counts as a "moral judgment" or as "moral reasoning" or as "justified ethical reasoning."

Discussions of utilitarianism in these two contexts are not as different as might at first appear. If some kind of utilitarian reasoning can be shown to be what reflective people do use, or if it can be shown to be the kind all ought to use, then presumably utilitarianism as a normative position—as the one "valid" principle in normative ethics—can be established, in the way we can expect to establish such things in ethics.

The formulation of utilitarianism I shall work out in this paper, then, can be viewed in either of two ways, corresponding with the persuasions of the reader. It can be viewed as a candidate for the status of normative "truth," or, for the noncognitivist, for whatever status is in his theory the analogue of truth in cognitivist theories. Or it can be viewed as a way of thinking or reasoning, as a rule of valid inference—the central theme either of considerations which play a role in the ethical inferences of reliable moral judges, or of considerations which would play a certain role in ethical thinking if we thought as we ought to do, in view of the functions (etc.) of ethical discourse. One way of putting the contrast is this: we can view our formulation either as a candidate for the status of being a true principle of normative ethics or as a rule for valid inferences in ethics. I am not, incidentally, suggesting that it is a merely terminological matter which view we take of it; I think it is *not* merely this, since the kinds of reasoning used to support one view may be quite different from those used to support the other view. My point is that the theory I wish to discuss may properly be considered in either light, and that the difficulties I shall raise are difficulties which must be taken seriously by philosophers who discuss utilitarianism in either of these contexts. Mostly, I shall talk for convenience as if utilitarianism were a normative principle; but everything I say, and all the difficulties I consider, can just as well be placed in the context of metaethical discussion.

The view to be discussed is a form of "rule-utilitarianism." This terminology must be explained. I call a utilitarianism "act-utilitarianism" if it holds that the rightness of an act is fixed by the utility of *its* consequences, as compared with those of other acts the agent might perform instead. Act-utilitarianism is hence an atomistic theory: the value of the effects of a single act on the world is decisive for its rightness. "Rule-utilitarianism," in contrast, applies to views according to which the rightness of an act is not fixed by *its* relative utility, but by conformity with general rules or principles; the utilitarian feature of these theories consists in the fact that the correctness of these rules or principles is fixed in some way by the utility of their general acceptance. In contrast with the atomism of act-utilitarianism, rule-utilitarianism is in a sense an organic theory: the rightness of individual acts can be ascertained only by assessing a whole social policy.

Neither form of utilitarianism is necessarily committed on the subject of what counts as "utility": not on the meaning or function of such phrases as "maximize intrinsic good," and not on the identity of intrinsic goods—whether enjoyments, or states of persons, or states of affairs, such as equality of distribution.

In recent years, types of rule-utilitarianism have been the object of much interest.[1] And for good reason. Act-utilitarianism, at least given the assumptions about what is valuable which utilitarians commonly make, has implications which it is difficult to accept.[2] It implies that if you have employed a boy to mow your lawn and he has finished the job and asks for his pay, you should pay him what you promised only if you cannot find a better use for your money. It implies that when you bring home your monthly pay-check you should use it to support your family and yourself only if it cannot be used more effectively to supply the needs of others. It implies that if your father is ill and has no prospect of good in his life, and maintaining him is a drain on the energy and enjoyments of others, then, if you can end his life without provoking any public scandal or setting a bad example, it is your positive duty to take matters into your own hands and bring his life to a close. A virtue of rule-utilitarianism, in at least some of its forms, is that it avoids at least some of such objectionable implications.

In the present paper I wish to arrive at a more precise formulation of a rule-utilitarian type of theory which is different from act-utilitarianism and which is not subject to obvious and catastrophic difficulties. To this end I shall, after an important preliminary discussion, begin by considering two formulations, both supported by distinguished philosophers, which, as I shall show, lead us in the wrong direction. This discussion will lead to a new formulation devised to avoid the consequences of the first theories. I shall then describe three problems which the new theory seems to face, and consider how—by amendments or otherwise—these difficulties may be met.

I

UTILITARIANISM AS A THEORY ABOUT THE OBJECTIVELY RIGHT

Before we can proceed there is a preliminary issue to be settled. It is generally agreed that utilitarianism is a proposal about which acts are *right* or *wrong*. Unfortunately it is also widely held—although this is a matter of dispute—that these terms are used in several senses. Hence, in order to state the utilitarian thesis clearly, we must identify which sense of these words (if there is more than one) we have in mind. Utilitarianism may be clearly false in all of its forms if it is construed as a universal statement about which acts are right or wrong, in some of the senses in which these words are, or at least are supposed to be, used.

It is plausible to say that "wrong" is sometimes used in a sense equivalent to "morally blameworthy" or "reprehensible," in a sense which implies the propriety of disapproval of the agent for his deed. Now, if utilitarianism is understood as a theory about right and wrong actions in this sense, I believe it is an indefensible theory in all its forms. For we have good reason to think that whether an act is wrong in this sense depends in part on such things as whether the agent sincerely believed he was doing his duty, whether the temptation to do what he did was so strong that only a person of very unusual firmness of will would have succeeded in withstanding it, and whether the agent's action was impulsive and provoked, or deliberate and unprovoked. If whether an act is wrong depends in part on any one of these factors, then it is difficult to see how the utilitarian thesis that rightness or wrongness is in some sense a function of utility can be correct.

We can, however, construe utilitarianism as a thesis about which acts are right or wrong in some other sense. It may, for instance, be taken as a theory about which acts are right or wrong in a forward-looking sense, which I shall call the "objective" sense. But what is this sense? It is by no means easy to say; and we must be careful not to describe some alleged sense of these words which in fact they never bear in common speech at all. Let me explain this possible second sense by means of an example.

Consider Eisenhower's position at the summit conference in 1960. Khrushchev demanded that Eisenhower apologize, as a condition for negotiation. Let us suppose that Eisenhower proceeded to ask himself the moral question, "What is the morally right thing for me to do now? Is it my moral obligation to apologize or to refuse to apologize?" Clearly, it would seem, this is a question he might have asked himself, whether he did or not. Obviously, if he did try to answer this question, he must have considered many things. One thing he must have considered was the state of Khrushchev's mind. Did Khrushchev really think there had been a breach of faith, an affront to the Russian people, which in decency called for at least an apology? Was

Khrushchev really willing to negotiate for peace if only this—which might relieve some political pressures at home—were done? Everything considered, would an apology, however personally distasteful (and perhaps politically unfortunate, at home), markedly promote the cause of peace? Let us suppose that Eisenhower surveyed these points as carefully as possible with his advisers and came to a conclusion on them. And let us suppose that he then moved to a moral conclusion. Presumably his conclusion (if he raised the moral question) was that it was not his duty to apologize, that on the contrary it was his duty *not* to apologize. But surely in a complex situation of this sort he must have put his conclusion in a qualified way; he must have said something like, "*Probably* it is my duty not to apologize." And, conceivably, he might some day change his mind about this, and say to himself, "It was my duty to apologize; my judgment then was mistaken." I think we shall all agree that he might well have expressed himself in this qualified way and that he might later revise his judgment in the manner suggested.

The crucial thing about understanding the sense in which "duty" (or "wrong") is here being used is whether the qualifying "probably" is introduced or whether the revision conceding a "mistake" may be made, for one reason or for another. Does he say "probably" because he does not and cannot know Khrushchev's real state of mind? Does he say a "mistake" was made because, as it turns out, Khrushchev's state of mind was really different from what at the time he supposed it to be? If the answer to these questions is affirmative, then evidently duty depends, at least to some extent, on what the facts really are and not merely on what one thinks they are, even after careful consultation with advisers. But if the answer is negative, then it is open to one to say that the qualification and mistakes come in only because it is so difficult to *balance* different considerations, and that what is one's duty does not depend on what the facts really are, but only on what one thinks they are, at least after properly careful reflection and investigation.

If we answer these questions in the affirmative and consequently say that "duty" is sometimes used in a sense such that whether something is one's duty depends on what the facts really are, then we are conceding that the word (and, presumably, "right" and "wrong" and "moral obligation") is sometimes used in an "objective" sense—the sense in which G. E. Moore thought it was sometimes used when he wrote *Ethics* and *Principia Ethica*. And if so, it is not entirely stupid to propose, as Moore did, that furthermore, an act is right, in that objective sense of "right," if and only if its *actual* consequences, whether foreseeable at the time or not, are such that the performance of the act produces at least as much intrinsic good as could be produced by any other act the agent could perform instead. It is this sense of these terms—the sense in which duty (etc.) depends on what the facts really are and not on what the agent thinks about them—which I am terming the "objective" sense. I shall construe utilitarianism as a proposal about which acts are right or wrong in this objective sense.

It would be foolish, however, to say that it is quite *obvious* that the answer to the above questions is in the affirmative; and consequently it would be foolish to affirm without doubt that there is a sense of "duty" in which duty depends on what the facts are and not on what the agent thinks they are—and much more foolish to affirm without doubt that there is *no* sense of "duty" in which duty depends, not on the facts, but on what the agent thinks the facts are, at least after properly careful investigation.

Philosophers who think these words have no "objective" sense at all, or who at least think there is still a third sense of these terms, over and above the two I have sketched, probably can mostly be said to think that these words are used in what we may call the "subjective" sense—and either that this is their only sense or that it is one ordinary sense. They do not agree among themselves about what this sense is. Some of them hold that "right" (etc.) is sometimes so used that—if I may identify their conception by my own terminology, which, of course, some of them would not accept—an act is right in that sense if and only if it would have been right in my objective sense, if the facts had really been what the agent thought they were, or at least would have thought they were if he had investigated properly. What is one's duty, on this view, depends on what the agent thinks about the facts—or would think if he investigated properly—not on what the facts really are. Naturally, if one has this (alleged) sense of "duty" or "right" in mind when formulating the principle of utilitarianism, one will say the principle is that an act is right if and only if the agent *thinks*—or would think, if he investigated properly—it will maximize utility (or have some such relation to utility). Or, perhaps, the principle will say that an act is right if and only if it will maximize expectable utility, or something of the sort.

The question whether there is an objective sense, or a subjective sense, or perhaps both such senses, is a difficult one. Although I think it plausible to suppose there is an "objective" sense, I do feel doubt about the matter. I propose, nevertheless, to discuss utilitarianism as a theory about right and wrong in this sense. I do so for several reasons. First, there are many philosophers who think there is such a sense, and an examination of utilitarianism construed in this way "speaks to their condition." [3] Second, even if there were no such ordinary sense of "right," we could define such a sense by reference to the "subjective" sense of "right" (assuming there is one); and it so happens that we could say all the things that we have occasion to say in ethics by using this defined "objective" sense of "right" and also terms like "blameworthy" and "reprehensible." We could say "all we have occasion to say" in the sense that any statement we make, and think important, could be put in terms of this vocabulary. Third, it is important to see how types of rule-utilitarian theory fare if they are construed as theories about which acts are right or wrong in this sense. Doubtless sometimes writers on this topic have not kept clearly in mind just which sense of "right" they were talking about; it is useful to see what difficulties arise *if* they are to be taken as talking of what is right or wrong in the objective sense. Finally, an assessment of utilitarianisms as theories about which acts are objectively right will enable us to make at least some assessments of utilitarianisms as theories about which acts are subjectively right, in view of the logical connection indicated above between "right" in the objective sense and "right" in the subjective sense.

2

ACCEPTED RULES VS. JUSTIFIABLE RULES AS THE TEST OF RIGHTNESS

It is convenient to begin by taking as our text some statements drawn from an interesting article by J. O. Urmson. In this paper, Urmson suggested that John Stuart Mill should be interpreted as a rule-utilitarian; and Urmson's opinion was that Mill's view would be more plausible if he were so interpreted. Urmson summarized the possible rule-utilitarian interpretation of Mill in four propositions, of which I quote the first two:

A. A particular action is justified as being right [in the sense of being morally obligatory] by showing that it is in accord with [is required by] some moral rule. It is shown to be wrong by showing that it transgresses some moral rule.
B. A moral rule is shown to be correct by showing that the recognition of that rule promotes the ultimate end.[4]

Urmson's first proposition could be taken in either of two ways. When it speaks of a "moral rule," it may refer to an *accepted* moral rule, presumably one accepted in the society of the agent. Alternatively, it may refer to a *correct* moral rule, presumably one the recognition of which promotes the ultimate end. If we ask in which way the proposed theory should be taken, in order to arrive at a defensible theory, part of the answer is that qualifications are going to be required, whichever way we take it. I think it more worthwhile and promising, however, to try to develop it in the second interpretation.

Various philosophers would make the opposite judgment about which interpretation is the more promising. And there is much to be said for their view, in particular the following points. First, we shall probably all agree that the moral rules accepted in a community often do fix real obligations on members of the community. For example, among ourselves it is taken for granted that primary responsibility for caring for an old man falls on his children, although in special cases it could fall elsewhere. On the other hand, suppose that our social system contained the rule—as that of the Hopi actually does—that this responsibility falls primarily on the children of a man's sisters, again with exceptions for special cases. It seems clear that in a social system like ours the children do have responsibility for their father, whereas in a social system like that of the Hopi they do not—the responsibility belongs to the children of the sisters. There are complications, to be sure; but in general we must say that when an institutional system specifies that responsibility falls in a certain place, then on the whole and with some exceptions and qualifications, that is where it really does lie. Any theory which denies this is mistaken; and if our second theory is to be plausible, it must be framed so as to imply this. Second, I think we should concede that if two persons are debating whether some act is right and one of them is able to show that it infringes on the accepted moral code of the community, the "burden of proof" passes to the other party. The fact that it is generally believed that a certain kind of action is wrong is prima facie evidence that it is wrong; it is up to persons who disagree to show their hand. Third, if a conscientious man is deliberating whether he is morally obligated to do a certain thing which he does not wish to do, I believe he will generally feel he must do this thing, even if he thinks that a correct moral code would not require him to, provided he concludes that many or most persons in his community would conclude otherwise. The reason for this is partly, I think, that a conscientious man will take pains to avoid even the appearance of evil; but the reason is also that a conscientious man will wish to make substantial allowances for the fact that he is an interested party and might have been influenced by his own preferences in his thinking about his obligations. He will therefore tend to hold himself to the received code when this is to his disadvantage.

Nevertheless, it is extremely difficult to defend Urmson's rule interpreted in this way, even when we hedge it with qualifications, as, for example, Toulmin did. In the first place, people do not *think* that anything like this is true; they think they are assessing particular cases by reference to objectively valid principles which they happen to know, and not simply by reference to a community code. Notice how we do not find it surprising that people with unusual moral principles, such as the immorality of killing and violence in all circumstances, come to distinctive conclusions about their own particular obligations, by no means drawing their particular moral judgments from the code of the community. The whole tradition emphasizing the role of conscience in moral thinking is contrary to the view that socially accepted principles are crucial for deciding what is right or wrong. In the second place, we frequently judge ourselves to have moral obligations either when we don't know what the community "standards" are, or when we think that in all probability there is no decided majority one way or the other: for instance, with respect to sexual behavior, or to declaration, to revenue officers, of articles purchased abroad or of one's personal income. Surely we do not think that in such situations the proper judgment of particular cases is that they are morally indifferent? Third, and perhaps most important, we sometimes judge that we have an obligation when we know that the community thinks we don't; and we sometimes think an act is right when the community thinks it wrong. For instance, we may judge that we have an obligation to join in seeking presidential clemency for a convicted Communist spy whom we regard as having received an unduly severe sentence because of mass hysteria at the time of his trial, although we know quite well that the communal code prescribes no favors for Communists. Again, we may think it not wrong to work on the Sabbath, marry a divorced person, perform a medically necessary abortion, or commit suicide, irrespective of general disapproval in our group. Were these things *ever* objectively wrong, in view of being proscribed—even unanimously—by the community of the agent? (It may be replied that the "code" does not legislate for complex matters of these sorts, but only for more basic things, like Ross's list of prima facie obligations. But it is not clear what can be the basis for this distinction; the acts in question may be prohibited by law and would be reported by a visiting anthropologist as proscribed by the code.)

One might argue that the existence of an accepted moral rule is not sufficient to make particular actions wrong or obligatory but is a necessary condition. To say this, however, is to say that men have no obligation to rise above the commonplace morals of their times. Whereas in fact we do not think it right for men to be cruel to animals or to slaves in a society which condones this.

We cannot well say in advance that no thesis like Urmson's can play an important part in a defensible theory of morals, if it is interpreted in this first way. But the difficulties are surely enough to encourage experimenting with versions of the second interpretation. Let us turn to this.

For a start, we might summarize the gist of Urmson's proposal, construed in the second way, as follows: "An act is right if and only if it conforms with that set of moral rules, the recognition of which would have significantly desirable consequences." A somewhat modified version of this is what I shall be urging.

One minor amendment I wish to make immediately. I think we should replace the second clause by the expression, "the recognition of which would have the *best* consequences." This amendment may be criticized on the ground that the business of moral rules is with commanding or prohibiting actions whose performance or omission would be quite harmful if practiced widely, but not to require actions which just maximize benefits, especially if the benefit concerns only the agent. It may be said, then, that the amendment I propose is possibly a clue to *perfect* behavior but not to right behavior. But this objection overlooks an important point. We must remember that it is a serious matter to have a moral rule at all, for moral rules take conduct out of the realm of preference and free decision. So, for the recognition of a certain moral rule to have good consequences, the benefits of recognition must outweigh the costliness of restricting freedom. Therefore, to recognize a moral rule restricting self-regarding behavior will rarely have the best consequences; rules of prudence should normally not be moral rules. Again, my proposal implies that moral rules will require services for other people only when it is better to have such services performed from a sense of obligation than not performed at all; so the amendment does not commit us to saying that it is morally obligatory to perform minor altruistic services for others.

But why insist on the amendment? The reason is that the original, as I stated it (but not necessarily as Urmson intended it), is insufficiently comparative in form. The implication is that a rule is acceptable so long as it is significantly better than no regulation at all. But the effect of this is tolerantly to accept a great many rules which we should hardly regard as morally acceptable. Consider promises. There are various possible rules about when promises must be kept. One such possible rule is to require keeping *all* promises, absolutely irrespective of unforeseeable and uncontemplated hardships on the promisee. Recognition of this rule might have good consequences as compared with no rule at all. Therefore it seems to satisfy the unamended formula. Many similar rules would satisfy it. But we know of another rule—the one we recognize—with specifications about allowable exceptions, which would have much better consequences. If we are utilitarian in spirit, we shall want to endorse such a rule but not both of these rules; and the second one is much closer to our view about what our obligations are. The amendment in general endorses as correct many rules which command our support for parallel reasons, and refuses to endorse many others which we reject for parallel reasons.

3

A SPECIOUS RULE-UTILITARIANISM

I shall now digress briefly, in order to bring out the importance of avoiding a form of rule-utilitarianism which seems to differ only insignificantly from our above initial suggestion, and which at first seems most attractive. It is worthwhile doing so, partly because two very interesting and important papers developing a rule-utilitarian theory may be construed as falling into the trap I shall describe.[5] I say only that they "may be" so construed because their authors are possibly using somewhat different concepts and, in particular, may not be thinking of utilitarianism as a thesis about right and wrong in the objective sense.

Suppose that we wrote, instead of the above suggested formulation, the following: "An act is right if and only if it conforms with that set of moral rules, general conformity with which would have best consequences." This phrasing is a bit vague, however, so let us expand it to this: "An act is right if and only if it conforms with that set of general prescriptions for action such that, if everyone always did, from among all the things which he could do on a given occasion, what conformed with these prescriptions, then at least as much intrinsic good would be produced as by conformity with any other set of general prescriptions." This sounds very like our above formulation. It is, however, different in a very important way: for its test of whether an act is right, or a general rule correct, is what would happen if people *really all did act* in a certain way. The test is not the consequences of recognizing a rule, or of acting with such a rule in mind; the test as stated does not require that people do, or even can, think of or formulate, much less apply the rule of a moral code. What is being said is simply that a rule is correct, and corresponding conduct right, if it would have best consequences for everyone actually to act, for whatever reason, in accordance with the rule. Of course, one of the consequences to be taken into account may be the fact that expectations of conduct according to the rule might be built up, and that people could count on conforming behavior.

This theory is initially attractive. We seem to be appealing to it in our moral reasoning when we say, "You oughtn't to do so-and-so, because if everybody in your circumstances did this, the consequences would be bad."

Nevertheless, the fact is that this theory—however hard it may be to see that it does—has identically the same consequences for behavior as does act-utilitarianism. And since it does, it is a mistake to advocate it as a theory preferable to act-utilitarianism, as some philosophers may have done. Let us see how this is.

Let us ask ourselves: What would a set of moral prescriptions be like, such that general conformity with it, in the sense intended, would have the best consequences? The answer is that the set would contain just one rule, the prescription of the *act-utilitarian:* "Perform an act, among those open to you, which will have at least as good consequences as any other." There cannot be a moral rule, conformity with which could have better consequences than this one. If it really is true that doing a certain thing will have the very best consequences in the long run, everything considered, of all the things I can do, then there is nothing better I can do than this. If everyone always did the very best thing it was possible for him to do, the total intrinsic value produced would be at a maximum. Any act which deviated from this principle would produce less good than some other act which might have been performed. It is clear, then, that the moral rule general conformity with which would produce most good is a rule corresponding to the principle of act-utilitarianism. The two theories, then, have identical consequences for behavior. I am, of course, not at all suggesting that everyone *trying* to produce the best consequences will have the same consequences as everyone *trying* to follow some different set of rules—or that everyone trying to follow some different set of rules may not have better consequences than everyone trying just to produce the best consequences. Far from it. What I am saying is that *succeeding* in producing the best consequences is a kind of success which cannot be improved upon. And it is this which is in question, when we are examining the formula we are now looking at.

To say that succeeding in producing the best consequences cannot be improved upon is consistent with admitting that what will in fact have the best consequences, in view of what other people in fact have done or will do, may be different from what would have had the best consequences if other people were to behave differently from the way in which they did or will do.

The behavior of others is part of the context relevant for determining the effects of a given act of any agent.

It may be thought that this reasoning is unfair to this rule-utilitarian view. For what this theory has in mind, it may be said, is rules forbidding classes of actions described in ways other than by reference to their utility—rules forbidding actions like lies, adultery, theft, etc. So, it may be said, the principle of act-utilitarianism is not even a competitor for the position of one of the rules admitted by this theory.

My reply to this objection is twofold. In the first place, it would be rather foolish to suppose that any system of moral rules could omit rules about doing good, rules about doing what will maximize utility. Surely we do wish to include among our rules one roughly to the effect that, if we have the opportunity to do a great deal of good for others at little cost, we should do it. And also a rule to the effect that we should avoid harming others. It is no accident that W. D. Ross's list of seven prima facie obligations contains four which refer to doing good, in one way or another. But the point would still stand even if we ignore this fact. For suppose we set about to describe a set of rules, none of which is explicitly to prescribe *doing good*, but general conformity with which will maximize utility. Now obviously, the set of rules in question will be that set which prescribes, by descriptions which make no reference to having good consequences, exactly that very class of actions which would also be prescribed by the act-utilitarian principle. And one can find a set of rules which will prescribe exactly this class of acts without referring to utility. We can find such a set, because every member of the class of acts prescribed by the act-utilitarian principle will have some other property *on account of which* it will maximize utility in the circumstances. Every act, that is to say, which maximizes utility does so because of some doubtless very complex property that it has. As a result, we can set up a system of prescriptions for action which refer to these complex properties, such that our system of rules will prescribe exactly the set of acts prescribed by the act-utilitarian principle. The set of rules may be enormously long and enormously complex. But this set of rules will have the property of being that set, general conformity with which will maximize utility. And the acts prescribed will be identical with the acts prescribed by the act-utilitarian principle. So, again, the prescriptions for conduct of this form of rule-utilitarianism are identical with those of the act-utilitarian theory.

4

RULE-UTILITARIANISM: A SECOND APPROXIMATION

The whole point of the preceding remarks has been to focus attention on the point that a rule-utilitarianism like Urmson's is different from act-utilitarianism only when it speaks of something like "*recognition* of a rule having the best consequences" instead of something like "*conformity* with a certain rule having the best consequences." With this in mind, we can see clearly one of the virtues of Urmson's proposal, which we interpreted as being: "An act is right if and only if it conforms with that set of moral rules, *the recognition of which* would have the best consequences."

But, having viewed the difficulties of a view verbally very similar to the above, we are now alert to the fact that the formulation we have suggested is itself open to interpretations that may lead to problems. How may we construe Urmson's proposal, so that it is both unambiguous and credible? Of course we do not wish to go to the opposite extreme and take "recognition of" to mean merely "doffing the hat to" without attempt to practice. But how shall we take it?

I suggest the following as a second approximation.

First, let us speak of a set of moral rules as being "learnable" if people of ordinary intelligence are able to learn or absorb its provisions, so as to believe the moral propositions in question in the ordinary sense of "believe" for such contexts.[6] Next, let us speak of "the adoption" of a moral code by a person as meaning "the learning and belief of its provisions (in the above sense) and conformity of behavior to these to the extent we may expect people of ordinary conscientiousness to conform their behavior to rules they believe are principles about right or obligatory behavior." Finally, let us, purely arbitrarily and for the sake of brevity, use the phrase "maximizes intrinsic value" to mean "would produce at least as much intrinsic good as would be produced by any relevant alternative action." With these stipulations, we can now propose, as a somewhat more precise formulation of Urmson's proposal, the following rule-utilitarian thesis: "An act is right if and only if it conforms with that learnable set of rules, the adoption of which by everyone would maximize intrinsic value."

This principle does not at all imply that the rightness or wrongness of an act is contingent upon the agent's having *thought about* all the complex business of the identity of a set of ideal moral rules; it asserts, rather, that an act is right if and only if it *conforms* to such a set of rules, regardless of what the agent may think. Therefore the principle is not disqualified from being a correct principle about what is objectively right or wrong, in Moore's sense; for it makes rightness and wrongness a matter of the facts, and totally independent of what the agent thinks is right, or of what the agent thinks about the facts, or of the evidence the agent may have, or of what is probably the case on the basis of this evidence.

An obvious merit of this principle is that it gives expression to at least part of our practice or procedure in trying to find out what is right or wrong. For when we are in doubt about such matters, we often try to think out how it would work in practice to have a moral code which prohibited or permitted various actions we are considering. We do not, of course, ordinarily do anything as complicated as try to think out the *complete* ideal moral code; we are content with considering whether certain specific injunctions relevant to the problem we are considering might be included in a good and workable code. Nevertheless, we are prepared to admit that the whole ideal code is relevant. For if someone shows us that a specific injunction which we think would be an acceptable part of a moral code clearly would not work out in view of other provisions necessary to an ideal code, we should agree that a telling point had been made and revise our thinking accordingly.

In order to get a clearer idea of the kind of "set of rules" (with which right actions must conform) which could satisfy the conditions this rule-utilitarian principle lays down, let us note some general features such a set presumably would have. First, it would contain rules giving directions for recurrent situations which involve conflicts of human interests. Presumably, then, it would contain rules rather similar to W. D. Ross's list of prima facie obligations: rules about the keeping of promises and contracts, rules about debts of gratitude such as we may owe to our parents, and, of course, rules about not injuring other persons and about promoting the welfare of others where this does not work a comparable hardship on us. Second, such a set of rules would not include petty restrictions; nor, at least for the most part, would it contain purely prudential rules. Third, the rules would not be very numerous; an upper limit on quantity is set by the ability of ordinary people to learn them. Fourth, such a set of rules would not include unbearable demands; for their inclusion would only serve to bring moral obligation into discredit. Fifth, the set of rules adoption of which would have the best consequences could not leave too much to discretion. It would make concessions to the fact that ordinary people are not capable of perfectly fine discriminations, and to the fact that, not being morally perfect, people of ordinary conscientiousness will have a tendency to abuse a moral rule where it suits their interest. We must remember that a college dormitory rule like "Don't play music at such times or in such a way as to disturb the study or sleep of others" would be ideally flexible if people were perfect; since they aren't, we have to settle for a rule like "No music after 10 P.M." The same thing is true for a moral code. The best moral code has to allow for the fact that people are what they are; it has to be less flexible and less efficient than a moral code that was to be adopted by perfectly wise and perfectly conscientious people could be.

Should we think of such a moral code as containing only

prescriptions for situations likely to arise in *everyone's* life—rules like "If you have made a promise, then . . ." or "If you have a parent living, then treat him thus-and-so"? Or should we think of it as containing distinct sets of prescriptions for *different roles or statuses*, such as "If you are a policeman, then . . ." or "If you are a physician, then . . ."? And if the ideal code is to contain different prescriptions for different roles and statuses, would it not be so complex that it could not be learned by people of ordinary intelligence? The answer to these questions is that the rule-utilitarian is not committed, by his theory, to the necessity of such special codes, although I believe he may well admit their desirability—admit, for instance, that it is a good thing for a physician to carry a rule in his mental kit, specially designed to answer the question, "Shall I treat a patient who does not pay his bill?" In any case, our rule-utilitarian theory can *allow* for such special rules. Nor is there a difficulty in the fact that people of normal intelligence could hardly learn all these special sets of rules. For we can mean, by saying that a code can be "learned" by people of ordinary intelligence, that any person can learn all the rules relevant to the problems *he* will face. A rule-utilitarian will not, of course, have in mind a moral code which in some part is secret—for instance, lawyers having a moral code known only to themselves, a code which it would be harmful for others to know about. For surely in the long run it could not have best consequences for a society to have a moral code, perhaps granting special privileges to some groups, which could not stand the light of public knowledge.

5

FIRST PROBLEM: MORAL CODES FOR AN IMPERFECT SOCIETY

Our "second approximation" to a rule-utilitarian principle has proposed that an act is right if and only if it conforms with the requirements of a learnable moral code, the adoption of which by *everyone* would maximize utility—and meaning by "adoption of a code" the learning and belief that the code lays down the requirements for moral behavior, and conformity to it to the extent we may expect from people of *ordinary conscientiousness.*

The italicized words in the preceding paragraph indicate two respects in which the proposed test of rightness in a sense departs from reality. In actuality moral codes are not subscribed to by everybody in all particulars: there is virtual unanimity on some items of what we call "the code of the community" (such as the prohibition of murder and incest), but on other matters there is less unanimity (in the United States, the "code" permits artificial birth-control measures despite disapproval by many Catholics), and it is a somewhat arbitrary matter to decide when the disagreement has become so general that we ought not to speak of something as part of the code of the community at all. There is probably some measure of disagreement on many or most moral matters in most modern communities (and, surely, in at least many primitive communities). Furthermore, our proposal, in an effort to be definite about the degree of commitment involved in the "adoption" of a code, spoke of an "ordinary conscientiousness." This again departs from reality. Ordinary conscientiousness may be the exception: many people are extremely, perhaps even overly conscientious; at the other extreme, some people act as if they have developed no such thing as a conscience at all. It is characteristic of actual communities that there is a wide range in degrees of conscientiousness.

As a result of these departures from reality, our test for rightness savors a bit of the utopian. We are invited to think of different worlds, each populated by people of "ordinary conscientiousness," all of whom are inoculated with a standard moral code. We are to decide whether given types of action are right or wrong by considering which of these hypothetical communities would realize a maximum of value.

There is force in the proposal. In fact, if we are thinking of sponsoring some ideal, this conception is a useful one for appraising whatever ideal we are considering. Just as we might ask whether large military establishments or a capitalist economy would be suitable for the ideal community of the future, so we can ask whether certain features of our present moral code would be suitable in such a community. It may be that such a conception should play a large role in deciding what ultimate ideals we should espouse.

Nevertheless, this conception may, from its very framework, necessarily be unsuitable for deciding the rightness of actions in the real world. It appears that, in fact, this is the case with both of the features mentioned above.

First, the proposal is to test rightness by the desirability of a rule in a moral code among people of ordinary conscientiousness. Now, in a community composed of people of ordinary conscientiousness we do not have to provide for the contingency of either saints or great sinners. In particular, we do not have to provide for the occurrence of people like Adolf Hitler. In such a community, presumably, we could get along with a minimal police force, perhaps an unarmed police force. Similarly, it would seem there would be no value in a moral prescription like "Resist evil men." In the community envisaged, problems of a certain sort would presumably not arise, and therefore the moral code need not have features designed to meet those problems. Very likely, for instance, a moral code near to that of extreme pacifism would work at least as well as a code differing in its non-pacifism.

More serious is the flaw in the other feature: that the test of rightness is to be compatibility with the requirements of the moral code, adoption of which *by everyone* would maximize utility. The trouble with this is that it permits behavior which really would be desirable if everyone agreed, but which might be objectionable and undesirable if not everyone agreed. For instance, it may well be that it would have the best consequences if the children are regarded as responsible for an elderly parent who is ill or needy; but it would be most unfortunate if the members of a Hopi man's native household—primarily his sisters and their families—decided that their presently recognized obligation had no standing on this account, since the result would be that as things now stand, no one at all would take the responsibility. Again, if everyone recognized an obligation to share in duties pertaining to national defense, it would be morally acceptable to require this legally; but it would hardly be morally acceptable to do so if there are pacifists who on moral grounds are ready to die rather than bear arms. And similarly for other matters about which there are existing and pronounced moral convictions.

It seems clear that some modification must be made if our rule-utilitarian proposal is to have implications consistent with the moral convictions of thoughtful people. Unfortunately it is not clear just what the modification should be. The one I am inclined to adopt is as follows. First, we must drop that part of our conception which assumes that people in our hypothetical societies are of ordinary conscientiousness. We want to allow for the existence of both saints and sinners and to have a moral code to cope with them. In order to do this, we had better move closer to Urmson's original suggestion. We had better drop the notion of "adoption" and replace it by his term "recognition," meaning by "recognition by all" simply "belief by all that the rules formulate moral requirements." Second, we must avoid the conception of the acceptance of all the rules of a given moral code by *everybody* and replace it by something short of this, something which does not rule out the problems created by actual convictions about morals. Doing so means a rather uneasy compromise, because we cannot sacrifice the central feature of the rule-utilitarian view, which is that the rightness of an act is to be tested by whether it conforms with rules the (somehow) general acceptance of which would maximize utility. The compromise I propose is this: that the test whether an act is right is whether it is compatible with that set of rules which, were it to replace the moral commitments of members of the *actual society* at the time, *except where there are already fairly decided moral convictions*, would maximize utility.

The modified theory, then, is this: "An act is right if and only if it conforms with that learnable set of rules, the recognition of which as morally binding, roughly at the time of the act, by all actual people insofar as these rules are not incompatible with existing fairly decided moral commitments, would maximize intrinsic value."[7]

The modification has the effect that whether an act is right depends to some extent on such things as (1) how large a proportion of the actual population is conscientious and (2) what are the existing fairly decided moral beliefs at the time. This result is not obviously a mistake.

6

SECOND PROBLEM: CONFLICTS OF RULES

The objection is sure to be raised against any rule-utilitarian theory of the general sort we are considering that the whole conception is radically misconceived. For the theory proposes that what makes an act right is its conformity to the set of rules, recognition of which would maximize utility; and it is proposed that if we are in serious doubt whether an action would be right, we should ask ourselves whether it would conform with a utility-maximizing set of rules. Now, the objection will run, the very conception of such a set of rules evaporates, or else appears to involve contradictions, when we try to get it in sharp focus. The very idea of a set of rules simple enough to be learned and different from act-utilitarianism, and at the same time sufficiently comprehensive and precise to yield directions for conduct in every situation which may arise, is an impossible dream.

The reason is that moral problems are often quite complex. There are pros and cons—obligations and counter-obligations—which have to be weighed delicately. For instance, a promise that has been made to do something is normally a point in favor of saying that doing it is obligatory; but just how much force the promise will have depends on various circumstances, such as when it was made, how solemnly it was made, whether it was fully understood by both parties, etc. The force of these circumstances cannot be stated and weighed by any set of rules. There is a moral to be drawn, it may be said, from W. D. Ross's theory of prima facie obligations: Ross could provide no general direction for what to do when prima facie obligations conflict; he had to leave the resolution of such conflicts to conscience or intuition. So, in general, no code simple enough to be written down and learned (and different from act-utilitarianism) can prescribe what is right in complex cases.

The difficulty is obviously a serious one. If the very concept of a complete code, the recognition of which would maximize utility, cannot be explained in detail, then the proposal that the rightness of every action is fixed by its conformity with the provisions of such a code must be abandoned.

What must be done to meet this charge? Of course, it cannot be demanded that we actually produce the ideal moral code for our society, or even a complete code of which the correct code might be supposed to be a variation. What can be fairly demanded is that we describe classes of rules or elements which may be expected in the ideal code, and that we make clear, in the course of this description, that the rules constituting the classes are simple enough to be learned, and that a person who had learned the rules of the several classes would be in a position to give an answer to all moral questions—or at least as definite an answer as can reasonably be expected. We may suppose that, if the theory is to be plausible, these classes of rules will be familiar—that they will be rules which thoughtful people do use in deciding moral issues. Let us see what can be said.

It is clear that a complete moral code must contain rules or principles of more than one level. The lowest level will consist of rules devised to cover familiar recurrent situations, presumably rather like those proposed by Ross in his formulation of prima facie obligations. Thus, it will contain rules like "Do not injure conscious beings," "Do what you have promised to do," etc. On reflection, we can see that such rules must be qualified in two ways. First, each of them must conclude with an exceptive clause something like "except as otherwise provided in this code." But second, they must be more complex than our samples; as Ross well knew, such simple rules do not state accurately what we think are our prima facie obligations—and presumably such rules are not the rules it would maximize welfare to have recognized as first-order rules. Consider for instance the rule I have suggested about promises. It is too simple, for we do not seriously believe that *all* promises have even a prima facie claim to be fulfilled; nor would it be a good thing for people to think they ought. For instance, we think there is no obligation at all to keep a promise made on the basis of deliberate misrepresentation by the promisee; and it is to the public interest that we should think as we do. Just as the law of contracts lists various types of contracts which it is against the public interest for the courts to enforce, so there are types of promises the fulfillment of which we do not think obligatory, and a moral requirement to fulfill them would be contrary to the public interest. The lowest-level group of rules, then, will include one about promise-keeping which will state explicitly which types of promises must be kept except when some more stringent obligation intervenes. And the same for the other basic moral rules.

I do not know if anyone would contend that it would be impossible to write down an exact statement formulating our total prima facie obligations—the kinds of considerations which to some extent make a moral claim on agents. I do not know if anyone would say that in principle we cannot state exactly the list of prima facie obligations it would maximize utility for everyone to feel. Whether or not anyone does say that a list of exact prima facie obligations cannot be stated, I know of no solid argument which can be put forward to show that this is the case. I do not believe a satisfactory list *has* been provided (Ross's statement being quite abbreviated), but I know of no sound reason for thinking that it cannot be. It would not, I think, be an impossible inquiry to determine what is the total set of distinct fundamental prima facie obligations people in fact do recognize in their moral thinking.

A set of first-level rules, however, is not enough. For moral perplexities arise most often where there are conflicts of prima facie obligations, where there would be conflicts of the first-level moral rules. If the rule-utilitarian theory is to work, it must provide for the resolution of such perplexities. How can this be done?

The problem can be partially met by supposing that a complete moral code will contain second-level rules specifically prescribing for conflicts of the basic rules. One second-level rule might be: "Do not injure anyone solely in order to produce something good, unless the good achieved be substantially greater than the injury." In fact we already learn and believe rules roughly of this kind. For instance, Ross suggested in *The Right and the Good* that we think there is normally a stronger obligation to avoid injury to others than to do good or to keep one's promises. A moral code can contain some such second-order rules without intolerable complexity.

But such rules will hardly be numerous enough to solve all the problems. And the rule we stated was not precise: it used the vague phrase "substantially greater," which is clear enough, in context, to decide for many situations, but it is by no means precise enough to legislate for all. I think, therefore, that if the very conception of a set of rules simple enough to be learned and adequate to adjudicate all possible cases is to be intelligible, it must be possible to formulate a consistent and plausible "remainder-rule," that is, a top-level rule giving adequate directions for all cases for which the lower-level rules do not prescribe definitely enough or for which their prescriptions are conflicting. We are not here called upon to identify the correct remainder-rule—although we know that the rule-utilitarian theory is that the correct one is the one the recognition of which (etc.) would do most good. What we are called upon to do is to sketch out what such a rule might well be like.

It is worthwhile to mention two possibilities for a remainder-rule.[8] First, such a rule might specify that all cases not legislated for by other clauses in the code be decided simply on the basis of comparative utility of consequences. For such cases, then, the remainder-rule would prescribe exactly what the act-utilitarian principle prescribes. Second (and I think this possibility the more interesting), the remainder-rule might be: "One is obligated to perform an action if and only if a person who knew the relevant facts and had them vividly in mind, had been carefully taught the other rules of this code, and was uninfluenced by interests beyond those arising from learning the code, would feel obligated to perform that action." Such a rule could decide cases not legislated for by the remainder of the code only if the explicit rules were taught so as to be connected with different degrees of *felt obligation.* In some cases such an association could be established by the very content of the rule, for instance, in the case of a rule stating that there is an obligation not to injure others, and that the obligation increases in strength with the amount of injury involved. Another example is that of second-level rules about the priorities of first-level rules. In other cases the association might be fixed simply by the relative insistence or firmness of the teachers, with respect to the rule in question. As a result of the rules being taught in this way, conscientious people would have established in them hesitations, of different degrees of strength, to do certain sorts of things—in other words, a sense of obligation to do or avoid certain things, the sense having different force for different things. Therefore, when persons so trained were faced with a situation in which lower-order rules gave conflicting directions (and where no higher-order rule assigned an explicit priority), they would hesitate to resolve the problem in various ways because of the built-in sense of obligation. Now, the proposed remainder-rule would in effect be a somewhat qualified prescription to take whatever course of action would leave morally well-trained people least dissatisfied. (I imagine that something like this is what Ross had in mind when he said that in complex situations one must rely on one's intuition.) The rule-utilitarian proposal is, of course, that the correct degree of felt obligation to be associated with a rule is, like the order of priorities expressed in the second-level rules, fixed by the relative utilities of the various possible arrangements —partly the utilities of the adjudications of complex cases by the remainder-rule.

It is after all possible, then, for a moral code different from act-utilitarianism to be simple enough to be learned and still able to decide for all problems which may arise.

7

THIRD PROBLEM: RELATIVITY TO THE AGENT'S SOCIETY

One final complication may be needed in the rule-utilitarian proposal. In place of saying that the rightness of an act is fixed by conformity with the prescriptions of the moral code, the recognition of which as morally binding by people (etc.) *everywhere* would maximize intrinsic good, we might say that the rightness of an act is fixed by conformity with the prescriptions of that moral code, the recognition of which as morally binding by people *in the agent's society* would maximize intrinsic good. This kind of complication should be avoided if possible, because it is difficult to assign a definite meaning to the phrase "in the agent's society." We should notice, incidentally, that it is *not* suggested that the test be the maximizing of intrinsic good only in the agent's society; such a thesis would promise quite dubious consequences.

A modification of this sort would admit a kind of relativism into ethics. For, while it is consistent with the rule-utilitarian principle itself being correct for everyone, it has the consequence that an act might be right in one society which would be wrong in another society. For instance, it might be a moral obligation for a man to support his elderly father in one society, but not his obligation in another society. Most philosophers, however, would probably view this kind of relativism as innocuous, since such differences in obligation could occur only when conditions in the two societies were different in such a way that recognition of one rule by one society would have best consequences, and recognition of a different rule by another society would also have best consequences.

But is there any reason for adopting this complicating feature? Why not say that, if a moral code is valid for anybody it is valid for everybody? Surely, it will be said, *some* moral rules are universally valid—perhaps, for instance, a rule forbidding a person from causing another pain merely in order to give himself pleasure. And if so, perhaps we can go on, with Ross, to say that the fundamental principles of obligation are universally true, although their application in special circumstances may give rise to an *appearance* of society-bound rules. For instance, Ross would say that "Keep your promises" is universally a true and important first-level rule. But in some places a thing is promised with certain mutually-understood but not explicitly stated conditions, while in other places the implicit conditions are different. As a result, the conduct required, in view of the explicit promise, by the universally valid principle is different in different societies. Or again, "Thou shalt not steal" or "Thou shalt not commit adultery" might be construed as universally valid injunctions, the first being not to take property which, according to the institutions of the society, is recognized as belonging to another, and the second, not to have sexual relations with any person if either party is, according to the custom of the society, the marriage partner of another. All fundamental moral principles, then, may be thought to have intersocietal validity; only the specific conduct enjoined or prohibited may vary from one society to another because of local conditions.

This view, however, faces serious difficulties. In order to bring these into focus, let us consider an example: the obligations of a father to his children. In the United States, I believe, it is thought that a father should see to it—within the limits of his financial capacities—that his children receive a good education, enjoy physical and mental health, and have some security against unforeseeable catastrophes. Contrast this with a society, like that of the Hopi, in which responsibility for children falls primarily on a household, "household" being defined primarily by blood-ties with the mother. In this situation, responsibility for children is primarily a problem for the mother and her blood relatives. (The factual accuracy of these assertions is not, I believe, a material consideration.) In the United States, the father is generally charged with responsibility for bringing the welfare, or prospects of welfare, of his children up to a certain rough minimum; in the Hopi society this responsibility falls roughly on other persons, although the father may share in it as far as affection dictates. Correspondingly, in the United States grown children have responsibility for their father, whereas among the Hopi the responsibility for the father belongs elsewhere—not on a man's own children but on the household of the father, the one to which he belongs through blood-ties with his mother and siblings.

I take it nobody is going to argue that fathers in the United States do not have the obligations they are generally thought to have, or that Hopi fathers do have obligations which are generally thought to fall elsewhere. (There may be some exceptions to this.) Therefore, if there is to be a *universal* moral rule locating obligations for the welfare of children, it will be one which roughly places it, at least for the present, where it is recognized to be in these societies. What kind of rule might this be? It is hard to say. Very possibly there is uniformity of assignment of such responsibilities in societies with a certain kind of social structure, and hence one could conceivably state a general rule prescribing that fathers do certain things in societies of a specified sociological description. It is doubtful, however, whether such a rule is simple enough to be learned. Moreover, social structures may be too much organic wholes to permit even such generalizations; if so, in respect of some kinds of conduct there can be no general, intersocietally valid moral rule at all.

There is another way of putting much the same point. Instead of asking whether we can frame a general rule which will have implications for particular societies coincident with what we should want to say are the actual locations of responsibilities in these societies, we might ask whether any universal rules can be framed, recognition of which as morally binding would have consequences comparably as good as local rules, devised on the basis of examination of individual institutional structures as a whole. Is the universality of moral rules to be so sacrosanct that we shall not recognize a moral rule as binding on a given society unless it can be viewed as a special case of some universally valid rule? A person who wishes to make utility the test of moral rules will, I think, wish to make the utility of local rules his test.

It may be supposed that the example of family obligations is untypically complex. But to do so would be a mistake. The responsibilities of physicians and teachers—or professional men in general—to the individuals whom they serve pose similar difficulties. So do the ethics of borrowing and the charging of interest. It is possible that the broad outlines of prohibited and required behavior will be rather similar in all societies. But when we come to the fine points—the exceptions, the qualifications, the priorities—we are in for difficulties if we must defend the view that statable universal rules are the best ones for everybody to feel bound by, or that they conform to serious opinions about the location of obligations in various types of society. This, I think, has been the conclusion of various "self-realizationist" philosophers like A. MacBeath and C. A. Campbell.

Let us then consider (without necessarily insisting that it be adopted) the view that the rightness of an act is fixed by conformity with the prescriptions of that moral code, the recognition of which as morally binding by people (etc.) *in the agent's society* would maximize intrinsic good. Can we propose a meaning of "in the agent's society" sufficiently definite that we can say the proposal is at least a clear one?

How shall we identify "the society" of the agent? This question could have been answered fairly simply in much earlier times when all societies were rather clearly demarcated atomic units, although when we remember the relationships of the *kula* reported by Malinowski, we can see that matters were not always so simple even among primitive peoples. The question is difficult in a modern civilization. What is a Columbia University professor who lives in the suburbs to count as his "society"? The faculty club? His suburb? New York City? The state of New York? Any choice seems a bit arbitrary. Or suppose Khrushchev makes a promise to Eisenhower. What society should we bear in mind as the one the utility of a set of rules in which sets the standard of right and wrong?

Very tentatively, I am inclined to suggest that we understand the "society of an agent" in the following way. An individual, I suggest, may live in several "moral worlds," and the rules for these several moral worlds may be different. For one thing, he is a member of a succession of local groups, each one more inclusive than the last: the local community, the metropolitan area, etc. Now a good part of one's life is lived as a resident, a neighbor, a citizen. Insofar as moral problems arise as part of one's life in this capacity, the problem is to be settled by reference to the rules best for the geographical community. How wide a geographical community should we pick? The best answer seems to be: the largest area over which common rules can be adopted without loss of utility. If it were costly in utility to apply to a borough the rules which were the best for the metropolitan area, then we had better consider our case in the light of rules useful for the smaller group. But a person has other roles besides that of citizen and neighbor. One may be a member of groups which transcend the local community—perhaps nation-wide associations, class, or caste. Most important, perhaps, are transactions resulting from the institutional involvement of the participants; for example, business transactions involving corporations or unions, or the affairs of the church, or educational affairs, or the activities of the press or radio. In these cases a segment of the life-relations of the individuals involved consists in their interactions with others who have the same role or who participate in the same institution. In such cases, I suggest that the moral rules governing behavior should be the rules adoption of which by the relevant group (for example, the group participating in a given institution) would be best, as governing the transactions of that group. It may be, of course, that we do not need some of these complications, that there is no need to distinguish the rules for businessmen in dealing with each other or with a union from the ones properly followed in one's relations with wife and neighbor.[9]

8

CONCLUDING REMARKS

The principle with which we end is this: "An act is right if and only if it conforms with that learnable set of rules the recognition of which as morally binding—roughly at the time of the act—by everyone in the society of the agent, except for the retention by individuals of already formed and decided moral convictions, would maximize intrinsic value."[10]

I wish to make three final comments on this principle.

First, one may ask whether a set of moral rules which would maximize intrinsic value in the way described would necessarily be a *just* set of rules. Surely, if the rules are not just, conformity with them will by no means guarantee that an action is right. A further inquiry must be made about whether additional requirements are needed to assure that moral rules are just. It may be that, as I have suggested elsewhere, none is called for if equality of some sort is an intrinsic good.

Second, if the proposed principle is correct, we can give at least a partial answer to a person who asks *why* he ought to perform actions he is obligated to perform, if they conflict with his self-interest. Perhaps a person who asks such a question is merely confused, and his query not worth our attention. But we can say to him that one reason for meeting his obligation is that by doing so he plays the game of living according to the rules which will maximize welfare. And this will be, at least partially, a satisfying answer to a man who is activated by love or sympathy or respect directed at other sentient beings generally.

Finally, some reflections on the employment of the principle. It is, perhaps, obvious that it is not necessary to advocate that everyone always bear the rule-utilitarian principle in mind in deciding what he ought to do. Not that it would be harmful—beyond the waste of time—to do so; for it is obvious that the clear moral obligations are prescribed by the principle. For example, only an instant's thought is required to see that it is socially useful to recognize the rule that solemn promises should be kept—doubtless with some qualifications. The rule's employment is important, however, in analyzing more difficult cases, in making clear whether a given moral rule should be qualified in a certain way. Of course, it would be foolish to suggest that application of the principle is an easy road to the resolution of moral problems. It may very often be that after most careful reflection along the lines suggested, the most that can be said is that a given action is probably the one which the principle requires. If so, if we accept the principle, we can go on to say that this action is probably the right one.

NOTES

1. In one form or another its plausibility has been urged by J. O. Urmson, Kurt Baier, J. D. Mabbott, Stephen Toulmin, R. F. Harrod, Kai Neilsen, A. MacBeath, C. A. Campbell, Jonathan Harrison, Marcus Singer, and, to some extent, John Rawls and P. H. Nowell-Smith. Mabbott has expressed the opinion that the essence of it is to be found in Francis Hutcheson.
2. In this paper I propose to ignore that form of act-utilitarianism which proposes to close the gap between what seems to be right and the implications of act-utilitarianism, by asserting that such things as promise-keeping are intrinsically good. This form of theory has most recently been defended by Oliver Johnson in his *Rightness and Goodness* (The Hague: Martinus Nijhoff, 1959).

   I am inclined to agree that there are some intrinsically good things which are not states of persons—for instance, equality of distribution of welfare. But act-utilitarians require to count further things—such as specific traits of character like truthfulness, or complexes like the-keeping-of-a-promise—as intrinsically good in order to square with reasonable convictions about what is right or wrong. But surely it is contrary to the spirit of utilitarianism to decide the issue, say, whether a promise should be kept by appeal to such intrinsic values. One would have thought the utilitarian would test the merits of traits of character like truthfulness by examining whether they have good consequences rather than decide that there is an obligation to tell the truth by considering the intrinsic goodness of truthfulness. Should not the issue of the intrinsic goodness of truthfulness wait upon reasoning to show that it is a good thing to tell the truth? One who denies this is far from traditional utilitarian thought. In any case, can we seriously claim that the-keeping-of-a-promise is an intrinsic good? It would be absurd to hold that we can add to the value of the world by the simple device of making promises and then keeping them, irrespective of what is effected by the keeping of them. Presumably, then, what is held is rather that the-breaking-of-a-promise is intrinsically bad. But how will it be shown that precisely this is intrinsically bad? Suppose I promise to do something no one wants done, and everyone is greatly relieved when I fail to perform. Is this intrinsically evil?

The kind of utilitarianism I propose here to discuss is one with narrower commitments about what is intrinsically good—one which does not claim that specific kinds of action or specific traits of character (like truthfulness or fidelity) are intrinsically good or bad. This kind of utilitarianism is worth assessment even if my reasons for ignoring other types are unsound.

3. Notice that such philosophers are not refuted by the mere consideration that sometimes we say "is right" and not "is probably right" even when we know we lack evidence about some facts that might be relevant to what is right in the objective sense. It would be a mistake to infer from such usage that we are not employing "right" in the objective sense. For, in general, we are entitled to make any assertion roundly without the qualifying word "probable" if we know of no definite grounds for questioning the truth of the assertion.
4. J. O. Urmson, "The Interpretation of the Philosophy of J. S. Mill," *Philosophical Quarterly*, III (1953), 33–39.
5. These articles are: J. Harrison, "Utilitarianism, Universalization, and Our Duty to be Just," *Proceedings of the Aristotelian Society*, Vol. LIII (1952–53), pp. 105–134; and R. F. Harrod, "Utilitarianism Revised," *Mind*, n.s. XLV (1936), 137–156.
6. To say that a moral code can be learned by a person is not to say he can learn to *recite* it. It is enough if he learns it well enough to recall the relevant rule when stimulated by being in a context to which it is relevant. Learning a moral code is thus like learning a complex route into a large city: we may not be able to draw it or explain to others what it is, but when we drive it and have the landmarks before us, we remember each turn we are to make.
7. This formulation is rather similar in effect to one suggested to me by Wilfrid Sellars. (I have no idea whether he now inclines toward it, or whether he ever did lean toward it strongly.) This is: "An act is right if and only if it conforms with that set of rules the *teaching of which* to the society of the agent, at the time of the action, would maximize welfare." This formulation is simpler, but it has its own problems. Teaching to which and how many individuals? By whom? With what skill and means? We should remember that it may be unwise to teach children the rules that are best for adults and that it may sometimes be desirable to teach ideals which are more extreme than we want people actually to live by, e.g., those of the Sermon on the Mount.
8. It will probably be clear why the remainder-rule cannot simply be the rule-utilitarian principle itself. For the rule-utilitarian principle states that an act is right if and only if it conforms with the rules of a certain kind of code. If one of the rules of the code were the rule-utilitarian principle, it would contain reference to a code which

presumably would itself contain again the rule-utilitarian principle, and so on ad infinitum.

9. The above discussion shows that the theory that what is right is behavior conforming with the *accepted* rules of the agent's society has complications which have not been adequately discussed.
10. As the principle now stands, a given individual might have to learn several codes, corresponding to his several roles in society.

5

ON THE NATURALISTIC FALLACY

George Nakhnikian *Wayne State University*

G. E. Moore's now classic discussions of the naturalistic fallacy are frequently unclear and imprecise, and in certain crucial places they are misleading. A thorough documentation of these charges would require lengthy exegesis and digressions into metaphysics and theory of meaning. I shall dispense with both. Instead of dwelling on defects, I shall try to formulate clearly and defend what I take to be Moore's perfectly correct warnings against certain mistakes in moral philosophy.

In Chapter I of *Principia Ethica*, while discussing the naturalistic fallacy, Moore either directly or obliquely calls attention to six distinguishable errors:

(1) Failing to see that no definition can be a moral or evaluative assertion.
(2) Failing to see that no analytic moral or evaluative statement can be a moral or evaluative assertion.
(3) Misidentifying two different but co-extensive properties.

(4) Supposing that an expression E is synonymous with an expression E′, while in ordinary discourse "This is E but not E′" is not self-contradictory.

(5) Defining "good" in terms of the very properties we would invoke if someone wanted to know the reasons why *x* is good.

(6) Thinking that a definition of "good" is the ultimate support or justification for any of our evaluations.

One gathers from the way Moore writes that although every one of these errors is either the result of the naturalistic fallacy or leads to it, still none of them is *the* naturalistic fallacy. In one place Moore says, that *the* naturalistic fallacy, the root error, is failing to see that it is in principle impossible to give a *correct* definition of "good," a term Moore uses to refer to "that which is at the same time common . . . and peculiar" to all ethical judgments. But elsewhere Moore tells us that he will call "the naturalistic fallacy" the error of confusing good, which is not a "natural" object, with any "natural" object whatever. He goes on to add that even if no "natural" objects were involved in the definition, there would still be a fallacy in defining "good" at all, although in that case he would not call it "the naturalistic fallacy." Moore thus presents two different formulations of what *the* naturalistic fallacy is. One formulation identifies it as the attempt to define "good" at all. The other identifies it as the misidentification of goodness with some "natural" object. To complicate matters further, we have the list of errors, (1)–(6), some of which at least qualify as species of the generic "fallacy" of trying to define "good" at all. For if it is a fallacy to define "good" at all, then (4) and (5) are specific ways of committing it, provided that in (4) the expression being miselucidated is "good."

My main object is to support Moore to the effect that (1)–(6) are pitfalls to be avoided by anyone who tries to clarify the nature of evaluation and obligation. Along the way I shall be saying that Moore has not proved the impossibility of explicating "good" in naturalistic terms. The point is not new, but the way I shall be making it may be. Moore has three main lines of attack against the definability of "good." In one line of attack, he seems to imply that anyone who sees that (1)–(6) are errors will see that "good" is indefinable. Moore is right that (1)–(6) are mistakes; but he is obviously wrong in supposing that this fact implies the indefinability of "good." The second and third lines of attack relate to Moore's view of analysis. The "open question" argument comes in at this point.

Moore has two distinguishable conceptions of analysis: a phenomenological-atomistic one and a "linguistic" one. According to the phenomenological-atomistic conception, we are supposed to see, as a result of holding before our minds the object goodness, that goodness is simple, not capable of being broken up into parts, hence indefinable. This recipe is dialectically inconclusive. Even with the best will in the world, most philosophers would be nonplussed if invited to take a phenomenological "look" at goodness. And the atomistic part of the recipe is inapplicable in principle. The notion of absolute simplicity is nonsense. Simplicity is always relative to some respect. Indivisibility into parts is not a respect. We have first to specify the respect in which the parts are to be distinguished from the whole.

It is only when Moore departs from the phenomenological-atomistic recipe and turns his attention to the contours and nuances of the language of evaluation in which the word "good" plays so central a role that we return to the philosophical dialectic. This brings us to the second conception of analysis, a conception which I have called the "linguistic" one. The paradigm here is the analysis of being a brother into being a male sibling. Although Moore explicitly disavows that analysis is concerned with the elucidation of linguistic expressions, in practice he defends his analytic elucidations by appeal to the logic of ordinary discourse. What, after all, is our final justification for identifying male siblinghood with being a brother except that in fact the English word "brother" is synonymous with the English expression "male sibling"? This ultimate appeal to ordinary discourse underlies the "open question" argument. Is pleasure, after all, good? This is an open question in ordinary English. Is a brother, after all, a male sibling? This is not an open question. The fact that the first is an open question shows that "good" cannot be defined as pleasure. To suppose that "good," as ordinarily used, means pleasure is to commit an instance of the error listed as (4) above. Although Moore never to his own or to anyone else's satisfaction gave a precise specification of what a "natural object" or property is, he has in mind such things as pleasure, the greatest happiness of the greatest number, fitness to survive, etc., the sorts of things that are, roughly speaking, empirical entities. He uses the "open question" argument hoping to show that *no* definition of "good" is possible, hence no naturalistic definition is possible. His reason for this is inconclusive. In Chapter I, Section 13, (2) of *Principia,* Moore says that anyone who runs through a number of attempted definitions of "good" and sees, on the strength of the "open question," that none of them works will come to see that *no* definition will work.

If we adhere to Moore's strict sense of "linguistic" analysis, his conclusion that "good" is indefinable is correct, but his reason for thinking that his conclusion is true is invalid. A better explanation than Moore's for why the appeal to ordinary discourse will not give us any secure grounds for claiming that "good" means so and so, in contrast to the "brother"-means-male-sibling case, is that ordinary discourse is not as precise about "good" as it is about "brother." And for this very same reason, the "open question" argument cannot work wholesale. For it can work only in those cases where ordinary discourse is quite clear as to whether or not an expression of the form "This is P but not good" is self-contradictory. Thus, Moore's discussions concerning the naturalistic fallacy lead us to admit that elucidatory analysis, in the "linguistic" manner, will not yield a naturalistic definition of "good." But so far we have no reason to despair of giving a naturalistic *account* of goodness as distinguished from an analysis in the sense in question.

At this point I must say something about the distinction I have in mind between analysis and giving an account. The vogue in contemporary ethical theory has been to assume that the analysis of ethical and evaluative concepts, in the sense of explicating their contours and nuances in ordinary discourse, exhausts the legitimate work of the critical moral philosopher. Some of the air of triviality in strict analytical ethics is, I think, a reflection of this methodological assumption. Although I am an analytic philosopher and much of what I do is straightforward philosophical analysis, I am convinced that analysis alone is insufficient to get to the bottom of the perplexities of moral philosophy. Analysis, be it in the style of Moore, Russell, Austin, or Wittgenstein, is indispensable as a propaedeutic. It clears away the conceptual confusions that plague all of us, philosophers and non-philosophers. For example, the Moorean techniques are adequate for dispelling certain purely conceptual fallacies, the avoidance of which is a necessary condition of an acceptable theory of goodness. But I believe that analysis alone cannot decide the issue between naturalists and their foes. Is this an "open question": After all, is a thing good which is so constituted that it would reinforce the desires, sustain the interest, and occasion the satisfactions and enjoyments of everyone who had a mature and comprehensive grasp of that thing's scientifically discoverable and imaginatively explorable properties and relations? An appeal to the logical contours of ordinary discourse cannot settle the issue as to the openness of this question. If we are inclined, as we are, to saying that a thing of that description might, without contradiction, be said not to be good, we are also inclined in the opposite direction of wondering what on earth more goodness could be. This type of ambivalence is not uncommon. And we cannot simply admit its existence in a given case and then drop the subject. We need to explain in some not *ad hoc* manner what is going on and what can be done to dispel the ambivalence.

At this juncture we could make a linguistic legislation. But this is improper in the case of goodness, for we are confronted with a philosophical perplexity arising out of the imprecisions of everyday talk about good and bad things. Any adequate account of goodness must accommodate the clearly discernible logical features of the ordinary use of "good." Otherwise we have evaded the problem with which we started. The obscurities of ordinary discourse cannot override what we can clearly discern.

To give an account of goodness, then, is to map out the clearly discernible features of the logical contours of "good" without being intimidated by the obscurities, and to justify the account by some means other than the claim that everything in our account can be seen to be an accurate transcription of everyday usage. This refusal to be intimidated by obscurities and the manner of justifying our results distinguish giving an account from "linguistic" analysis.

To provide an account of goodness we begin by asking: What general principles or standards do we employ in deciding that our evaluations are not spurious? This is not a question that can be answered by sorting out entailments, equivalences, synonymies, contradictions in ordinary discourse. It is a matter which presupposes clarity about substantive matters, such as the fact that immediate likings, enjoyments, approvals are not always sustained in the light of further experience and knowledge; that a fool's evaluations are not as trustworthy as those of an informed and intelligent man; that evaluating is an activity possible only to creatures who are rational and capable of conative responses and affective states. In denying these facts, one would not be contradicting himself or making unintelligible noises. He would be simply expressing materially false beliefs. Those who recognize such substantive facts would see that the legitimacy of evaluations is a function of their satisfying principles or standards validated by just those extra-linguistic facts. When Dewey characterizes his discussion of the nature of value as "the construction of good," he may be trying to convey that what he is doing is neither stipulative analysis nor analysis in the sense of describing ordinary linguistic usage. He may be trying to say that he is doing the sort of thing which here I am calling "giving an account." (This has to be stated with reservations because Dewey is not always too clear as to what he thinks he is doing. In fact, in "The Construction of Good" Chapter X of *The Quest for Certainty*, he says things which sound as if he were stipulating a meaning for "good" and justifying it on the grounds of its pragmatic utility.) An account of goodness in naturalistic terms would be neither a stipulation nor simply a description of how the word "good" is used in ordinary discourse. It would be a formula which specifies the principles or standards whose fulfillment is necessary and sufficient for correctly ascribing goodness to things. And to locate these standards it is not enough to examine the logical properties and relations of evaluative statements. We must also become clear as to certain relevant substantive facts. However, a detailed exploration of these issues is beyond the scope of this paper.

The other formulation of the naturalistic fallacy, that it is the misidentification of good and some "natural" object or other, is a hint worth clarifying and developing. I suggest in passing that (5) may be a first step toward unpacking Moore's hint. We would further need to study the logical status of the properties we would invoke in giving valid reasons for calling something "good." We would have to understand the ways in which these properties differ from goodness as well as among themselves. I shall not do anything along these lines in this paper.

I now begin my defense of Moore's warnings against (1)–(6).

In the last paragraph of Chapter I, Section 6 of *Principia*, Moore says that "propositions about the good are all of them synthetic and never analytic; and this is plainly no trivial matter. And the same thing may be expressed more popularly, by saying that, *if I am right*, then nobody can foist on us an axiom as that 'Pleasure is the only good' or that 'The good is the desired' on the pretense that this is 'the very meaning of the word' " (my italics). Just before this quotation, Moore states the main thesis, that "good" is indefinable. If we take the italicized phrase to be referring to that thesis, then the quotation gives an outline of an argument, later to be elaborated, for the thesis that "good" is indefinable. I have already argued that the argument is inconclusive against the possibility of a naturalistic account of goodness. However, it is true that if propositions about the good are synthetic, then nobody can state it as a principle that, e.g., pleasure and only pleasure is good, and at the same time defend it *as a moral principle* on the ground that "good" means pleasure. The argument proving the truth of *this* hypothetical is quite independent of the question whether or not "good" is amenable to a naturalistic account, although if the indefinability thesis were proved, the consequent of the hypothetical would be a corollary of it.

Moore says that the indefinability thesis "amounts to this: That propositions about the good are all of them synthetic and never analytic. . . ." By "amounts to" Moore seems to intend identity. If this is what he means, he is wrong. The indefinability thesis does not entail the syntheticity thesis. Even if "good" is indefinable, it is possible to formulate analytic statements "about the good," viz., the good is the good. Because Moore mistakenly thinks that indefinability implies syntheticity and also that indefinability is proved, he does not bother to argue independently for the proposition that assertions "about the good," which I take to mean evaluations, are never analytic. There is, however, a proof of this proposition. I shall give the proof immediately after this word of caution: The proof of the syntheticity of evaluations and moral assertions does not entail the indefinability of "good." "Propositions about the good" may be either evaluations or analytic statements. The fact that all evaluations are synthetic is consistent with the possibility that there are analytic evaluative statements which are not evaluations and whose analyticity is owing to a definition of "good."

Now for the argument that definitions and analytic statements cannot be moral or evaluative assertions or principles. This is in two steps. First, no definition can be an evaluative or moral assertion. Second, no analytic statement can be an evaluative or moral assertion.

No definition can be a moral assertion. Regarding two expressions as being definitionally equivalent is tantamount to holding that whenever, and only whenever, the one expression is correctly used, the other may be used with equal propriety. Underlying this permissive rule is a stronger one to the effect that the two expressions must be used in accordance with the same set of rules. These remarks obviously do not provide anything like a complete analysis of definitions. For that we need a thorough investigation of what language rules are and what constitutes using two expressions in accordance with the same set of rules.

I am simply assuming that what I have said about definitions is correct as far as it goes.

Moral assertions are also "rulish." A moral assertion must satisfy at least two conditions. It must mention an identifiable action and say of it that it ought to be done or that it ought not to be done. A moral assertion can be satisfied or violated. Secondly, a moral assertion should be capable of being construed as an answer to: "In these circumstances (actual or imagined), ought I or ought I not to do such and such?"

Although definitions and moral assertions are "rulish" in that they are all directly action-guiding, there is a crucial difference between them. Definitions are relative to a language. Whenever we invoke, report, or stipulate a definition, we let it be known that *if* or *as* one wants to speak correctly in a given language, one must use a certain expression of that language in accordance with the very same rules by which one uses another expression (of that or of another language). No moral assertion relates to a language in this way. A moral assertion formulates an unconditional requirement or an unconditional prohibition to do a certain act. Therefore, no definition can be a moral assertion. Hence, no definition of a moral expression can be a moral assertion.

Similarly, no evaluative assertion is relative to a language in the way that definitions are. An evaluative assertion must mention an identifiable entity and ascribe merit to it or rank it in order of merit relative to something else. Therefore, no evaluative assertion is a definition. Hence, no definition of an evaluative expression can be an evaluative assertion.

There is a similar sharp distinction between moral assertions and analytical moral or evaluative statements. Again, I shall formulate first the argument proving that no moral assertion can be an analytic moral statement. Its extension to evaluative assertions is easy.

Examples of analytic moral statements are:

(*a*) The wrongful killing of a human being is wrong.
(*b*) All wrong actions are wrong.

(*c*) All actions which everyone in circumstances C ought to do are actions which no one in circumstances C is permitted to refrain from doing.

I call such statements as these "analytic moral statements" because they are analytic statements containing words like "ought," "right," "permitted." It is evident that not all analytic statements can be construed as being alternative ways of invoking or reporting in the material mode a definition normally formulated in the formal mode. For example, if "The wrongful killing of a human being is wrong" were construed as being a definition of "wrong" in the material mode, the assertion that lying is wrong would be a misuse of language, which it is not in ordinary discourse. Because some analytic statements could not possibly be mistaken for definitions, to show that no analytic moral statement can be a moral assertion we need an argument independent of the one proving that no definition can be a moral assertion.

Recall that a moral assertion must satisfy at least two conditions. It must mention an identifiable action and say of it either that it ought to be done or that it ought not to be done. Moreover, it must be capable of being construed as an answer to: "In these circumstances, ought I to do or ought I not to do such and such?" Analytic moral statements fail to satisfy both of these conditions. Consider (*a*) "The wrongful killing of a human being is wrong." We might be tempted to think that (*a*) is telling us not to kill human beings wrongfully and that it is an answer to: "In these circumstances, ought I or ought I not to kill this or that human being wrongfully?" But what is killing a human being wrongfully? (*a*) does not say. The statement fails to mention an action which we can identify independently of judging it to be right or wrong to do. Otherwise put, an answer telling me that such killings of human beings as are wrongful are wrong does not tell me which killings it is that I am to refrain from doing. I cannot guide my actions by such a statement. Contrast this with (*d*) "Killing human beings is wrong." This is a moral assertion. It tells us that an identifiable action, killing a human being, is not the thing to do. It can also be construed as an answer to: "In these circumstances ought I or ought I not to kill this or that human being?" Kill one human being and you violate (*d*). You do what it prohibits. Kill as many people as you will, wrongfully or not. You are not doing anything (*a*) says you are not to do. All (*a*) says is that any killing of a human being you are not to do is an action you are not to do.

For similar reasons, no evaluative assertion can be analytic. Examples of analytic evaluative statements are:

(*e*) The good wines of France are good.

(*f*) All good things are good.

(*g*) If a thing is good, then it merits being sought, realized, and perpetuated.

Recall that an evaluative assertion must mention an identifiable entity and say of it that it has merit or rank it in order of merit relative to something else. No analytic evaluative statement can do either one of these things. Take (*e*), for example. It says that the meritorious wines of France are meritorious. But this does not tell us which French wines it is that are meritorious (have value). The statement fails to mention an entity that we can identify independently of judging it to be good. Contrast this with (*h*) "The wine in the cellar is good." This is a genuine evaluation. It tells us that a certain identifiable entity has value.

To sum up, an evaluative assertion must perform one of two related linguistic acts, neither of which is performed by analytic evaluative statements. Therefore, no analytic evaluative statement can be an evaluative assertion. In fact, no analytic statement whatever can be an evaluative assertion, but this needs no emphasis because no one would be tempted to confuse an evaluative assertion with an analytic statement which did not contain at least one value word.

Anyone who argued that pleasure and only pleasure is good because "good" means pleasure *might* be in a complete muddle if he were not on guard against (1) or (2) or both. If he thought that he was defending "Pleasure alone is good" as an evaluative principle, he would be contradicting himself. If we take " 'Good' means pleasure" as a definition, it cannot be an evaluative principle. Moreover, the definition entails that "Pleasure alone is good" is analytic. But the statement is being defended as an evaluative principle. Hence it is being defended as being at the same time analytic and non-analytic, which is self-contradictory. The trouble here is not that we have a faulty definition. Even if the definition were correct, this way of arguing would implicate us in logical absurdities. And this shows that if propositions about the good are synthetic, and we have seen that they are, then regardless of whether or not "good" (or "right") are indefinable, nobody can establish it as a moral or evaluative principle that all and only F are good (or right) on the ground that "good" (or "right") means F.

The next question that naturally suggests itself is this. Are there definitions of "good" which can be shown to be inadmissible? The errors numbered (3), (4), and (5) are directly concerned with this question. Even if "good" were definable, no definition of it could count as correct unless it avoided these particular errors. It seems safe to say that (3) is a description in "the material mode" and (4) is a description in "the formal mode" of one and the same error. For to confuse two different properties is tantamount to regarding as synonymous two predicates which are not in fact synonymous. Whichever way we put it, the error is egregious, and it is not peculiar to moral contexts. It can occur even when the misidentified properties and expressions are of the same type, both "natural" or both "non-natural." In this generic form, the error is not interesting. Moore himself, in Chapter I, Section 12 of *Principia*, mentions them only to dismiss them without further ado. On the other hand, (5) is an interesting species of this error. It specifically involves at least one moral or evaluative property or expression. Any instance of (3), (4), or (5) can be successfully demolished by the "open question" argument.

The mistake in (5) would be to treat goodness as being on the same level of discourse as the properties of things we have to take account of correctly in judging that a thing does or does not have value. In short, to proscribe (5) is to lay down a negative condition for a satisfactory definition of "good." It does not provide a criterion of being a property which we have to take account of in judging that a thing has value in the sense of providing a test by which we could unerringly pick out from any context these properties of things. It simply rules out all definitions of "good" whose definientia list the very properties we would invoke if we had to give the reasons why X is good; and for a very good reason. If "X is good" is defined as "X is a, b, c, . . . n," then a, b, c, . . . n cannot be the properties we invoke to support our evaluation of X as good. If someone required to be shown why X is good, it would be no answer to tell him "because X is a, b, c, . . . n." To say that X is a, b, c, . . . n would be just another way of saying that X is good. This, however, does not imply that "good" is indefinable.

We now come to (6) on our list of errors.

In the first sentence of the last paragraph in Chapter I, Section 14 of *Principia*, Moore writes: "My objections to naturalism are then, in the first place, that it offers no reason at all, far less any valid reason, for any ethical principle whatever. . . ." He means to be attacking any ethical theory which defines "good" at all and uses the definition as the ultimate support for all evaluations. Now Moore is right when he suggests that justification by definition is a fatuous enterprise. But he seems to be arguing from this fatuousness to indefinability. This inference is invalid. First let us see why Moore is right, and then we shall see why his inference is wrong.

It is easy to see that justification by definition is fatuous. Consider this example. I am trying to show you that doing A is your duty. You are not convinced. But A *is* your duty, I say, because your doing A would contribute to the welfare of the community. But suppose that I define "A is your duty" to mean that your doing A will contribute to the welfare of the community. In that case, "A is your duty" is just another way of saying "Your doing A will contribute to the welfare of the community," and I have not provided a reason why doing A is your duty. In asserting "A is your duty" and "Your doing A will serve the welfare of the community" I have simply used two different expressions to say the same thing. This is illuminating only to those who need a lesson in language. It is of no help whatever to anyone who requires to be shown that doing A is his duty.

Moore says that naturalism—the view that "good" is definable—offers no reason whatever for any ethical principle. But ethics must provide valid reasons for ethical truths. Therefore, Moore intimates, naturalism is false; "good" is indefinable. But all that Moore's argument against fatuous validation proves is that the *defining* property of goodness cannot serve as a *reason* why X is good. An ethical theory which defines "good" need not also use the defining property of goodness in this illegitimate manner. In other words, from the fact alone that an ethical theory has a definition of "good" it does not follow, *pace* Moore, that the theory makes nonsense of giving good reasons to back up evaluations.

The failure of Moore's charge that naturalism cannot offer any reasons for any evaluation or ethical judgment whatever leaves him only the "open question" argument. I have already given my reasons for saying that this works against definitions one at a time. It cannot prove that "good" is in principle inexplicable in naturalistic terms. This, however, is not the main point of this paper. My principal objective has been to argue on the side of Moore against those who might be tempted to commit errors (1)–(6).

6

IMPERATIVES, INTENTIONS, AND THE LOGIC OF "OUGHT"

Wilfrid Sellars *Yale University*

INTRODUCTION

My purpose in this paper[1] is to explore the logic of "ought," with a view to determining the relations which obtain between it and certain other key terms of practical discourse. In particular, I shall be concerned with the relation between "I ought to do X" and "I shall do X"; "You ought to do X" and "Do X!"; "He ought to do X" and "He shall do X"; and between "I ought to do X" and "He ought to do X." I shall also be concerned with the relation between "Everybody ought to do A, if in C" and "Would that everybody were happy!" on the one hand, and "Would that I were happy!" on the other.

Put in more traditional terms, this paper is about the relation between "*thinking oneself* under an obligation to do something" and "(*ceteris paribus*) deciding to do it for the reason that one ought to do it," and between "*being* under an obligation to do something" and "having a reason for doing it, namely, the reason that one ought to do it." Insofar as I have a thesis to defend it is the twofold one that to know that there are certain things that one ought to do *is* to have a sense of duty, and that obligation, by its very nature, is intersubjective. And if, thus baldly stated, neither component of this thesis is new (for the first smacks of emotivism and second of intuitionism), some interest may attach to the way in which this joint thesis is developed, and the consequent clarification of the relation between the sense of duty on the one hand, and the impartial love of humanity on the other.

If one were to ask a convinced student of *The Right and the Good*,[2]

> Could a person "apprehend a principle of prima-facie obligation" to the effect that one ought, for example, to keep promises—that is, *Anglice*, could one know that, other things being equal, one ought to keep one's promises—and yet have no tendency to be moved to act on specific occasions by the thought that one ought to do *this* as being the keeping of a promise?

—would he not answer (though I must qualify this in a moment) that there is no contradiction in the idea of such a person, or (if he should think that tending to be so moved is a defining trait of a *person* [3]) at least in the idea of such an intelligent animal? But if he finds no contradiction in this idea, would he be content to say that it is a contingent *empirical* fact about human nature that people who know what they ought to do tend to be moved to act by the thought that they ought so to act? Or would he not be more likely to subsume this fact under the heading of the "synthetic a priori"?

It must be admitted, and this is the qualification mentioned above, that some intuitionists, notably H. A. Prichard, seem to think that it is not a merely empirical mistake but, rather, an absurdity to suppose that one might apprehend what he ought to do, yet have no tendency whatever to be moved to act by the thought that he ought to do it. Thus, when Prichard writes, "To feel that I ought to pay my bills is to be moved towards paying them," [4] the context makes it clear that he is not thinking of the feeling that I ought to pay my bills as something distinguishable from (but built upon) the apprehension that I ought to pay them, but rather as being this apprehension itself. In comparing the apprehension of obligation to the apprehension of mathematical truths, Prichard writes that "in both [cases] insight into the nature of the subject leads me to recognize its possession of the predicate," [5] but he nevertheless insists that the apprehension of an obligation is different from the apprehension of a mathematical truth. My difficulty with Prichard on this point (as with the many philosophers who have insisted that moral thinking qua thinking is "conative," no "mere blend" of thinking and "emotion") is that he offers not even the beginning of a satisfactory analysis of this phenomenological insight, an analysis which would account for the fact that moral thinking differs from, but resembles, other forms of thinking, by relating both to the fundamental categories of an adequate philosophy of mind. Prichard's grasp of the distinctive traits of moral thinking exhibits the combination of thinness and acuteness which is characteristic of his philosophy. It is because Sir William David Ross has turned thin truth into quick error by forcing Prichard's insights into the procrustean bed of neo-Aristotelian theory, that we could picture, as we did, the response of the student of *The Right and the Good* to our question about ought and motivation.

If, now, we turn to a convinced student of *Language, Truth and Logic* [6] and ask,

> Can a person know that he ought to do *this* action without being moved to do it?

I think it reasonably clear that his answer would take the form of a commentary on the question. The upshot would be some such statement as the following: "The so-called thought that one ought to do A here and now is not, strictly speaking, a thought at all, but rather a specific way of being moved to do A. With this qualification the answer to your question is no, for the simple reason that to 'know' that one ought to do A here and now is to be moved to do it." If we press him to say just how the specifically moral character of the "being moved" is to be understood, if it is not a matter of being moved by the *thought* that one ought to do A, it is unlikely that we would get a satisfactory answer. For in its early stages emotivism, naïve or sophisticated, views as *analytic* the connection between "thinking that one ought" and "having a motive" which classical intuitionism, with the exception we have noted, takes to be either *empirical* or *synthetic a priori.* On the other hand, as is well known, it tends to view *thinking* that one ought as "*thinking*" that one ought.

It was the signal merit of intuitionism, particularly of the deontological variety, to have insisted on the uniqueness of prescriptive discourse, as over and against traditional naturalism's attempts at reduction, and on the truly propositional character of prescriptive statements, as over and against the emotivist contention that ethical concepts are "pseudo-concepts" and the logic of moral discourse a "pseudo-logic." But the epistemological and metaphysical commitments of ethical intuitionism, which precluded it from understanding the logical connection between "thinking that one ought" and "being moved to do," thus forced it to make a mystery both of the conduct-guiding role of moral discourse, and of the uniqueness of prescriptive discourse which it had so happily emphasized.

The situation seems clearly to call for a theory which, without denying that ought-statements stand, as such, in logical relation to one another, makes the connection between moral thinking and doing *analytic*, a matter of strict logic. That attempts along these general lines are in the air is clear. One of these, the neo-imperativist approach of R. M. Hare,[7] is, in my opinion, sufficiently close to the truth to be a useful point of departure for the ideas I wish to develop. While I think that something *like* his account of the concept of ought is true, I do not think that it will do as it stands. Indeed, I think that its very closeness to the truth has enabled it to obscure essential points about the concept of obligation.[8]

Universality and the Logic of Imperatives

I

A person who says, "X ought (morally) to do *this*," commits himself to supporting this statement with a statement of the form, "Doing this, in these circumstances, is doing A in circumstances C, and anyone ought always (*ceteris paribus*) to do A in C." [9] This fact is sometimes put by saying that singular ought-statements imply universal ought-statements. This is true, however, only in a special sense of "imply." Nor will it quite do to speak of "presupposing," for though one who makes a singular ought-statement is committed to support it with a universal ought-statement, it is not necessary that he have the latter "up his sleeve." If a wise man tells Jones that he ought to do a certain action, he has a reason to think that he ought to do it, and that the action could be subsumed under a moral principle, even though he is not in a position to do so. It is for this and related reasons that I have elsewhere [10] characterized this sense of implication as dialectical. Yet, though it is a "looser" relation than presupposing, let alone ordinary implication, it is, like the latter, a logical, as opposed to psychological, relation.[11]

Now even if there is no plausibility at all to the suggestion that "You ought to do B" is simply the imperative "Do B!" with or without psychological embellishments, the claim that the ought-statement is equivalent to a singular imperative which is implicitly universal in the above sense is something to be reckoned with. This claim can be construed as the idea that "You ought to do B" is equivalent to "Do B!*" where the asterisk is a signal of a dialectical commitment to support it with an "argument" of the form,

Let everyone universally do A in C!
Doing B is doing A in C
So, do B!

Thus, the claim is that in "You ought to do that," the ought plays the dual role of (1) giving the infinitive ("to do") which follows it the force of a verb in the imperative mood ("Do!"), and (2) embodying a commitment to support this singular imperative in the manner indicated above.

Now this claim (which is, of course, only a rough approximation to more sophisticated analyses of the imperativist type) is open to many objections, some of which, in my opinion, are sufficiently compelling to call, at the very least, for a substantial revision. It will be useful to begin our exploration of the logic of ought by raising one of these objections, the full force of which will not emerge until a later stage of our argument. This objection is that the "ought" in the universal ought-statement "Everybody ought always to do A in C" does not seem to be redundant. Yet it cannot be accounted for in terms of the two roles of ought specified above. For the latter, (2), that of signaling a dialectical commitment to back up the sentence in which it appears with a sentence having the logical form of universality, is on the face of it irrelevant, in the case of the first principles of obligation, while the purpose of the former, (1), can easily be achieved by using the imperative mood to start with, that is, by simply saying, "Let everyone always do A in C!"

The answer of one imperativist to this objection is to be found in the concluding pages of *The Language of Morals.* There Hare argues that in addition to playing roles which are essentially the same as those indicated above, the ought also gives the imperative it signalizes a truly universal force. He points out that in actual usage, "Let everybody always do A in C!" means "Let everybody *from now on* do A in C!" (it being silly to say, for example, "Let everybody wear blue suits yesterday!"). "Everybody ought always to do A in C" has, as Hare sees it, an imperative force which is suggested by the absurdity of "Let everyone do A in C throughout the past as well as the future!" in actual usage.

2

To evaluate Hare's reply, we must begin by considering certain features of the logic of commands.

The issuing of commands (i.e., commands only, not sentences in the imperative mood generally) is not a promiscuous activity. Not everyone on every occasion can properly command another to do a certain action. There must be something about one person's relationship with another which authorizes him to issue the command; and a relationship which authorizes one person to command another to do something may not authorize him to command something else. I referred above to the issuing of commands as a *performance,* and this is, of course, the heart of the matter. The parallel with promising is instructive. As Austin has pointed out,[12] making a promise is a performance which creates a presumptive prima-facie obligation to do A on the part of the person who says, "I promise to do A." It "creates" this obligation by virtue of the moral principle which can, for our purposes, be formulated as follows:

If X appropriately says "I promise to do A" to Y, then
X owes it to Y to do A.

Now, whereas promising is a performance which binds the speaker, issuing a command binds the person to whom it is issued. Thus, issuing a command within the limits of one's authority "creates" a presumptive prima-facie obligation to do the action commanded on the part of the person to whom it is addressed. And this performance "creates" an obligation, *binds*, only because, like promising, it rests on a principle, in this case:

If X appropriately says to Y "I command you to do A!" then
Y owes it to X to do A.

Thus the claim which commands have on our obedience is but a special case of the claim which our obligations have upon us. Obeying a command, like keeping a promise, is a special case of doing one's duty—though to characterize any particular obeying or promise-keeping as a doing of one's duty is, of course, a defeasible matter.[13]

There is another, if closely related, respect in which the logic of commands resembles the logic of promises, and it is this respect which is directly relevant to our argument. Consider the sentence:

I promise to call you, if it rains.

There is no such reasoning as

I promise to call you tomorrow, if it rains tomorrow
It will rain tomorrow
So, I promise to call you tomorrow

or, in general,

I promise to do A in dt, if p
p
So, I promise to do A in dt.

It is, for reasons which will be developed in a moment, nonsense to suppose that one performance of promising can, as performance, be a conclusion from another. A person who believes that *p* and intends to do A, if *p*, may promise to do A, or, more cautiously, to do A, if *p*. His reasoning *in foro interno* as far as his intentions are concerned may perhaps be represented by the schema:

I shall do A in *dt*, if *p*
p
So, I shall do A in *dt*.

But while there would be an absurdity in saying "*p and* I shall do A, if *p but* I shall not do A," there seems to be no such absurdity in the saying "*p; and* I promise to do A, if *p; but* I do not promise to do A." (NB: "do not promise" must not be confused with "have not just promised.") It would, however, for reasons pertaining to the relation between promising and intending, be absurd to say "*p; and* I promise to do A, if *p; but* I promise not to do A."

3

The opening remarks of the preceding section make it clear (if it was not already clear) that there would be a logical howler in any attempt to "reduce" ought-statements to commands. It might seem equally clear that to show this is not to show that ought-statements cannot be "reduced" to imperatives. For although commands, like promises, presuppose principles of obligation, surely, it will be said, simple imperatives do not. Telling someone to do something does not as such appear to create an obligation on his part to do it. On the other hand, the fact that you told him to do it (as contrasted with the possibility that he might merely have overheard you "intend out loud" that he do it, or even that you might have told him of your intention that he do it) is relevant in a special way to his deliberations on his rights and duties, particularly vis-à-vis you, and on whether he has good reasons for doing what he proposes to do. Intending out loud, telling *of* your intentions, and telling someone *to* do something are all of them pieces of conduct. They must, however, be carefully distinguished from one another, for they enter in different ways into the web of prescriptions and norms which govern our relations with our fellow men. Indeed, while it may be literally true that the fact that you tell someone to do something does not create an obligation on his part to do it, it may well presuppose a context of obligations for its significance as *telling*. While simply telling someone of your intention to do something does not create an obligation on your part to do it—at least in that simple way which characterizes the institution of The Promise, nevertheless it would be misleading to say that telling one's intentions to somebody is logically prior to or independent of practical principles. Again, if X stands in certain relations to Y, the fact that X tells Y to do A generates a claim on Y to do A. It can even be argued that in the case of the highwayman who, brandishing a pistol, says, "Give me your money!" the ought of prudence is being mobilized, and that, in general, there are no proper imperatives without some connection with practical principles, or, at least, that in such cases telling degenerates into merely making manifest one's desires and intentions.

I have contrasted "intending out loud" that X do A with telling someone (perhaps X himself) of one's intention that X do A. Both of these seem to be covered by the ambiguous phrase "expressing one's intention," though I think it is properly limited to the latter, or "telling of," case. A similar danger of confusion is to be found in the case of the "expression of belief." Here too we must draw a threefold distinction between "thinking out loud that *p*" (thinking out loud being the basic form of all thought), "telling someone of one's belief that *p*" (i.e., expressing one's belief that *p*), and "telling someone that *p*." For our purposes, the crucial distinction in each case is that between *telling of* (or expressing) one's intention or belief on the one hand, and *telling to* or *telling that* on the other. Telling of one's beliefs or intentions, as we are using this phrase, is not to be confused with describing oneself as having these intentions. It should not be overlooked, however, that the self-description "I intend that X do A" (though not its cognates in other persons, tenses, and moods) has the force of an expression of intention in addition to its descriptive role, just as "I think that *p*" has the force of an expression of "the thought that *p*" in addition to its autobiographical role.

Before continuing with the argument, there are two terminological conventions I should like to adopt in this paper. The first, a simple matter of convenience, is that whether the subject of a sentence of the form

X shall do A

is "I" or "you" or "Jones," it always expresses the speaker's intention or resolve that X do A. Although this stipulation does minor violence to correct English usage, the awkwardness is more than offset by the gain in simplicity of formulation. Correspondingly, sentences of the form

X will do A

even in the first person are to be understood as expressions of the speaker's belief that the person referred to by "X" will do A.

My second stipulation is that an utterance which not only expresses the speaker's intention that the person referred to by "X" do A, but plays the *telling to* role as well, is to be represented by the form

X shall do A!

where the "!" signalizes this role. Thus, in terms of this convention, the utterance

X shall do A

simply expresses the speaker's intention that the person referred to by "X" do A. It may be overheard by this person, but it is not, as overheard, a telling him to do A. It might appear that the form

You shall do A (as contrasted with "You shall do A!")

must be ruled out on the ground that utterances in the second person are not overheard by the person addressed as "you." That this is not the case will become clear from what follows.

The concept of telling someone to do something is to be distinguished from that of telling someone one's intention that someone (perhaps the same person) do something. Thus, to say "I shall do A" to X is to tell X *of* one's intention to do A, but is not to tell anybody, even oneself, *to do* A. Correspondingly, to say to X "You shall do A," while it is at least a telling X of one's intention that he do A, need not have the force of "You shall do A!" i.e., the force of telling X to do A. Again, while

Tom shall do A

simply expresses the speaker's intention that Tom do A,

Tom shall do A!

said to Tom tells him to do A, and said to Dick, will, according to the conventions of this paper, have the force of the *imperative*, "Let Tom do A!" which not only tells Dick of one's intention that Tom do A, but tells Dick *to do* something, roughly what he reasonably can to ensure that Tom does A, and is, therefore, the equivalent, in terms of our convention, of

You (Dick) shall do what you reasonably can to ensure that Tom does A!

Furthermore, imperatives of the form

Let it be the case that *p!*

will be represented in terms of our convention as

It shall be the case that *p!*

which, as *telling to*, would differ from both

It shall be the case that *p*

as addressed to certain persons and advising them of one's intention that it be the case that *p*, and

It shall be the case that *p*

as a simple expression of one's intention that it be the case that *p*.

A parallel convention will enable us to distinguish

S is P!

as telling someone that S is P, from "S is P" as a *telling of* (or expressing of) one's belief that S is P, and, a fortiori, from an utterance of "S is P" as a mere thinking out loud that S is P.

We are now in a position to clarify our intuitive feeling that there is no such reasoning as

I promise to do A in *dt*, if *p*
p
So, I promise to do A in *dt*.

This clarification will also make manifest that there is no such reasoning as

Do A in *dt*, if *p!*

p
So, do A in *d*t!
i.e., in terms of our convention,
You shall do A in *d*t, if *p!*
p
So, you shall do A in *d*t!

Also that there is no such reasoning (in terms of our "telling that" convention) as

q if *p!*
p!
So, *q!*

Though there are, of course, the reasonings

X shall do A in *d*t, if *p*
p
So, X shall do A in *d*t

and

q if *p*
p
So, *q*.

The point is a simple one about the concept of reasoning. Promising, telling to, telling that, and telling of are all public performances which require an audience. Reasoning is something which can go on *in foro interno;* and if it goes on out loud, it is the sort of thing which is overheard. It can also be expressed in a sense which parallels the expressing or telling of one's beliefs and intentions.

Is there anything which stands to reasoning and to the expression of reasoning as "telling that" stands to "thinking that" and to "expressing the thought that," and as "telling to" stands to "intending" and to "expressing one's intention"? A plausible candidate is "arguing." But before we ask whether there are imperative arguings, let us note that not only are there no imperative reasonings *in foro interno* (which is obvious), there are also no expressions of reasonings which have imperatives as premise or conclusion. Only a confusion between a "telling to" and a "telling of" (or expressing) one's intention that X do A could lead to the contrary conviction. (The current practice of speaking of imperatives and resolutives as though they were co-ordinate from a logical point of view or even related as genus to species—"to resolve" being to tell *oneself* to do something—involves this confusion). It makes sense to suppose that an expressed reasoning could have occurred without being expressed; and if so, there cannot be such things as expressed reasonings the premises or conclusions of which are promisings, tellings to, or tellings that. In particular, there is no such thing as imperative inference.

Is there, perhaps, such a thing as imperative *argument?* An argument is a performance in which a conclusion is defended by offering reasons which give it logical support or purport to do so. Is there, perhaps, such an argument as:

You shall do A!
because you shall do A and B!

Is there, perhaps, an argument of the form

I promise to do A
because I promise to do A and B

There are, of course, the arguments

I told you to do A
because I told you to do A and B

and

I promised to do A
because I promised to do A and B

but, of course, in the latter there is no telling to or promising. Again, there are the supported performances

I promise to do A
because you have been so kind

and

You shall do A!
because you have been naughty

but these are obviously not arguments of which the promising and the telling to are the conclusions. Rather they point to practical reasonings which have as their conclusions

I shall promise to do A

and

I shall tell X to do A

It is tempting to suppose that since an argument is a performance analogous in certain respects to a telling that or a telling to, its conclusion can be a telling that or a telling to. That this is not the case becomes clear when we reflect that what is defended by the argument

q
because *p* and (*p* implies *q*)

is not the *telling someone that q* (for while there is a sense in which logic provides a reason for telling people that *q* when we have told them that *p* and that [*p* implies *q*], it does so via practical principles about "telling that" which compete with other practical principles about "telling that"), but rather the *thought (expressed or unexpressed) that q*. And once we see that not even the performance of telling someone that *q* is defended by the argument

q
because *p* and (*p* implies *q*)

so that there is no such thing as the argument

q!
because p and (*p* implies *q*)!

it becomes equally clear that there simply are no such things as the arguments

I promise to do A
because I promise to do A and B

and

You shall do A!
because you shall do A and B!

Let me try to make my point in terms of Hare's example, which runs,

Take all the boxes to the station!
This is one of the boxes.
So, take this box to the station!

I do not wish to deny that, as Hare [14] has stressed, these three sentences are so related that a person who candidly said to Jones

Take all the boxes to the station! By the way, this
is one of the boxes.

and yet, though insisting that he had not changed his mind, refused to tell Jones to take *this* box to the station, would have convincingly shown that he did not understand either one or the other of these sentences. (This point is not unrelated to one made above about the logical absurdity of "*p and* I promise to do A, if *p but* I promise not to do A.")

4

We have been arguing that the "telling to" signal, "!," like "I promise," does not belong within the context

—, so . . .

and that the only tellings which are appropriate to this context are tellings of. The fact that it does not make sense to speak of imperative inference ("telling to" inference) has been almost as potent a factor in leading people to suppose that there cannot really be such a thing as practical inference, as the fact that expressions of intention are neither true nor false.

Let me begin a more detailed examination of the logic of practical reasoning by proposing the following analysis of the example of the boxes. The analysis breaks the reasoning down into the following moments:

M(1) This is one of the boxes
So, (Jones will shortly take all the boxes to the station) implies (Jones will shortly take this box to the station)

M(2) So, (Shall [Jones's shortly taking all the boxes to the station]) implies (Shall [Jones's shortly taking this box to the station])

M(3) Shall [Jones's shortly taking all the boxes to the station]
So, Shall [Jones's shortly taking this box to the station]

These moments are to be explained as follows. M(1), when made more explicit, turns out to be the second moment of the sequence:

M(1-1) (Jones will shortly take all the boxes to the station *and* This is one of the boxes) implies (Jones will shortly take this box to the station)
So, (This is one of the boxes) implies ([Jones will shortly take all the boxes to the station] implies [Jones will shortly take this box to the station])

M(1-2) This is one of the boxes
So, (Jones will shortly take all the boxes to the

station) implies (Jones will shortly take this box to the station)

Two remarks are necessary: (1) "Implies" means that relation between propositions which authorizes inference.[15] It will be assumed without argument that implication in this sense includes physical or natural implication as well as logical implication in the narrower sense. Nothing in this paper hinges on the treatment of inductive generalizations as principles of inference. The reader may, if he prefers, press the analysis to a "deeper" level in which laws are introduced as premises. (2) A distinction must be drawn between "independent" and "dependent" implication. Thus, in the conclusion of M(1-1), the first occurrence of "implies" is as independent implication, while the second occurrence is as dependent implication. A dependent implication is one which presupposes a state of affairs to obtain which is not explicitly asserted by the implication statement itself.

P dependently implies Q

presupposes that there is an R such that

P and R independently imply Q

Thus M(1-1), by a correctly interpreted use of the principle of exportation, as it applies to implication proper (as contrasted with "material" implication), takes us from one logical truth to another, where the second logical truth has as its consequent the dependent implication which, by virtue of the next moment to be considered, becomes the principle in accordance with which M(3) proceeds.

M(2) has the form

(P) implies (Q)

So, (Shall [P]) implies (Shall [Q])

a move which holds where P and Q have a content appropriate to practical reasoning. Leaving aside for the moment considerations of tense and the question whether P and Q admit of analytic or self-contradictory values in the context "Shall [—]," we can lay down as a formation rule for shall-statements that one moves from an indicative statement to a shall-statement by turning the indicative statement into a gerund and prefixing it with the shall-operator. Thus, for example, we would go from

Tom will shortly cross the road

to

Shall [Tom's shortly crossing the road].

Notice that the latter does not imply

Tom will shortly cross the road.

We can, in effect, note a parallel in this respect between the shall-statement and the modal statement

Possible [Tom's shortly crossing the road].

On the other hand, it seems proper to stipulate that

Shall [*my* shortly crossing the road]

implies

I will shortly cross the road

i.e., that it contains the prediction, just as

Necessary [Tom's shortly crossing the road]

contains

Tom will shortly cross the road.

It is important to note that according to the proposed formation rule, a shall-operator operates on only one verbal noun. Thus the conjunctive statement [16]

Tom will shortly cross the road *and* Dick will shortly sit down

gives rise to

Shall [*its being the case that* Tom will shortly cross the road and Dick will shortly sit down].

This means that for simplicity of representation we can leave the job of turning indicative statements into verbal nouns to the brackets and write the shall-statements corresponding to a given indicative as

Shall [(indicative)]

Since we are representing shall-statements as a matter of an operator operating on a gerund, it might seem appropriate to follow Hare by interpreting indicative statements as a matter of an operator operating on a gerund also. This, however, is not only unnecessary, but seriously mistaken. Let us consider the indicative counterpart of the practical reasoning about boxes dissected above.

M′(1) This is one of the boxes

So, (Jones will shortly take all the boxes to the station) dependently implies (Jones will shortly take this box to the station)

M′(2) Jones will shortly take all the boxes to the station
So, Jones will shortly take this box to the station.

The important thing to note is that the "implies" of M′(1) is a relation word which takes singular terms for its arguments. In the present context we are using it to take verbal nouns for its arguments. In other, but related, uses "implies" takes that-clauses or quoted expressions for its arguments. These singular terms are derivative from the corresponding indicative statements. One operates on an indicative statement to get the corresponding singular term. Thus in

(S is P) implies (S is Q)

the indicative statements "S is P" and "S is Q" have been turned into the singular terms "(S is P)" and "(S is Q)." Thus an inference in accordance with this license is to be understood not as

S being P, yes
So, S being Q, yes

which *adds* a yes-operator to a "phrastic," but rather as simply

S is P
So, S is Q

which *subtracts* the singular term operator which "suspends" "S is P" and "S is Q" in the inference ticket. Correspondingly, M′(2) is not to be "reconstructed" as

(Jones's being about to take all the boxes to the station) yes
So, (Jones's being about to take this box to the station) yes

for it is "perspicuous" as it stands.

I have chosen my examples and oriented my discussion so as to imply that "shall" inference tickets are always of the form

(Shall [—]) implies (shall [. . .])

and rest on a corresponding indicative inference of the form

(—) implies (. . .)

Whether or not this is always true will be discussed at a later stage in the argument.

5

To sum up the argument of the past few sections:
(1) There is no such thing as imperative inference, i.e., inference involving tellings to as tellings to. There is, however, practical reasoning, and there is argument involving *tellings of intentions*.
(2) We have emphasized that the only sense in which there is a special logic of imperatives is that exhibited by the reasoning

X tells Y (to do A if *p*)
p
So, X tells Y (to do A)

which is the counterpart of

X tells Y (that *q* if *p*)
p
So, X tells Y that *q*.

That these arguments are valid (with some requirement as to the ascertainability of *p*) is analytic of the concept of *telling* as a performance. Note that while

X tells Y to do A
Doing A entails doing B
So, X tells Y to do B

and

X tells Y that *p*
That *p* entails that *q*
So, X tells Y that *q*

are valid arguments, the same is not true if a less restricted use of "implies" is substituted for "entails." Indeed, it can be argued that this is the locus of the difference between what statements *entail* and what they *imply* without *entailing*. A related point concerns the validity of the arguments

X intends Y to do A
Doing A *entails* doing B
So, X intends Y to do B

and

X believes that *p*
That *p* entails that *q*

So, X believes that *q*

But to follow up the point would take us too far afield.

(3) We have suggested that "shall" inference tickets have the form

(Shall [—]) implies (shall [. . .])

where the shall-operator appears in both antecedent and consequent, and that they are parasitical upon indicative inference tickets of the form

(—) implies (. . .)

where the square brackets of the "shall-" tickets are understood to make participial expressions of the statements mentioned by the indicative inference ticket. It is important to note, though the full significance of the fact lies outside the scope of this essay, that although in the context "(—) implies (. . .)" gerund expressions are to be construed as singular terms, in the simple context "shall [—]" they are not. In other words, shall-statements, unlike implication statements, are in the object-language. In this respect "shall" resembles truth-functional connectives.

Universality and the Logic of Intentions

6

It will be useful to conclude these animadversions on the logic of imperatives and resolutives with some remarks on the hypothetical imperative.[17] My main point is that to say "If you want A, do B!" is not a special case of telling someone to do something. Here, again, we find the imperative mood serving as the vehicle of a performance, but the performance is that of giving advice, rather than telling someone to do something.[18] The "want" of "If you want A, do B!" like the "want" of "What does he want me to do?" is roughly equivalent to "intend."[19]

It might seem plausible to interpret the hypothetical imperative

If you want the red one, take *that!*

uttered by Jones to Smith, as having the force of

(Since *that* is the red one and you (Smith) want the red one).
"You (Smith) take the one you want!" implies "You (Smith) take *that!*"

and hence as the principle of the argument

You (Smith) take the one you want!
The one you want is the red one
That one is the red one
So, you (Smith) take it.

But, as we have already pointed out, the hypothetical imperative belongs to the category of advice, and in advice the imperative mood is used in answer to the question,

What shall I (Smith) do?

It is, therefore, concerned with the *questioner's* intentions, whereas the *telling to* use of imperatives answers the question,

What do you want me to do?

and expresses the intention of the person who uses the imperative. When Jones advises Smith by saying "Do A!" in answer to the question "What shall I do?" Smith accepts this advice by forming the intention expressed by "I shall do A." It is as though Smith handed to Jones the incomplete sentence,

I (Smith) shall do . . .

and Jones had added "A" to complete it.

In the case of the hypothetical imperative, "If you want the red one, take *that!*" Jones is telling Smith that *that* is the red one. He is, however, giving this information in a way which reflects the deliberative role it would play in Smith's thinking if, indeed, he does intend to take the red one. This role can be represented by

(1) *That* is the red one
So (I take the red one) implies (I take *that*)
So, (Shall [I take the red one]) implies (Shall [I take *that*])

(2) Shall [I take the red one]
So, shall [I take *that*]

Thus, to advise Smith with the hypothetical imperative in question is to answer, by anticipation, the question

I (Smith) shall take the red one, *so which* shall I take?

The answer, however, though verbally similar to the *telling to* "You (Smith) take *that!*" conveys the information that *that* is the red one for use as a premise in Smith's reasoning as outlined above.

7

Let us now look at the implications of the above considerations for the analysis of ought-statements. At the end of Section 4 we were preparing to examine the idea that ought-statements are truly universal imperatives; that they have a force which it takes what is, from the standpoint of actual usage, the absurdity "Everybody do A in C throughout all past and future time!" to represent. We are now in a position to understand this absurdity and to see that it just won't do to suppose that by a simple extension (for analytic purposes) of the ordinary imperative mood, we can represent ought-statements as truly universal imperatives. Reflection on the fact that imperative utterances are practical performances to which appeal can be made in justifying or excusing our conduct, makes it clear that they presuppose *publication* to those who are to do what the imperatives tell them to do. It is no accidental feature of imperatives that one can only tell people to do things in the future. And it is no accidental feature of imperatives that they are formulated by the use of tensed verbs in which the tense has its full and ordinary force. There can be no counterpart here of the "tenseless" *is* which philosophers use to formulate truly universal matters of fact. Only God at the time of creating Adam could have sensibly used the imperative "Everybody at all times and places do A in C!" for only then was all relevant time all future time.

But if we cannot *tell* past people to do A in C, we can *wish* that they had done so. If moral principles cannot be interpreted as truly universal imperatives, may they not be the expression of truly universal wishes? "Everybody ought to do A in C," then, would have the force of "Would that everybody had done A in C, and did A in C from now on"—a wish which we may abbreviate to

Would that everybody *universally* did A in C!

This suggestion has the advantage (over the imperativist account) that

Would that everybody universally did A in C!
X is (was, will be) in C
So, would that X did (had done) A!

has the feel of deliberative reasoning. And though there are fairly obvious reasons to mistrust this suggestion, let us refuse, for the moment, to entertain them, for it will be useful to let it grow before it is modified or abandoned.

Let us suppose, then, as a working hypothesis, that

Everybody ought to do A in C
X doing B in these circumstances is X doing A in C
So, X ought to do B

has the force of

Would that everybody universally did A in C!
X doing B in these circumstances is X doing A in C
So, would that X did B!

and let us suppose, again as a working hypothesis, that

Would that I did B

has the force of

I shall do B

and

Would that X did B!

the force of

X shall do B

where the shall-sentences are used in accordance with the stipulations of Section 3. Now let us add the logical point, which derives from the analysis of what it is to have an intention, that, other things being equal, a person who candidly says

I shall do B

and is not a victim of self-deception, and is not mistaken about the circumstances, and does not change his mind, *will do* B; and that, with similar qualification, one who candidly says

Tom shall do B

will do that which he believes would bring about Tom's doing of B. If we add this logical point, can we not claim that the above is at least a first approximation to an analysis of what it is to *have* a moral principle and act on it?

8

But if this account has the merit of freeing ought-statements from "telling to," while preserving the connection with "intending" which was the sound core of the imperativist analysis, it won't do as it stands. Much more remains to be said about the universality represented, in this account, by "Would that everybody universally did A in C!" Then, when and if this hurdle has been crossed, the account must be freed from its stress on sentences having the special force of the form "Would that X did A!" Of these tasks, the former will prove decisive.

Consider the case of someone who has a universal wish in a more ordinary and restricted sense of "universal." Suppose that Jones wishes that "everybody" do a certain kind of action, where the scope of "everybody" is, say, the people who are with him on a particular occasion. We who reflect on Jones's intention may ask ourselves

Why (for what reason) does Jones wish that everybody do A? and we may arrive at an answer of one of the following types:

(*a*) Because if everybody does A, this would have as its *joint* result the state of affairs S (which he wishes to exist for its own sake).

(*b*) Because each doing of A has a consequence of a certain kind K (which he wishes to exist for its own sake), and if everybody does A, this would bring about the maximum number of K states of affairs.

(*c*) Because if everybody does A, everybody does A (i.e., *everybody doing A* is a state of affairs which he wishes to exist for its own sake; he is interested in single doings of A only as logically necessary conditions of everybody doing A.

(*d*) Because if everybody does A, there are that many individual doings of A. (He would wish any A-doing to exist for its own sake).

I do not wish to imply that this list exhausts the possible types of answer to the above question. There is also the answer

(*e*) Because they ought (as he thinks) to do A.

This answer, however, only poses all over again the puzzles we are seeking to solve.

Answers of type (*a*) and (*b*) would seem to be clearly irrelevant to the analysis of action *on principle*, and I shall just assume, for the time being, that there is no sense in thinking that having the principle *Everybody ought to do A in* C is a matter of wishing that everybody did A in C *for the sake of the consequence of such action.* Answers (*c*) and (*d*) are useful points of departure for the solution of our first problem, that concerning the universality of ought-statements. Let us consider them in reverse order.

The first thing to note is that while (*d*) grants that Jones wishes that everybody did A, it emphasizes that it is individual cases of A-doing in which he is interested; his wish that a given case of A-doing exist is not a wish that it exist *in order that* a set of A-doings exist. Rather, his wish that everybody do A sums up, so to speak, his wishes that this, that, and the other person do A. He "just likes" individual cases of A-doing to exist, the more the merrier. He does not deliberate

Would that "everybody" did A!

So, would that Tom did A!

If anything, he deliberates

Would that Tom, Dick, Harry, indeed that "everybody" did A!

Case (*c*), on the other hand, provides us with an example of

Would that everybody did A!

So, would that Tom did A!

Yet it clearly does not give us what we are looking for, as it specifies that Jones is interested in Tom's A-doing only as a necessary condition of the state of affairs *everybody doing A*, that is to say, as one component in the state of affairs

Tom doing A and Dick doing A and. . . .

But action on principle is not *silly*, as it would be if it were a matter of wishing that I keep this promise as a logically necessary condition of a world-long and world-wide keeping of promises.

If only we could combine that feature of (*c*) which is expressed by

Would that "everybody" did A!

So, would that Tom did A!

with that feature of (*d*) which is expressed by

Whether or not the others do A, would that Tom did A!

Now the moral of the above example is that to understand action on principle, it is not enough to invoke *separately* the ideas of *universality* and *not as a means*. The universality of the intention of action on principle *is* the manner in which the action is not intended as a means. To understand the universality of the intention in action on principle is to understand the sense in which a particular action, done on principle, is done for the sake of the action itself.

The point at which I am driving is, perhaps, best brought out by making a somewhat parallel point in another context, though to make it in such brief compass I must skate hurriedly over thin ice. To acknowledge that

All M's are *universally* N's

is to be prepared candidly to say such things as

This is an M, *therefore* it is an N

That is an N *because* it is an M

If this *were* an M, it *would be* an N

If this *had been* an M, it *would have been* an N

If *anything* were an M, it would be an N.

The point of the parallel is that

Would that everybody *universally* did A in C!

is the expression of commitment to a *principle*, only if it expresses a readiness to such reasonings as

Would that Tom did A, *for* he is a person in C

I am a person in C, *so* would that I did A!

Since Dick was a person in C, would that he had done A!

Once again, let us permit the suggestion to grow before submitting it to a closer scrutiny. If it is sound, then to represent the deliberation which culminates in "I ought to do this" by the form

Would that everybody universally did A in C!
I am in C
So, would that I did A!

would be to make the mistake of treating an expression of the principle *in accordance with which* one reasons about particular cases as though it were the major *premise* of such reasonings. The corresponding mistake in the case of theoretical (as contrasted with practical reasoning) is represented by the form

All M is *necessarily* N
This is M
So, it is N

We shall come back to this point in a moment. In the meantime we can see why, if the suggestion is sound, approving *on principle* of a doing of A in C is not the same thing at all as favoring it simply because one recognizes it to be a doing of A in C. To say of Jones that he favors an item simply because he thinks of it as being of a certain description is to say that it is the fact that Jones thinks of the item as being of that sort which explains why he favors it. We can represent this by the reasoning

Jones thinks that x is f
So, Jones approves of x

and the inference ticket which authorizes this reasoning as

Whenever Jones thinks that an item is f, he approves of it.

But the fact that *we* reason about Jones's approval of x along these lines must not be confused with the idea that *Jones's* approval of x is a *reasoned* approval. That is, we must avoid the assumption that because *we* can correctly argue as above, Jones must have reasoned

x is f
So, would that x were defended, etc.

It is simply not true that if Jones's thought that x is f is the *explanation* of the approval, then his approval must be a *reasoned* approval. It *may* be, or it may not. And if it is a reasoned approval, then the explanation of his approval of *x* is, strictly speaking, not

Jones approves of *x* because he thinks that it is f

but rather,

Jones approves of *x* because he thinks that *x* is f *and* accepts the practical principle "If anything is f, would that it be defended, etc."

To represent Jones as thinking

Would that *x*, which is f, were defended, etc.

is not the same thing at all as representing him as reasoning

x is f

So, would that *x* were defended, etc.

even though we add to the former the information that *whenever* Jones thinks of an item as f, he thinks (*ceteris paribus*)

Would that it were defended, etc.

As a parallel it may be pointed out that (as Prichard has emphasized)

(1) Jones thought that it would thunder *because he thought* that lightning had just occurred

is authorized by "Whenever *Jones thinks* that lightning has occurred, *he thinks* that it will thunder," and can be a mere matter of the "association of ideas," whereas

(2) Jones thought that it would thunder because lightning had just occurred (Jones thought "It will thunder because lightning has just occurred")

cannot. A psychological commentary on Jones's thinking in the latter case would have to mention Jones's acceptance of the principle "One may infer the occurrence of thunder from that of lightning" (Jones thinks "Whenever lightning occurs it will thunder"). Notice that (2) endorses the idea that lightning has just occurred. If the speaker does not wish to endorse Jones's thought that lightning has just occurred, he would say

(3) Jones thought that it would thunder because (he thought) lightning had just occurred.

This parenthetical use of "he thought" must not be confused

with the "he thought" of "*because he thought* that lightning had just occurred."

Thus, we see, it is essential not to confuse

> Smith did B because he thought his doing B would be doing A in C

with

> Smith did B *because*, he thought, *his doing B would be doing A in* C.

The difference in punctuation highlights the difference between asserting that the occurrence of thoughts of the form "my doing B would be a case of doing A in C" constitutes a (partial) explanation of the occurrence which was Smith's doing of B, and asserting that it was practical thinking of the form "I shall do B because my doing B would be a case of doing A in C" which accounts for Smith's doing of B. In the second case, the "he thought" is a parenthetical comment by the speaker on Smith's reason for doing as he did. It must, of course, be granted that reasons are causes, i.e., that *in general* we can move from statements of the second form to statements of the first, and vice versa. But these moves are not without their dangers. For, as is well known, in causal explanations we are content to single out one aspect of the total relevant situation within which the explanandum occurs, dub it the cause, and relegate the presupposed remainder to the category of *condition*. On the other hand, we have not given a person's reason for acting as he did, unless we have given the whole reason in its proper form. Thus, in attempting to indicate that Smith has acted on principle, we may begin by saying, in the order of causes

> Smith did B because he thought that to do B in his circumstances would be to do (an action of kind) A in (circumstances of kind) C.

This, however, leaves it open whether, in our statement of Smith's *reason* for acting as he did, we should say

> (A) Smith did B because, he thought, doing B in his circumstances would be doing A in C

or

(B) Smith did B because, he thought, doing B in his circumstances would be a case of *anybody* doing A when in C.

It is only (B) which represents Smith as reasoning (roughly),

(B′) Would that I did A, if I am in C
(In the case of anybody, would that he did A when in C)
To do B in these circumstances is to do A in C
So, would that I did A.

On the other hand, (A) is satisfied if Smith's decision is of the form,

(A′) Would that I did A, if I am in C
To do B in these circumstances is to do A in C
So, would that I did B

provided only that if Smith were to think of *any* action of *any* person as a doing of A in C, he would wish it done for its own sake, and hence reason *in each case*

(A″) Would that Y did A, if Y is in C
To do B in Y's circumstances is to do A in C
So, would that Y did A

Even with this proviso, however, (A) does not acquire the force of (B). To reason *in each case* as in (A″) is not the same thing as to reason in each case *in terms of a principle applicable to each case*. Yet we will not have clarified the difference, in the case of practical reasoning, until we understand the status of the bracketed move in reasoning (B) above.

Notice, also, that if this proviso is not added, and if, for example, the doing of A in C by other people would not be approved by Smith, then we would have to revise the statement of Smith's reason for doing what he did to read, correspondingly,

(A‴) Smith did B because, he thought, doing B in his circumstances would be a doing of A in C by Smith

and the original causal statement to read

Smith did B because he thought doing B in his circumstances would be a case of Smith doing A in C.

Approving *on principle* is not the same as being disposed to "just like" each item which one comes to think of as being of a certain kind.[20] This is not, for the moment at least, to be construed as a denial that people *might* arrive at the espousal of a principle of doing A when in C by a process which began with "just liking" (however this might come about) individual cases of people doing A in C; nor that, regardless of how we come to espouse it, the principle, when challenged, *might* be "justified" by the fact that when all the chips are down and all the information in, we find that we "just like" any case of doing A in C, in a sense of "just like" which is not the espousal of the principle all over again.

9

Let us now return to the topic of universality. We had arrived at the point of suggesting that "Would that everybody *universally* did A in C!" expresses the espousal of a principle of conduct, as expressing a readiness to reason in accordance with the form

X is (was, will be) a person in C
So, would that X did (had done) A

where X is a variable which ranges over persons, that is to say, *us*.[21] But before we proceed, we must, as already noted, free our account from its overly close connection with *wishing*, which stems, it will be remembered, from its genesis in a critique of the imperativist analysis. But instead of examining the logic of "to wish" and showing how "would that . . ." is related to other forms of practical discourse in order to show how wishes can embody the same principles as other practical "attitudes," I shall limit myself to pointing out that while neither "X should have done A" nor "It should have been the case that *p*" can be said to express intentions, any more than "X did A" or "It was the case that *p*" can be said to express expectations; nevertheless, intending may have its past tense (and subjunctive) counterparts, as expecting has its counterpart in historical thinking. A person who thinks at 10:00 A.M.:

Shall [X doing A ten minutes from now]

can be said to intend that X do A in ten minutes. Is there no practical thought that he can think about X doing A at 10:20, assuming that he has not changed his mind? It is surely plausible to interpret

Should [X doing A ten minutes ago]

as a differently tensed counterpart of the former. But what role might such thoughts play? It is worth noting that "X should have done A" is much closer to "X ought to have done A" than are simple "shalls" to "oughts." If we throw more light on the relation of "ought" to "shall," we may then be in a position to appreciate practical discourse in the historical mode. But first let us continue with our attempt to build "shall" into "ought" without letting that problem distract us.

At the end of Section 4 we argued that reasoned decisions involving "shall" were ultimately of the form

Shall [—]

So, shall [. . .]

where the implication authorizing this inference, namely,

(Shall [—]) implies (shall [. . .])

rests on an implication between the indicative statements "—" and ". . ." which, by being bracketed, i.e., turned into participial expressions, serve as operands which the shall-operator turns into shall-statements. A not too complex example of practical reasoning of this kind would be

I shall do A, if I have the money

I have the money

So, I shall do A

which, on the above analysis, breaks down as follows:

(1) Shall [my doing A, if I have the money]

(2) (I have the money) implies ([I will do A, if I have the money] implies [I will do A])

(3) I have the money

(4) So, (my doing A, if I have the money) implies (my doing A)

(5) (Shall [my doing A, if I have the money]) implies (Shall [my doing A])

(6) So, Shall [my doing A]

In this "breakdown" of the original inference, the antecedents and consequents of implication statements (2), (4), and (5) are either *both* indicatives or *both* resolutives. In other words, whereas the original formulation suggests that the reasoning proceeds in accordance with the principle

(I have the money) implies (Shall [my doing A])

or, perhaps,

"(If I have the money, then shall [my doing A]) *and* I have the money)" implies (Shall [my doing A])

in neither of which is the antecedent a shall-statement, the proposed breakdown separates the reasoning into separate stages which are either pervasively indicative or pervasively resolutive.

Against this background what are we to make of the reasoning, characteristic of action on principle,

Jones is a person in C
So, Jones shall do A

Our first attempt may well be to construe this reasoning as authorized by the general inference ticket

(X is a person in C) implies (X shall do A)

But as this ticket has a shall in its consequent, but no shall in its antecedent, we may be tempted to think of it as a *derivative* inference ticket, one which must be explicated in terms of an inference ticket moving from shall to shall, and which, in its turn, rests on an inference ticket which moves from indicative to indicative. Thus, we might be tempted to reconstruct the argument as follows:

(1) Shall [(X) (X doing A, if X is in C)]
(2) "(X) (X does A, if X is in C)" implies (Jones does A, if Jones is in C)
(3) "Shall [(X) (X doing A, if X is in C)]" implies (Shall [Jones doing A, if Jones is in C])
(4) Shall [Jones doing A, if Jones is in C]
(5) (Jones is in C) implies ([Jones doing A, if Jones is in C] implies [Jones doing A])
(6) Jones is in C
(7) (Jones doing A, if Jones is in C) implies (Jones doing A)
(8) (Shall [Jones doing A, if Jones is in C]) implies (Shall [Jones doing A])

(9) Shall [Jones doing A]

But this suggestion, according to which moral principles are universal resolutives of the form

Shall [(X) X doing A, if X is a person in C]

runs up against the objection that it would be silly to espouse such resolutives knowing full well that in a great many cases people who are in C simply have not done, nor will they do, A.

A more plausible approach, which has the advantage of interpreting the universality of moral principles in terms of *each* case rather than the totality of cases, draws on the concept of an *axiom schema.* According to it, instead of saying that

Shall [(X) (X doing A, if X is a person in C)]

is an axiom, we should rather say that every statement derived from the schema

Shall [X doing A, if X is a person in C]

by replacing X with the name of a person is an axiom or first principle of moral reasoning. According to this approach, the first three steps of the above breakdown are to be replaced by the characterization of (4) as an axiom conforming to the above axiom schema.

But what is the difference between the following two conceptions of espousing a moral principal pertaining to people doing A in C?

(A) to espouse such a moral principle is to accept as a first principle of practical reasoning any resolutive conforming to the schema

Shall [X doing A, if X is in C]

(B) to espouse such a moral principle is to accept the general inference ticket,

(X is a person in C) implies (Shall [X doing A])

To choose between these interpretations requires a closer look at conditional intentions, i.e., at the logical form of "X shall do A, if *p*" and its relation to the inference

X shall do A, if *p*

p

So, X shall do A.

It has often been argued that the closest that ordinary language comes to exhibiting the truth-functional connective of *material implication* in its pure form is in the expression of conditional intentions. Or, to put the point the other way around, that whereas most ordinary uses of "if . . . , then—" give expression to basic or derivative relations of inferability, the "if . . . , then—" of conditional intention has nothing to do with inferability, but rather is material implication pure and simple. But this way of putting the point is too strong; for if a person says

I shall do A, if *p*

and we subsequently find that in spite of becoming convinced that *p*, he does not do A, we shall infer either that he has changed his mind, or that he was mistaken about his frame of mind, or that he was deceiving us. Thus there is a logical connection between "I shall do A" and "*p*" stronger than material implication, and it would be incorrect to say that the force of "I shall do A, if *p*" has *nothing* to do with inferability. On the other hand, the inferability seems clearly to relate to the force of "shall" as governing the entire conditional, and not only to be compatible with the absence of an *independent* intentional connection between *p* and the doing of A but also to require that there be none. The inferability is exhibited by the following schema, in which (and hereafter in this essay) "*if* . . . , *then*—" stands for material implication.

X candidly says (thinks) "Shall [*if p, then* my doing A]"
X candidly says (thinks) "*p*"
So, X will do A

If so, then it is a mistake to interpret the "if . . . , then—" of conditional intention as anything more than material implication, even though one must grant that a relation stronger than material implication obtains between the corresponding biographical statements concerning intentions, beliefs, and actions.

These considerations throw light on the difference between interpretations (A) and (B) above of what it is to espouse a moral principle. For it enables us to dispel the feeling that these proposals are *equivalent*. This feeling rested on the rough equivalence between accepting the *inference ticket*

(x is f) implies (x is g)

and accepting the *schema*

If x is f, then x is g

as defining a class of *axioms* (i.e., unconditionally assertable statements). Thus, if to espouse a moral principle *were* to accept the schema

If X is in C, then X shall do A

as defining a set of axioms, one might well conclude that to speak instead of accepting the inference ticket

(X is in C) implies (X shall do A)

would be to say essentially the same thing in other words. But if, as we have argued, it is a mistake to interpret expressions of conditional intention as having the form

If p, then X shall do A

and if they must, instead, be attributed the form

(Shall [if p, then X doing A]), i.e., (Shall [*if* p, *then* X doing A])

as must be done to bring the condition within the intention, the parallel disappears. Thus, (B) must be rejected, and (A) so interpreted as not to confuse

X accepts as a first principle of practical reasoning any resolutive conforming to the schema: (Shall [*if* X is in C, *then* X doing A])

which is (in first approximation) the correct account, with

X accepts as a first principle of practical reasoning any resolutive conforming to the schema (*if* X is in C, *then* shall [X doing A])

which is not.

This account of espousing a principle has the additional merit of making clear *why* it won't do to interpret such espousal as a matter of having a *general* intention, thus:

X accepts as a first principle of practical reasoning the universal resolutive, "Shall [(X) (*if* X is in C, *then* X doing A)]."

For to intend *in this sense* that everybody do A in C, knowing, as one does, that "(X) (*if* X is in C, *then* X *does* A)" is false, would be, if not (as it seems to be) logically impossible, at least silly.

Let me now suggest as the next step in the analysis of ought-statements that

X (as being a person in C) ought to do A

has the force of

Shall [X doing A] *because* X is in C and shall* [*if* X is in C, *then* X doing A]

where the asterisk attached to the second "shall" is a *signal* that the speaker recognizes resolutives of the form

Shall [*if* X is in C, *then* X doing A]

as first principles of practical reasoning. Needless to say, this answer is oversimplified in a number of respects, not the least of which is its presupposition that the A and C of the ought-statement are the action and circumstance categories of a principle at hand. For the relation between ought-statements and principles is more flexible than indicated above. To make an ought-statement one need not, as we saw in Section 4, have a principle up one's sleeve; rather, one commits oneself to the idea that "there is" an explanation having the form of the above because-statement, X's circumstances being of kind C and the action in question of kind A.

A more radical defect in the above "analytical model," as we shall see, is its neglect of that dimension of moral principles which is the fact that they are *our* principles (not merely *my* principles) though it does justice to the fact that they are principles *about* us.

10

There is a consideration pertaining to intentions and their expression which, though not strictly a part of the argument of this paper, indicates how it might fit into the broader framework of an empiricist philosophy of mind.[22] It is that to *intend* that person P do A is to *think* "P shall do A," i.e., to be disposed to have *thoughts* of the kind "P shall do A" where these thoughts are inner episodes construed on the model of the overt utterances which, in candid discourse, are *initiated by* these inner episodes, and in this sense, express them. (To *believe* that *x* is f is, correspondingly, to *think* "*x* is f," i.e., to be disposed to have thoughts of the kind "*x* is f," where these thoughts are inner episodes construed on the model of the overt utterances which, in candid discourse, are initiated by these inner episodes, and would be said to express this belief.) And if we must add that in a certain sense one can think "P shall do A" without really intending that P do A, this is not because intending that P do A is thinking "P shall do A" *plus* something else, but because that which appears to introspection as the thought "P shall do A" is only *presumptively* this thought. Thus, if someone candidly assures us "I shall do A," and it turns out at the appropriate time that, although he assures us that he has not changed his mind, the thought of doing A has no power to move him to act, then it would be proper to deny not only that he had really intended to do A, but also that the presumptive thought "I shall do A," which he had introspected, really was such.

Notice that I am not saying that *intending,* for example, to do B in order to bring about A, is identical with the *power* of the thought "My doing B would bring about A" to move one to act. I am, however, insisting that the power, in the causal order, of thoughts of the form "My doing B would bring about A" to move one to act is a presupposition of the language of "shall" and the order of reasons—indeed, that "I shall do B in order to bring about A" embodies this presupposition.[23]

It follows from the above conception of the status of intentions and beliefs, together with the interpretation of ought defended in this essay, that to *believe* "P ought to do A" is, in part, to *intend* "P shall do A."

II

We must now face up to the fact that "shall" and its kindred express the intentions of the *speaker*. Thus, and the point is an obvious one,

Jones shall do A

differs from

Jones intends to do A

in that whereas the speaker uses the latter to ascribe to Jones the intention to do A, the former expresses *the speaker's intention that Jones do A*. Thus, if I say to Jones

You shall do A

I have no logical right to expect him to concur by saying

Yes, I shall do A.

And if he should reply

No, I shall not do A

the logic of "shall" makes no demand that one or other of us change our mind by abandoning our intention—though logic does assure us that these intentions are incompatible in that they cannot both be realized. Consequently, if my statement

You (Jones) ought to do A

were simply

You (Jones) shall* do A

where the asterisk signals the presupposition of practical reasoning of the form

Shall [*if* Jones is in C, *then* Jones doing A]

So, Jones being in C, shall [Jones doing A]

in which the major premise is an axiom of the type discussed in Section 9, there would be no logical reason to expect Jones, given that he agrees that he is indeed a person in C, to meet *my*

You (Jones) ought to do A

with

Yes, I (Jones) ought to do A.

My point is that the language of morals differs from the language which simply expresses the speaker's intentions, not only by expressing or implying reasoning of the kind we have been exploring, but also by presupposing (in one sense of this much abused expression) that all disagreements of the form

A: Jones ought to do one thing

B: No! He ought to do another

are "in principle" reducible to disagreement *about matters of fact* and not to disagreement *in intention.*

How is this presupposition to be understood? The explanation centers around a simple fact about the grammar of the word "ought": that *ought, unlike shall, has a proper negative.* Whereas shall is characterized by the two forms

Shall [X doing A]
Shall [X not doing A]

ought enjoys the full complement

Ought [X doing A]
Ought [X not doing A]
Not-ought [X doing A]
Not-ought [X not doing A]

In short, one person can *contradict* another person's ought, whereas shalls *conflict* but do not *contradict.*

Let us introduce the concept of the *biographical counterpart* of a shall-statement. Thus, corresponding to Tom's shall-statement

Shall [X doing A]

there is the biographical counterpart

Tom intends that X do A

which, given that Tom speaks candidly and without self-deception, will be true. Using this concept we can pair off the following shall-statements and biographical counterparts:

(1*a*) Tom intends that X do A
(1*b*) Tom: Shall [X doing A]
(2*a*) Tom intends that X not do A
(2*b*) Tom: Shall [X not doing A]
(3*a*) Tom: intends that X do A or not do A as X pleases
(3*b*) Tom: Shall [X doing A, if X so wishes *and* X not doing A, if X so wishes]
(4*a*) Tom has formed no intention with respect to X doing A
(4*b*) Tom: Shall [X doing A]? [24]

It is clear that these relationships do not require the form

Not-shall [X doing A]

because the one case which might seem to call for it, namely (3*a*), simply gives us another example of a shall-statement. But what of biographical statements of the form "Tom does *not* intend that X do A"? Do we not have

(5*a*) Tom does not intend that X do A
(5*b*) Tom: Not-shall [X doing A]

and is not (5*b*) equivalent to

(5*c*) Tom: May [X not doing A]

The answer is that (5*a*) is compatible with (4*a*), whereas (5*c*) clearly expresses the outcome of a deliberation, and is, indeed, the expression of an intention. In fact, it would not be implausible to regard (5*c*) as a variant form of (3*b*).

Against the equation of (5*c*) with (3*b*), however, there are important considerations pertaining to the role of "may" in *telling to* discourse. It is, I believe, illuminating to regard the fundamental role of "may" as that of *withdrawing a telling to*. We have already called attention to the difference between expressing the intention that X do A, and telling X to do A, a difference which is represented in our symbolism by the difference between "Shall [X doing A]" and "Shall [X doing A]!" If, now we pair off *tellings to* with *their* biographical counterparts, we have, for example,

(6*a*) Tom tells X to do A

(6*b*) Tom: Shall [X doing A]!

Here the fact emerges that if Tom has told X to do A, he may subsequently (subject, of course, to certain conventions) withdraw this performance by saying "May [X not doing A]!" This direct withdrawal is not to be confused with the "implicit" withdrawal which is performed by "contramanding,"[25] i.e., presenting X with a new telling to, one which *conflicts* with the old, as,

Tom: Shall [X doing A]!

Tom (subsequently): Shall [X doing B]!

where doing B entails not doing A; or, in a weaker form,

Tom: Shall [X doing A]!

Tom (subsequently): Shall [X not doing A, if *p*]!

Withdrawing a telling to is the practical counterpart of withdrawing a telling that. Therefore, it is important to distinguish between *withdrawing* a telling that, and *contradicting* a telling that. The difference is illustrated by the dialog,

Tom: S is P

Tom (subsequently): S is not P

Dick (chiming in): S is not P

Tom has both contradicted and by implication withdrawn his earlier telling that. Dick obviously cannot withdraw Tom's telling that; but he can, and does, contradict it. Notice that Tom might have withdrawn his earlier telling that by saying "S may not be P after all." This use of "may" is not to be confused with notions pertaining to possibility or probability in those uses which do have proper contradictories.

The fallacy I am attempting to expose is exhibited by the following sequence of statements:

(1) *Countermanding* is the counterpart of *contradicting*

(2) To contradict is to assert the negative of what was asserted

(3) "May [X not doing A]!" countermands "Shall [X doing A]!"

(4) "May [X not doing A]!" = "Not-shall [X doing A]!"

The fallacy lies in the third step. "May [X not doing A]!" countermands "Shall [X doing A]!" in a sense which *is* the counterpart of contradiction, only if it is interpreted, roughly, as saying "Shall [X doing A, if X so wishes *and* X not doing A, if X so wishes]!"; in which case it is not a "not-shall" statement (whatever that might be) but simply another shall-statement which implicitly *withdraws* the original telling to. If, on the other hand, "May [X not doing A]" is taken to play the direct withdrawal role, then it is not the counterpart of a contradiction. and the argument also breaks down.

Universality and Intention: A Second Mode

12

I pointed out above that whereas one person can *contradict* another person's ought, shalls *conflict* but do not *contradict.* But to make it intelligible how ought can "at bottom" be a shall, and yet have this radical intersubjectivity, we must bite a bit deeper. Consider the following exchange:

D(1) Tom: S is P

Dick: S is not P

Dick has contradicted Tom; and supposing candor on all sides, we can correlate with this dialog the following biographical counterparts:

BD(1) Tom thinks that S is P
Dick thinks that S is not P

Consider, next, the dialog,

D(2) Tom: I (Tom) shall do A
Dick: You (Tom) shall not do A

This time the biographical counterparts are

BD(2) Tom intends that Tom do A
Dick intends that Tom not do A.

If we reflect on these two pairs, we notice a point of resemblance and a point of difference. The point of resemblance is that in each of the dialogs what each speaker says expresses *his* frame of mind—in the one case the thought that S is (or is not) P, in the other the intention that Tom do (or not do) A. The difference consists in the already noted fact that whereas in the first dialog Dick has contradicted Tom, in the second he has simply expressed an intention which is not co-realizable with Tom's intention.

Consider, next, the two dialogs,

D(3) Tom: I (Tom) ought to do A
Dick: You (Tom) ought *not to do A*

D(4) Tom: I (Tom) ought to do A
Dick: *It is not the case* that you (Tom) ought to do A.

Our analysis suggests the following biographical counterparts for the first of these dialogs,

BD(3) Tom intends that Tom *do A* because he has such and such an "axiomatic" intention and such and such factual beliefs
Dick intends that Tom *not do A* because he (Dick) has such and such an "axiomatic" intention (about Tom) and such and such factual beliefs.

But it leaves us puzzled as to just what to offer as the counterpart of D(4). For if our aim is to reconcile the idea that in D(4) Dick is contradicting Tom with the idea that the ought is a special case of shall, we can scarcely be satisfied with

BD(4) *Tom* intends that Tom do A
It is not the case that *Dick* intends that Tom do A.

For whereas in the biographical counterpart of D(1) the contradictory statements "S is P" and "S is not P" *reappear in the guise of that-clauses;* in BD(4) the supposedly contradictory statements have simply disappeared. On the other hand, if we simply represent the biographical counterpart of D(4) as

BD(4′) Tom thinks that Tom ought to do A
Dick thinks that not-(Tom ought to do A)

we say what is true, but lose contact with the "analysis" of ought in terms of shall.

I suggest that (to put it in a radically oversimplified manner) the *auto*biographical counterpart of an ought-statement is not simply

I intend that X do A because I have such and such an "axiomatic" intention with respect to X, and such and such factual beliefs

but rather

We intend that X do A. . . .

Thus, corresponding to the statements,

D(5) Tom: I (Tom) ought to do A as being a person in C
Dick: You (Tom) ought to do A as being a person in C
Harry: He (Tom) ought to do A as being a person in C

we have as counterparts *not*

BD(5) Tom "axiomatically intends" that Tom do A as being a person in C
Dick "axiomatically intends" that Tom do A as being a person in C
Harry "axiomatically intends" that Tom do A as being a person in C

but, rather, the autobiographical counterparts,

ABD(5) Tom: *We* "axiomatically intend" that Tom do A . . .
Dick: *We* "axiomatically intend" that Tom do A . . .
Harry: *We* "axiomatically intend" that Tom do A. . . .

And if, with this in mind, we form the autobiographical counterpart of D(4), we have something like,

ABD(4) Tom: *We* "axiomatically intend" that Tom do A . . .
Dick: *We* do *not* "axiomatically intend" that Tom do A. . . .

What is the force of such phrases as "*we* intend . . ." and "*we* are committed to the intention . . ."? Here we touch on the "institutional" aspect of morality. For "We intend . . ." is clearly not the logical sum, so to speak of "Tom intends . . . ," "Dick intends . . . ," "Harry intends . . . ," etc. Nor does

Tom (who is one of *us*) does *not* intend that X do A

contradict

We intend that X do A

any more than

Tom (who is one of *us*) doesn't mind women smoking

contradicts

We disapprove of women smoking.

Nor (I need scarcely add) does the fact that this is so involve the existence of a "group mind," capable of having beliefs and intentions, in a sense incompatible with empiricist principles. Empiricism has properly stressed the logical dependence of concepts pertaining to the beliefs and attitudes of groups on the corresponding concepts pertaining to individuals. This dependence, however, as the above examples make clear, involves a certain flexibility. Nevertheless, the fewer the people in the group who believe that *p* or intend that X do A, the less defensible becomes the statement that the group believes that *p* or intends that X do A. These are familiar considerations. I wish to emphasize that when the concept of a group is "internalized" as the concept of *us, it becomes a form of consciousness* and, in particular, a form of *intending.*

We saw above that "We intend that X do A" does not entail "Tom (who is one of us) intends that X do A." On the other hand, it is clear that a person who shares none of the intentions of the group could scarcely be said to be one of *us*. There is a particularly close logical connection between "We intend . . ."

and "I intend. . . ." This does not mean that it can never be proper to say "We intend . . . , though I, for myself, do not." On the contrary, this makes perfectly good sense. Yet there is clearly a tension between them. If to intend that X do A is, as I have suggested, to think "X shall do A," then we must distinguish between two shalls, one corresponding to "We intend . . ." and one to "I, for myself, intend. . . ." Let us represent them, respectively, as "shall*w*" and "shall*I*." *I suggest that ought, as an expression of intention, is a special case of shall*w. There are, in this case, two dimensions to the universality of moral principles as universal intentions: (1) the formal universality, or universality of application which can be represented by the formula, "All of us shall do A in C"; (2) *the universality of the intending itself*, which can be represented by modifying the above formula to read, "All of us shall*w* do A in C."

Let me now bring all these considerations together. I suggest that the fact that ought-statements, unlike ordinary shall-statements, have a proper negation is built on the shared intending expressed by "ought." In other words, the *syntactical* intersubjectivity of ought-statements which permits Dick to contradict Tom as in D(4) above, and which *consists in* the existence of the form "not-ought [X doing A]" in addition to the form "ought [X *not* doing A]" rests on the intersubjectivity of the intention expressed by ought-statements.

Notice that I am not saying merely that the existence of shared formally universal intentions is a sociological condition of the existence of intersubjective ought-talk. I am saying that intersubjective ought-talk *contains* within itself the "symbolic form" which is the very existence of *intending-as-one-of-us*. (Just as "I shall do A," in its candid, un-self-deceived use, is the very existence of a personal intending.) For this reason, a person who said "People ought to do A in C" but denied "We intend that people do A in C" would be like a person who said "I shall do A" but denied "I intend to do A." The truth of "X intends to do A" is a necessary condition of the "genuineness" (candor and absence of self-deception) of X's "I shall do A," much as the truth of "X believes that S is P" is a necessary condition of the "genuineness" of X's "S is P." Similarly, the truth of "Group G intends that people do A in C" is a necessary condition of the "genuineness" of "People ought to do A in C" said by a member of the group. Here, however, "genuineness" is a more complicated matter than the candor and absence of self-deception of an individual. One can know that *he* intends that people do A in C, and yet be deceived about the group's intention. The group has shared intentions by virtue of the fact that its members intend in the mode "shall*w*." But that the members intend in this mode does not guarantee that in point of fact there are shared intentions. Intending in the mode "shall*w*" is a "form of life," a conceptual framework within which moral discourse exists and without which it is impossible. Yet the actual existence of shared universal intentions is no more an antecedent condition of participating in moral discourse than actual agreement on matters of fact is an antecedent condition of participating in factual discourse. In each case the forms of discourse set this agreement as a *task*. To abandon the idea that disagreement on moral matters is even in principle capable of resolution is not to retreat to a moral solipsism; it is to abandon the moral framework itself, and to retreat to the language or "form of life" of purely personal intention.

13

We have argued that moral consciousness is a special form of *we*-consciousness, and, in effect, that one who does not intend in the *we*-mode, i.e., has no "sense of belonging to the group," cannot be said to have more than a "truncated" understanding of ought. The reader may be prepared to grant that something like a Darwinian natural selection of primitive cultures might bring it about that in the cultures which survive the internal and external dangers which beset them, people decide certain matters of conduct, *ceteris paribus*, on principles of the form

Shall*w* [*if* X is (was, will be) a person [26] in C, *then* X (not) doing (having done) A]

where these principles are *unexamined*, and the fact that people acknowledge them a matter of "social inheritance." But what of *examined* morality? How can we combine the conception of moral action as action on principle, with the idea that the principles in question are *reasonable* principles? Why "Everybody ought to do A in C" rather than ". . . A′ in C" or ". . . A″ in C"? And if we have a reason, and if this reason is a state of affairs, does one not therefore act in order to realize this state of affairs, and no longer on principle?

Now one line of thought is that to justify a set of principles is to find that, all things considered, one wishes doings of A in C, A′ in C′, etc., *as such* to exist. But, as we saw in Section 8, this might have either of two meanings. The first is that to speak of such wishes is a misleading way of referring to the acknowledgment of these very principles themselves, in which case the "justification" amounts to the *fact* that we still espouse them after the factual heights and depths of the world have been explored. The bearing of "all things considered" on the continued espousal of the principles is left completely in the dark. The second is that "One wishes doings of A in C, etc., *as such* to exist" is intended to refer not to an approval of such doings on principle, but rather to a liking of these ways of doing things which, though general, is not on principle, and can be compared to other naturalistic (or, in Kant's sense, pathological) likes and dislikes, in which case the suggestion is most implausible. Is our favoring of promise-keeping *as such* a naturalistic one?

A more plausible line of thought is that which finds the reason for *these* principles rather than *those* in a relation they have to the general welfare. But if we have regard for the general welfare, and find it to be such a reason, does this not mean that we now act in order to promote the general welfare, and envisage doings of A in C, A′ in C′, etc., as means to this end? And does this not, in turn, mean that we are no longer acting *on principle?* Can a person have a reason for his principles, and yet, without having to forget this reason, act *on* these principles? Indeed, can there be such a thing as having principles *and* having a reason for them at all?

Now once the question is posed in these general terms, the

source of the puzzle becomes clear. It lies in a failure to distinguish two senses in which a person may, at the time of acting, be said to *have a certain intention.* In the first place, there is the intention of the action, i.e., what he intends to do *as doing that particular action.* Then there are the purposes and intentions which, though he has them in mind, in an appropriate sense, at the time of acting, and though they may be closely relevant to that action, cannot correctly be said to be part of what he intends to do as doing that particular act. Plans, purposes, policies and the like do not have to be consciously entertained in order to be "in mind" and not forgotten. What I want to emphasize, however, is that even when they are consciously entertained, and as intimately related as they can be, after their own manner, to the intention of the action, they need not, for that reason, be part of the intention of the action.

I shall first develop this point in a way which oversimplifies the logical relations involved. Suppose that Jones, however he may have come to do so, loves his neighbor as his brother, and his brother as himself. "Would," he says, "that men, generally, were happy!" A study of the hearts of men and the ways of the world convinces him that an essential condition of the general welfare is that people generally do A in C, A′ in C′, etc. It also convinces him that for this to be the case, it is necessary that people, generally, act *on* the corresponding principles. (It may also convince him that general action *on* principle, in addition to being an indirect condition of the general welfare, is a direct condition, even, in some sense, a component, of it.)

Now it cannot be true that Jones intends that *everybody* act *on* these principles, unless it is also true that Jones intends that he himself act *on* these principles.

Would that everybody acted *on* P_1, P_2, . . . P_n!

So, would that I acted *on* P_1, P_2, . . . , P_n!

But his decision to acknowledge these principles is the decision to acquire (or, if already acquired, to reinforce and maintain) the character trait of arriving at decisions on matters of conduct by reasoning which, for our present purposes, can be represented by the form

Doing *this* would be a case of a person's doing A in C
(or A′ in C′, etc.)
So, I shall do it

and while his efforts to acquire (and maintain) these dispositions have the *purpose* of doing that which is conducive to the well-being of men generally, these traits, once acquired, manifest themselves in doings of A in C, A′ in C′, etc., of which, in an important sense, the *complete* intention has the form represented immediately above. Or, to put it in the language of ought,

Doing this would be a case of a person's doing A in C
So, I ought to do it.

In other words, these dispositions manifest themselves in actions of which, in an important sense, the motive is *not* the love of one's fellow men, but the sense of duty.

Yet if, in an important sense, Jones does A because it is what he ought to do rather than because it will further the well-being of his fellow men, there is still a sense in which he can be said to have both intentions in doing this action. They are not, however, cooperating intentions on the same level. We must say, rather, that each particular case of conscientious action on the part of Jones is supported by his abiding intention to develop and maintain in himself the dispositions to act *on* the principles, i.e., to espouse them; and this intention, in turn, is part and parcel of his abiding intention that these traits of character be a common possession of men generally, which, in turn, is a consequence (given his beliefs about the hearts of men and the ways of things) of his intention that men generally be happy, a state of affairs which he wishes to exist for its own sake.

Let us take a closer took at the move from "Would that men generally were happy" to "Would that I espoused such and such principles of conduct." The logical bridge between these statements can be schematically represented (in a way which obviously oversimplifies the empirical dimension of the reasoning) as follows:

Would that men generally were happy!
(Men generally being happy) implies (men generally doing A^1 in C^1)

So, would that men generally did A^i in C^i
(Men generally doing A^i in C^i) implies (men generally espousing P^i)
So, would that men generally espoused P^i
(Men generally espousing P^i) implies (my espousing P^i)
So, would that I espoused P^i

Two objections can be raised against this reasoning. The first is that if we interpret "men generally" as "everybody," the argument founders on the fact that we know that not everybody will do A^i in C^i and also that not everybody will espouse P^i. The justification of moral principles is not soft-headed sentimentality. While if we interpret "men generally" as "most people," the conclusion simply does not follow.

This objection is too strong as it stands, for it can be countered by taking the second horn and pointing out that from "Most A is B" to "(probably) this A is B" *valet consequentia*—given, of course, that we have no reason to suppose that this A is one of the exceptions. Yet the objection does prepare the way for a more penetrating objection. This objection is that the empirical facts do not discriminate between "most men" and "most men with the exception of myself," and, in particular, between "most people espousing P^i" and "most people (with the exception of myself) espousing P^i." The way seems open for a compromise between benevolence and self-love which undercuts the above reasoning. One who raises this objection will grant that a person fraught with benevolence but lacking in self-love would, on sitting down in a cool hour, be in a position to reason as above. But, it is argued, surely one who combines a modicum of self-interest with even a substantial amount of benevolence would find a loophole for a compromise. That this compromise would itself be the espousal of a general policy or plan of life is no answer, for it would not be the espousal of universal principles impartially applicable to all.

To rebut this objection we must take a closer look at the concept of benevolence. For, as might be expected, the bridge between benevolence and the life of principle requires a sense of "benevolence" which logically precludes the above compromise. Is there such a sense? Once again the answer lies in reflection on the force of "we" and its relation to "I." For the sense of "benevolence" that is required is not the impartial love of everybody, which is, as Kant saw, the espousal of a principle of conduct (roughly that one ought to help other people realize their ends), but the simple recognition of people generally as *we*. We have already seen that moral principles involve the consciousness of *us*. In fact, we have found it to play a dual role in principles, as can be brought out by representing them by the form "We shall*w* do A if in C." We can now add a third role to our list, the role which relates to the cool hour in which we rise above the level of conscientiousness as the unreflective fruit of "good upbringing." By now the direction of my argument should be obvious. For if we replace "*most people* but not I" by "*we* but not I" in the formulation of the objection, we move from consistency to incoherence. There is no *logical* place for a compromise between benevolence and self-love, where "benevolence" is understood as the consciousness of oneself and one's fellow men as *we*.

It is particularly important to distinguish the "loyalty" to people generally, the recognition of each man everywhere as one of *us*, from the impartial love of one's fellow men which is itself a matter of principle. For if one confuses these two, one will suspect that to defend principles in terms of impartial love is to reason in a circle. The recognition of each man everywhere as one of *us* was the extension of tribal loyalty which exploded it into something new. It has a precarious toehold in the world, and *we* are usually a far smaller group. Kant's conception of each *rational being* everywhere as one of us is a still more breath-taking point of view which may yet become a live option.

14

We have seen that, and how, the idea that the prime mover of reflective moral consciousness is benevolence can be reconciled with the idea that moral action is action *on principle*. It must be admitted that the character trait of acting on principle can exist without loyalty, as the fruit of training, precariously reinforced by praise and blame, and, on a larger scale, as a factor making for the selective survival of social groups and communities. Nevertheless, a conscience of this "chilly" kind must be threatened by every "cool hour" of critical reflection. For while self-love can find reasons for doing the things which good men do, it is unlikely to find reasons for maintaining the dispositions to act on moral principles which make good men good.

Self-love could, indeed, support the effort to acquire and maintain the disposition to arrive at a decision on certain matters of conduct by reasonings which are ultimately of a form represented by the schema

Shall [*if* I am in C at t, *then* my doing A]

that is to say, by reasoning which is built on an *ego-centric* intention, universal only with respect to time. Self-love could support such self-discipline on the ground that it is by being disposed to act *on* these principles that I shall be most likely to achieve my happiness.

But even the prudential ought is not to be confused with such egocentric rulishness. For ought, as we have seen, signalizes the presupposition of agreement. And the distinctive feature of the prudential ought is not its restriction in *scope*, but rather the fact that it is reflectively acknowledged that the reason for being prudentially conscientious is the fact that it is a means to one's own happiness. The prudential ought encompasses individual differences by bringing them into the content of its legislation, and, in this way, adds realism to its presupposition of intersubjectivity.

If this is correct, we should not expect the distinction between moral and prudential principles to have been made until men were on the threshold of reflective morality and had seriously begun to sit down in cool hours and raise the familiar groping questions which gave rise to moral philosophy. This does not mean, of course, that to have arrived at a reasonably clear conception of a certain class of principles as justified by self-love, and, hence, to have set these apart as "principles of prudence," one must have arrived at an equally clear conception of moral principles as justified by benevolence.

I have emphasized in the foregoing that [27] the only frame of mind which can provide direct support for moral commitment is what Royce called Loyalty, and what Christians call Love of Neighbor (*caritas*). This is a commitment deeper than any commitment to abstract principles. It is a precious thing, the foundation for which is laid in earliest childhood, though it can arise, in adult years, by a phenomenon known, in other contexts, as conversion. Recent psychological studies make clear what has always, in a sense, been known, that the ability to love others for their own sakes is as essential to a full life as the need to feel ourselves loved and appreciated for our own sakes, unconditionally, and not as something turned on or off depending on what we do. Thus, in a deeper sense, really intelligent and informed self-love supports, and can be an incentive to forming, the love of neighbor which, nevertheless, alone gives *direct* support to the moral point of view when we are alone in that cool hour.

APPENDIX

Since submitting this paper to the editors of *Methodos* I had an opportunity to read, in mimeograph, Chapter IV of Professor Castañeda's forthcoming important book on the logic of prescriptive discourse. While I disagree with certain aspects of his argument, and, in particular, with his defense of the concept of imperative inference, I do agree that the manifold of practical discourse is illuminated by viewing it against the model of a single mode of practical discourse variously enriched. Indeed, it is largely to him that I owe my possession of this insight, around which have clustered such additional insights as I have accumulated since I began my attempt to reconcile Prichardian intuitionism with naturalism some twenty years ago.

Until I read this chapter it had not occurred to me that

promising and *commanding* ("I command . . .") admit of being viewed as specific enrichments of basic practical sentence forms. Thus, while I would have explained the fact that there are no such reasonings as

(1) I promise to do A, if p
p
So, I promise to do A

or

(2) I command you to do A, if p
p
So, I command you to do A

as opposed to

(1*a*) I promised to do A, if p
p
So, I promised to do A

and

(2*a*) I commanded you to do A, if p
p
So, I commanded you to do A

by saying that the *signals* "I promise" and "I command" do not belong in the scope of "—, *so* . . . ," this claim, sound in essence though it is, would have been scarcely more than the report of an isolated "logical intuition."

In the terminology of this paper, "I promise to do A, if p" differs from "I shall do A, if p" (and, similarly, "I command you to do A, if p" from "You shall do A, if p!") in that they are not only *tellings* but tellings which, by virtue of the presence of the phrases "I promise" and "I command" are (if appropriately performed) subsumed under specific moral principles, as explained in Section 2. "I promise to do A, if p" has, therefore, the form "I shall do A, if p*," and "I command you to do A, if p" has the form "You shall do A, if p**," where "*" and "**" represent, respectively, the promise-making and the command-issuing signals. Like the telling-to signal "!", these signals are not, as such, ingredients in practical reasoning. But if there are no such practical reasonings as (A) and (B) above, there is the reasoning

First step: p
So, (its being the case that *if* p, *then* X does A) implies (X doing A)
Second step: So, (Shall [its being the case that *if* p, *then* X does A]) implies (Shall [X doing A])
Third step: Shall (its being the case that *if* p, *then* X does A)
So, Shall (X doing A).

I also wish to take this opportunity to thank Dr. Karl Potter, whose helpful criticism of the previous version of this paper led me to substitute the convention according to which "X shall do A" is the sheer *expression* of an intention, whereas "X shall do A!" is a *telling to* as well, for a considerably less perspicuous representation of this distinction.

NOTES

1. This paper is a revised version of a paper which appeared in *Methodos*, VIII (1956), 227–268.
2. W. D. Ross, *The Right and the Good* (Oxford: Clarendon Press, 1930).
3. For an interesting discussion of a parallel point, see Professor C. D. Broad's animadversions on the concept of a "rational being" in "Some Reflections on Moral Sense Theories in Ethics," *Proceedings of the Aristotelian Society*, Vol. XLV (1944–45), pp. 131–166.
4. "Does Moral Philosophy Rest on a Mistake?" (1912), in *Readings in Ethical Theory*, ed. W. S. Sellars and J. Hospers (New York: Appleton-Century-Crofts, 1952), p. 154.
5. *Ibid.*, p. 155.
6. A. J. Ayer, *Language, Truth and Logic* (London: Victor Gollancz, 1936).
7. *The Language of Morals* (Oxford: Clarendon Press, 1952). My understanding (to the extent that it is not misunderstanding) of Hare's view has been enhanced by an exchange of ideas in correspondence and personal conversation for which I am grateful.
8. May I take this occasion to acknowledge my indebtedness to my friend and former student, Dr. Hector-Neri Castañeda, whose dissertations for the M.A. and Ph.D. degrees from the University of Minnesota contain important and original contributions to the imperativists' approach to practical discourse. I have also had the benefit of several lengthy discussions with him in the early spring of 1956. The present paper contains many traces of his influence, though I do not know how much of its detail he would find acceptable.
9. I am concerned in this section with the "implicit universality" of the moral ought. I do not wish, therefore, to be taken to deny that there might be varieties of ought which have a lesser scope than *all persons at all times*. An ought, however, which simply reflected one person's intentions here and now would be no ought at all.

   Even the sense in which the moral ought applies to all persons requires careful analysis. It should not be assumed that the "everybody" in a moral principle has the force of "all human beings" in a purely descriptive, so to speak biological, sense of this phrase. It means, roughly, *all of us*, where *we* are those who accept each other as relevant participants in a discussion of what ought or ought not to be done, rather than simply belonging to the stage-setting of conduct. Today, *we* are men generally.

10. "Presupposing," *Philosophical Review*, LXII (1953), p. 214, n. 9.
11. It is, perhaps, worth noting that singular cause-statements are also, in this same sense, "implicitly universal." Thus a person who says, "Doing *this* to *that* in *these* circumstances caused it to behave *thusly*," commits himself to support his remark with a statement of the form, "*This* is an X, and doing *that* to an X is Y-ing it, and *these* circumstances are of kind C, and behaving *thusly* is Z-ing, and Y-ing an X in C causes it to Z. Singular cause-statements, then, like singular ought-statements, are not *merely* singular. Both are, so to speak, singular "after their own kind." Notice also that one can claim with reason that *this* caused *that* in *these* circumstances even though one does not have a causal universal "up one's sleeve" to cover one's claim. One can have reason to believe that the circumstances are such, and *this* and *that* of such kinds, that "there is" a causal universal under which they could be subsumed.
12. John Austin, "Other Minds," *Proceedings of the Aristotelian Society*, Suppl. Vol. XX (1946), pp. 169–174.
13. For an explication of the concept of defeasibility, see H. L. A. Hart, "The Ascription of Rights and Duties," *Proceedings of the Aristotelian Society*, Vol. XLIX (1948–49), pp. 171–194.
14. *Op. cit.*, pp. 24ff.
15. Since we are concerned with modal contexts, it is important not to suppose that if P strictly implies Q, then (Shall [P]) implies (Shall [Q]). Stronger requirements are necessary to avoid paradox. As far as I can see, something like A. R. Anderson's reconstruction of "entails" is necessary.
16. It will be noticed that I am referring to statements of intention as statements. This seems to be in accordance with ordinary usage, although logicians have tended to restrict the term to items which are either true or false.
17. Hypothetical imperatives, represented by the form "If you want A, do B!" are, of course, not to be confused with the conditional imperatives we were discussing a moment ago. The latter have the form "Do B, if *p!*" where *p* is any relevant statement of fact. Hare has made it clear that "if you want A" is not a descriptive-psychological condition serving as a special case of *p*, but rather specifies a resolutive premise which is thought to be (possibly) operating in the practical reasoning of the person to whom the hypothetical imperative is addressed.
18. Hare, of course, construes "imperative" so inclusively that it covers "I shall do A" as well as "Do A!" Yet, since he construes all imperatives as *tellings to,* he construes "I shall do A" as telling oneself to do

A, which it clearly is not; though, of course, there is such a thing as "telling oneself to do A."

19. There are, of course, differences. It makes sense to say of a person that he intended to do or bring about something which he did not *want* to do or bring about. If one does B in spite of the fact that it brings about A, then one does not want to bring about A, although one intends to do so. It should also be clear that one may intend and, indeed, *want* that X do A although one does not *desire* that X do A. We do not use the word "desire" (or its cognates) in the case of action on principle.

20. For an earlier statement of this point, see my "Obligation and Motivation," *Philosophical Studies*, II (1951), 21–25. In the Introduction to the second edition of his *Language, Truth and Logic*, Ayer criticizes his earlier formulation of the emotive theory as follows: ". . . I fail to bring out the point that the common objects of moral approval or disapproval are not particular actions so much as classes of actions; by which I mean that if an action is labeled right or wrong, or good or bad, as the case may be, it is because it is thought to be an action of a certain type." Ayer is here on the point of recognizing the existence of practical reasoning as a genuine form of reasoning. But by failing to draw the above distinctions, he remains within the limits of his earlier formulation.

21. If we suppose that this principle can be put in the form

    If anybody were in C, would that he did A!

    we notice that if this is confused with

    Would it were the case that (if anybody were in C, he did A)!

    one arrives at the Kantian formulation,

    Would that it were a law of nature that people in C did A!

22. For an elaboration of such a framework, see my "Empiricism and the Philosophy of Mind," in *Minnesota Studies in the Philosophy of Science*, Vol. I (Minneapolis: University of Minnesota Press, 1956), pp. 253–328. See also "Some Reflections on Language Games," *Philosophy of Science*, XXI (1954), 204–228.

23. To appreciate at least the general force of this point, one has only to reflect that one has not learned to use "shall" unless, *ceteris paribus*, candid utterances of "I shall do A" are followed by the actual doing of A. "I shall do A" is, so to speak, "My doing of A in the future" as signalizing a forthcoming doing of A. Furthermore, the forthcoming doing of A which it signalizes is not a *blind* doing of A, and this in two respects: (1) the doing is, in a sense, brought about by the idea of doing A; (2) the bringing about itself is a *self-conscious* fact, and not a mere triggering of the action by the idea. This self-consciousness consists in the fact that the thought responsible for the action is "I shall do A," and can be traced to the fact that one hasn't learned the

use of "shall" unless "I shall do A" is not only the signal of a forthcoming doing of A, but is understood to be such a signal.

These and other points concerning the interrelationships of the order of reasons and the order of causes will be developed in a separate paper which began as a section of an early draft of the present paper.

24. I am assuming, of course, that the possibility of X doing A has occurred to Tom, and that he has been deliberating about it.
25. I am coining this expression because "countermanding" as ordinarily used appears to cover both simple withdrawal and what I am calling "contramanding."
26. See note 8 for an interpretation of "person" as "one of us."
27. These concluding remarks were taken from an unpublished paper, "Ethics and Philosophy," which was read to the Phoebe Griffin Noyes Library Association, Old Lyme, Connecticut, on January 26, 1960.

7

IMPERATIVES, DECISIONS, AND "OUGHTS": A LOGICO-METAPHYSICAL INVESTIGATION

Hector-Neri Castañeda *Wayne State University*

INTRODUCTION

The fundamental problem of moral philosophy has been to produce a clear understanding of the nature, i.e., the function and structure, of morality. Great progress has been accomplished since Socrates made the subject his professional business, and we ought to be grateful to the method used by most philosophers in trying to produce that greater understanding. It has consisted in a frank or qualified assimilation of moral judgments to commands, to descriptions of one's own mental states, to expressions of approval, to reports of a group's actions or someone's behavior, (more recently) to pieces of advice, etc. The tacit assumption has been some idea of simplicity which has moved the philosopher to "draw" a tidy theory or "picture" of the conceptual framework of morality. The leading argument rests, of course, on the similarities actually encountered by the insightful philosopher. But there is no longer any reason to assume any simplicity of that sort.

My purpose here is twofold. In the first place, I want to offer a systematic and comprehensive account of part of the underlying structure of the language of action, by exhibiting the complex relationships among some of the basic types of conceptual (or linguistic) units which make it up: formulations of command, request, advice, etc.; formulations of resolve; and norms, rules, and assertions about oughts, rights, wrongs, obligations, and prohibitions. (There are, obviously, other important conceptual units, such as formulations of goals or ends, value judgments, and moral judgments, which also constitute our normal language of action. Thus, the present investigation is nothing more than just one prolegomenon for the fundamental task of moral philosophy: a complete analysis or elucidation of the nature of morality.) In the second place, I want to examine the vexing question concerning the sense in which statements about obligations or rights, wrongs, or oughts, as well as their denials, are true or false. This metaphysical examination is the ultimate purpose of this essay, the tight logical analysis of the structure of part of the language of action being its only access.

It is notorious that ordinary ethical statements, as well as ordinary non-ethical ought-assertions, are said to be true or false. It is true, for instance, that we ought to pay our debts, that killing is generally wrong, and that in this country one ought to drive on the right-hand side of the road. The word "true" does not ostensibly have in those assertions a meaning different from the one it has in clearly empirical statements. And one is easily tempted to think that, for example, the rightness of an action is a characteristic, whose only peculiarity lies in being a characteristic of an action as opposed to something else, like a physical object or a sense-datum. But a little reflection establishes that it is difficult to make out what sort of characteristic rightness can be. For one thing, an action which is right (or wrong) may very well fail to exist, i.e., to be performed, and yet somehow its rightness is just as "real" as if it had been performed. For another, the obvious connection between statements about rights (or wrongs) and the other utterances that constitute the language of action seems destroyed when that language is divided into, on one side, statements about some peculiar characteristics and, on the other side, commands, requests, entreaties, decisions, which are neither true nor false and apparently have nothing to do with any special characteristics. To say that the rightness of an action is a non-natural property of the action, or a non-natural relationship between an agent and certain circumstances, and leave it at that, is little more than merely christening the perplexity and deciding to live with it, rather than seeking to unravel it.

The way out of this perplexity lies in a close examination of the systematic relationships among the different elements of the language of action (or practical reason), rather than in the contrast and analogy between given sentences in specified respects. The concern with the latter activity is very fashionable, and it has yielded rewarding results, some of which will be used here. However, one of my Kantian prejudices makes me feel confident that the simultaneous examination of several *types* of linguistic (or conceptual) units can provide a different, complementary insight. This prejudice is that at least some elements of the language of action do not each have an indivisible meaning (or use) of their own, such that we can get all the clarity that is to be got by asking "How do we use *this sentence?*" or "In what circumstances and for what purpose do we use *it?*" To suppose the latter is to assume a sort of logical atomism: that language is a collection of sentences each having its own isolable use. On the contrary, I assume that words (or concepts) as well as sentences (or judgments, or propositions) gain their meaning (or status), *inter alia*, by belonging to a system; they all have a systematic dimension or range within which they "revolve," as it were, along some axis resting on other words and sentences with which they belong in a system. Thus, for instance, I do not feel the need for assuming that every deontic assertion, or every sentence containing the word "ought," must have one and the same common feature for us to say that it is evaluative, or that it belongs in the language of action or of morals. Some ought-sentences may have certain features, others may lack them, and yet the word "ought" appearing in them all may have the same meaning, insofar as the sentences in question are related in certain different manners (to be specified) to other sentences which are typical of the language of action.[1]

The investigation of the systematic relationships among the elements of the language of action begins with a discussion of the most important contemporary views on the meaning of ought. Many philosophers have held, with minor variations of detail, that a characteristic function of sentences containing the word "ought," insofar as they belong to the language of action, consists of their being used to tell somebody to do something, or in Hare's terminology, of their entailing an imperative. In Sections 4–7 and 18–24, it is shown that the view is untenable. But the view arises from two valuable insights, one of which is embodied in a rigorous definition of "normative" formulated in Section 16; the other insight is discussed in Section 24. Other philosophers have claimed that to say "X ought to do A" *is* to say that there are reasons for X's doing of A. Often that claim involves the silent presupposition that the phrase "reason for doing" possesses a crystal-clear meaning, which is far from being the case. This is shown in Sections 10–13. But in one sense of that crucial term the view comes quite close to the heart of the meaning of ought, as is pointed out in Sections 18–20. In Sections 21–22 a long discussion (given elsewhere) of the meaning of what makes up the reasonableness of an action is outlined. It furnishes the materials for an analysis of the phrase "reason for doing," as is suggested in Sections 22–24. Finally, in Section 25, intuitionism is revisited; its insights are pointed out and reevaluated as background for a discussion of the contribution of the language of ought to practical experience.

My claim is that the language of oughts, rights, or obligations (whatever their sort) is dispensable, in the sense that the language of action has otherwise all the mechanisms for performing its characteristic functions. The main reason for that dispensability lies in the fact that the language of oughts (etc.) is a first-order "reflection" or "image" of the second-order language about the justification of imperatives and assertions of decision. That "reflection" is peculiar in that it contributes a "picture" of the latter language into the first-order language of imperatives and assertions of decision as a language of properties.

Thus, the rightness or wrongness of an action is a wholly objective property which the action possesses in the language of oughts, rights, and wrongs. It is a non-natural property in that it is the "reflection" of a logical (sematical) property of an imperative or a statement of resolve. But it is not an absolute property because it is eliminable, since it is dependent on a language which is in principle dispensable. Hence, it is not an ultimate constituent of the universe.

1 *The Analysis of "Ought" in Contemporary Philosophy*

I

CURRENT VIEWS

Recent discussion in moral philosophy has concentrated more and more on the question about the nature of morality as a whole, or on the not exactly equivalent question about the general characteristics of moral judgments, i.e., the criteria for the morally right action or the moral oughts. More or less implicitly, it is often assumed that the elucidation of the concepts of right, wrong, and ought is complete. Nowadays only an occasional shot breaks the prevailing silence over the distinctive meaning of the pivotal terms of the language of action, regardless of whether they are moral or non-moral. That distinctive meaning, however, is part of what deeply disquiets me.

At this date few philosophers would suggest that moral judgments or ought-assertions (whether moral or non-moral) are (like) commands, or expressions of approval, or ejaculations of desire or wish, or autobiographical statements of mental fact. If anything is clear from the last decades of controversy in moral philosophy, it is that ordinary ought-statements, inasmuch as they belong essentially to the language of action, are characteristically (like) none of those things. When it comes to explaining the distinctive meaning of the words "ought," "right," and "wrong," many philosophers nowadays would take one of three important lines of analysis, or some combination of them. First, there is the imperative approach, which locates the peculiar character of an assertion in one of those words uttered essentially with the purpose of telling someone (particularly in the form of advice) to do something on a certain occasion, or on several similar occasions. Second, there is the decision or resolutive approach, which identifies the distinctive meaning of an assertion of that sort with its being an expression of, or uttered somehow in essential connection with, a resolve or decision to do something. Third, there is the good-reasons approach, which establishes some equivalence in meaning between an assertion of the form "X ought to do A" and a corresponding assertion of the form "There are good reasons for X to do A," or at least some necessary involvement of the meaning of the latter in the meaning of the former.

Obviously, a combination of the three approaches is capable of yielding a powerful analysis of the concepts of ought, right, and wrong. But I contend that regardless of how correct each of the three lines of analysis is, they (alone, or together) do not provide an elucidation of the distinctive character of the language of oughts, rights, and wrongs, i.e., of its distinctive contribution to the language of action or of its peculiar structure. This is so because each of those approaches, especially the first two, are contrived from the very beginning to focus mainly on isolated assertions; they do not pay enough attention to the systematic structure of the whole language of oughts or to its connections with the other segments of the language of action, with which it forms a unitary complex. Now, to see why these contentions are plausible is at once to gain some insight both into the strength of those approaches and into the perplexing peculiarities of the language of oughts. An examination of those views is thus a most useful preliminary inquest.

A. The Imperative Approach

2

THE COMMON IMPERATIVE CORE

The old assimilation of assertions containing the word "ought" (or "right" or "wrong") to commands, the recent assimilation to exhortation, and the current assimilation to pieces of advice, have all a common denominator. They are all variations on the one theme of telling somebody, in one way or another, what to do. For that reason, it is one of Richard M. Hare's great contributions to moral philosophy to have proposed that general theme as one of two defining features of ought-utterances qua utterances of the language of action. Hare's proposal is, by its very generality, the most plausible that may come out of the whole family of imperative approaches. Every one of its deficiencies as well as some of its merits can be transferred to the other members of that family. Its examination is at bottom the examination of all imperative views on the analysis of ought.

3

HARE'S VIEW

The word "ought" is ambiguous. But in some of its meanings it is part of assertions which belong typically to the language of action. That happens (to put it vaguely, pre-philosophically, so to speak) when the assertion containing the word "ought" is made somehow with the purpose of making or helping somebody, including oneself, to come to do some action. This is a very inadequate, vague description of the character of ought. Its very unclarity makes it a practical term, and therefore the starting point of the philosophical investigation. It is our datum; and our problem is to elucidate it. So, let us write down as the point of departure, which, a fortiori, will also serve as a criterion of success for any proposed elucidation:

(O*) An ought-assertion is practical or belongs essentially to the language of action if it is proffered somehow with the purpose of making, or guiding somebody else's, choices of persons, objects, or actions.

In his *The Language of Morals* [2] (hereafter cited as *LM*), Hare offers a series of definitions and propositions which involve an analysis of (O*). Here we shall discuss only the minimal set containing the elucidation of (O*). The other parts of his view are just as interesting, some even more so, but if this minimal set involves a contradiction or other inadequacy, the entire view, of course, will involve this contradiction or inadequacy. D1–D3 below are the definitions and P1–P4 are the propositions making up this minimal set of Hare's view.

D1. *Sentence* (in the sense relevant for a logical discussion) = (grammatical) "sentence as used by a particular speaker on a particular occasion" (*LM*, p. 25).

D2. A sentence is imperative = its main verb is in what grammarians call the imperative mood (*LM*, pp. 4–5).

P1. A sentence is imperative if and only if it is used to "*tell* someone *to* make something the case" (*LM*, p. 5), i.e., to "*tell* someone *to* do something" (*LM*, p. 13).

P2. A sentence is indicative if and only if it is used to "*tell* someone *that* something is the case" (*LM*, p. 5).

P3. (*Poincaré's rule*) "No imperative conclusion can be validly drawn from [i.e., is entailed by] a set of premises which does not contain at least one imperative" (*LM*, p. 28).

P4. (The role of) telling to and (the role of) telling that are mutually independent and distinct.

D3. An ought-sentence is *used evaluatively* (or, is *evaluative*) = (1) it entails at least one imperative (*LM*, pp. 164, 168–169), and (2) it is properly universal (*LM*, pp. 175ff., 190ff.).

These definitions and propositions constitute the substance of Hare's view, which is the central core of the imperative approach to the analysis of "ought." Hare, of course, complements his view with other theses, among which the following are noteworthy:

P5. (*Hare's rule*) "No indicative conclusion can be validly drawn from a set of premises which cannot be validly drawn from the indicatives among them alone" (*LM*, p. 28).

P6. An imperative "X, do A" and its corresponding indicative "X does A" can be analyzed in terms of a common core "X doing A" (called the *phrastic*) and a special sentence-sign "please" or "yes" (called the *neustic*) (*LM*, pp. 16–17).

That is, "X, do A" is the complex "X doing A, please," and "X does A" is the complex "X doing A, yes."

P7. The logical words "if," "and," "or," "not," and even "all," and "some" belong (normally) to the phrastics; that is, they link phrastics to other phrastics, not sentences to other sentences (*LM*, pp. 21–22, 189).

According to P6 and P7, "Peter, don't come" is to be analyzed as "Peter not coming, please," and "Peter, either come or write" as "Peter either coming or writing, please." By P6 and P7 Hare seems to be committed to analyzing "If Peter comes, give him this book" as "(If Peter coming, you giving him this book) please," where the parenthetical expression is a conditional phrastic made up of two phrastics. So he might say that neither an imperative nor an indicative sentence appears in the antecedent of that conditional, even though "(If) Peter comes" looks like an indicative. This would be a conclusion of great importance to Hare, as we shall see in Section 5. But unfortunately it is based on P7, which seems to me to be false.

Let us note, with Hare, that "the two sentences 'You are going to shut the door' and 'Shut the door' are both about your shutting the door in the immediate future; but what they say about it is quite different." The former is an indicative, the latter an imperative (*LM*, pp. 5, 17). Now, we can distinguish from each other the following sentences, which I take to be, on the whole, imperatives:

(*a*) You, Paul, are going to shut the door, or you, Abel, shut it.

(*b*) You, Abel, are going to shut the door, or you, Paul, shut it.

(*c*) You, Abel, or you, Paul, shut the door.

The differences are quite clear. (*a*) tells Abel that he is to shut the door if Paul does not; (*b*) does not tell Abel to shut the door at all. Moreover, (*b*) tells Paul to shut the door if Abel does not, while (*a*) does nothing of the kind. (*c*) does not tell either Paul or Abel individually to shut the door. Yet, within Hare's view, by virtue of P6 and P7, either (*a*) and (*b*) are both meaningless, or both are indistinguishable from each other as well as from (*c*). Both (*a*) and (*b*) are meaningless if they are regarded as made up of two sentences linked by the logical word "or." All three are indistinguishable from one another if they are regarded as being made up of the neustic "please" attached to a complex of two phrastics connected by the logical word "or," namely: "(You, Paul, going to shut the door, or you, Abel, going to shut the door) please." Of course, they would also be meaningless, by P7, if they were to be analyzed as having an "or" connecting a phrastic to a sentence. Hence, P7 is false.

P5 (Hare's rule) also seems to me to be false of ordinary imperatives. It seems to me that from (*a*) together with the negative command "Abel, don't shut the door," Abel, or any other hearer for that matter, may correctly infer the indicative "Paul is going to shut the door." If this inference is correct, there is no indicative premise, let alone a set of indicative premises which by itself entails the conclusion "Paul is going to shut the door." In particular, if P7 is true, Hare's rule is false. For instance, the indicative (*e*) below follows validly from the command (*d*):

(*d*) Somebody, bring the book (which is) on the table

(*e*) There is a book on the table.

According to P7, all the logical terms of (*d*) belong to its phrastic, so that (*d*) in no way includes an indicative component. (*d*) is to be analyzed as "Somebody bringing the book on the table, please." Hence, Hare's rule P5 is false. But even without P7, Hare's rule is indefensible. Suppose that (*d*) is a complex of indicative and imperative: "There is one and only one book on the table, somebody, bring it." (*d*) cannot be divided into two premises, one being an indicative which by itself entails (*e*). The division which suggests itself would be:

(*d*1) There is one and only one book on the table, and
(*d*2) somebody, bring it.

But (*d*2) is not by itself a complete imperative, since it does not contain the referent of the pronoun "it." It cannot, therefore, be a premise. Hence this division is incorrect. (*d*) is simply just one indivisible imperative premise, which entails (*d*1) as well as the indicative (*e*), in spite of Hare's rule to the contrary.

In sum, Hare's logical theses P5 and P7 are false. It is not necessary, however, that Hare's central theses P1–P4 and definitions D1–D3 be made to depend upon P5–P7. Hare could very well have formulated an adequate systematization of the logic of imperatives. From now on I will assume that the logical words connect sentences or sentence forms to other sentences or sentence forms (as is customarily supposed), and not phrastics to phrastics. We can then proceed to examine the adequacy of the central core of Hare's view.

One small point is worth clarifying here. Hare's formulation of Poincaré's rule does allow of an immediate refutation. Ordinarily we regard, just as Hare does, that an assertion of the form "P or Q" is validly derivable from the assertion P, which is part of it. Thus, from the indicative "It is not raining" we could derive "It is not raining, or go home." Since the latter is logically equivalent to "If it is raining, go home," this should be derivable from "It is raining." Clearly, in ordinary language the conditional "If it is raining, go home" is taken unquestionably as an imperative. Hence, we have here an imperative derivable from an indicative. However, I will not press this example as an objection against Poincaré's rule. To allow Hare the use he wants of Poincaré's rule, I will add to his view the following:

P4*. At least for imperatives, the rule "From P, infer P or Q" is replaced by the rule "From P and Q, infer P or Q."

Since even in the ordinary logic of statements, doubts have been expressed from time to time about the wisdom of the rule "From P, infer P or Q," it is not unjustified to allow Hare a weaker rule.

Now, definition D3, part (1) is Hare's elucidation of (O*), substituting the phrase "practical or belonging essentially to the language of action" by the term "evaluative." Requirement (2) can be regarded as complied with as a matter of course (see *LM*, pp. 176ff., 190ff.). We shall assume that it is always satisfied. Hare's view, as so far characterized, includes the following propositions, which I shall call corollaries:

C1. No set of sentences every one of which is not used to tell someone to do something entails an imperative. (From P1, Poincaré's rule, P4*.)

C2. If a sentence entails an imperative, it is used to tell someone to do something. (From C1.)

C3. If a sentence is used to tell someone to do something, it entails an imperative. (From P1, since every sentence entails itself.)

C4. An ought-sentence is evaluative only if it is used to tell someone to do something. (From D3 and C2.)

C5. An ought-sentence is evaluative only if it is imperative. (From C4 and P1.)

The last corollary, C5, is important because it allows the application of all the rules of logic governing imperatives, in particular Poincaré's rule and P4*, to ought-assertions. Let us notice, however, that C5 does not say that every imperative is an ought-assertion. Hare is quite careful and lengthy in his discussion of the second defining feature of practical assertions about oughts (rights or wrongs). That feature is a complete universality, for which there is no analog in the other imperatives (see *LM*, Chaps. X–XII). Furthermore, Hare could easily have avoided C5 by accepting only one-half of P1, namely, "A sentence is imperative only if it is used to tell someone to do something." He would have then distinguished sharply between imperatives (which he defines anyway as sentences in the imperative mood) and ought-assertions; but C4 ("An ought-sentence is evaluative only if it is used to tell someone to do something") would still hold.

4

LIMITATIONS OF HARE'S VIEW: NEGATION

The preceding analysis of ought-assertions is clearly insightful. It fits very well our use of single second-person ought-statements about future actions, e.g., "You, Emil, ought to stop wasting your talents; you ought to finish your great symphonies." It takes some twisting to show its relevance to past-tense ought-statements. With some adequate remarks it may be shown to fit (more or less) also first-person statements about one's own obligations or oughts, and similarly for third-person statements (see *LM*, pp. 155–162). Even when the omitted parts are added, the view or theory is beautifully simple. Of course, I am not implying that no insurmountable difficulties will be found if the uses of single ought-sentences are examined. My point is that regardless of how well the view can be defended in the case of isolated ought-assertions, it shows certain important deficiencies when examined in the context of segments of the language of action, which include ought-sentences as parts. It is not that the occasions of use, or of utterance, are different. The only difference lies in the purely logical or linguistic context. But let us start with a definition:

Definition. Sentence S′ is *a negation of sentence S* = (1) S′ is a correct English sentence having all the terms of S with the same meaning they have in S, and S′ differs from S only by having exactly one—or, if S has negative terms, one more—of the following negative terms: "not," "does (do, did) not," and "it is not the case that"; (2) S′ is synonymous with, or logically equivalent to, a sentence S″ which is a negation of S of type (1).

Many ordinary imperatives have only one negation; for instance, "Write him a letter" has only the negation "Don't write him a letter," which can also be formulated as "Write him no letter." Many imperatives, however, have more than one negation; for instance, "Think that she loves you" has two negations: "Don't think that she loves you" and "Think that she does not love you." In general, an imperative of the form "X, do A" has the properly imperative negation "X, don't do A" and all the negations accruing to it from the several places in the description "A" which a negative term can occupy.

Let us suppose, then, that an imperative of the form "X, do A" has n negations. Obviously, the corresponding ought-assertion, i.e., the assertion of the form "X ought to do A" has $n + 1$

negations: the $n - 1$ negations accruing to it from the description "A," and the two properly "oughtish" negations: "It is not the case that X ought to do A" and "X ought not to do A." Now, the former may be said to entail an imperative, namely, "Don't do A." But the latter in no way entails an imperative, nor can it be said to be used in its normal sense (when uttered or written) to tell somebody to do something, or what to do on a given occasion. Hence, in accordance with corollary C4 ("An ought-sentence is evaluative only if it is used to tell somebody what to do") or with definition D3, part (1) ("An ought-sentence is evaluative only if it entails an imperative"), assertions of form F(1) below are not evaluative in Hare's sense:

F(1) It is not the case that X ought to do A.

Yet assertions of form F(1) do belong to the language of action, since they are the negations of assertions which belong to the language of action. Specifically, the word "ought" has, in an assertion of form F(1), the same meaning it has in the corresponding assertion of form F(2):

F(2) X ought to do A.

The word "ought" *has to have* the same meaning in the two assertions, for each of them to be the contradictory of the other. Since the assertion of form F(2) (let us suppose) entails an imperative, while its contradictory of form F(1) does not, entailing an imperative is not part of the common meaning of the word "ought" present in both assertions. Hence, Hare's definition D3, part (1) does not furnish a partial analysis of the meaning of the word (or concept of) "ought," as it appears in assertions belonging to the language of action.

Here we have not only a serious limitation of Hare's view, but also a distortion of the logical relationships among ought-assertions. The two assertions below, for instance, are logically equivalent in ordinary language:

(*a*) If you ought to graduate in June, you ought to take the examination;

(*b*) If it is not the case that you ought to take the examination, it is not the case that you ought to graduate in June.

In formal logic (*b*) is said to be the contrapositive of (*a*). Often the whole of (*a*) is used as a practical utterance. It may then entail the conditional imperative:

(*c*) If you ought to graduate in June, take the examination. Now, in ordinary language an unabbreviated conditional (or disjunction or conjunction) made up of purely non-imperative components is non-imperative. Since the components of (*b*) are of form F (1), they are not imperative; thus, (*b*) itself is not an imperative. By Poincaré's rule, (*b*) cannot entail any (non-analytic) imperative. Hence, (*b*) cannot entail (*a*), much less be equivalent to (*a*).

Hare's natural mode of defense would be an appeal to his principle P7 ("The logical words 'if,' 'and,' 'not,' 'or,' etc., combine phrastics to phrastics, not sentences to sentences"). He could then say that (*b*) is not made up of two non-imperative sentences, but of one conditional phrastic and one imperative neustic. But since in Section 3, P7 was shown to be false, there is no point in pursuing this line of defense.

It might be thought that Hare could preserve the entailment of (*a*) by (*b*) together with the rest of his view by rejecting my premise that a conditional made up of purely non-imperative component is not an imperative. If this were the case, Hare could reply that (*b*) is imperative, since it entails the same imperative (*c*) entailed by (*a*), for clearly (*a*) and (*b*) are logically equivalent. This reply, however, is not open to Hare; his own principles P6 and P7 get in his way. According to these principles, in every sentence there is one neustic for each phrastic; thus, if it is granted that (*b*) is a compound of two non-imperative sentences, each sentence has its own phrastic and its own non-imperative neustic. There is then no vacant phrastic in (*b*) for an over-all imperative neustic to govern. Hence, Hare can regard (*b*) as imperative in order to make the equivalence between (*a*) and (*b*) conform with Poincaré's rule, only at the cost of destroying his own principles P6 and P7.

Moreover, Hare stands to gain little by giving up P6 and P7 and allowing (*b*) to be imperative in spite of its two non-imperative components. On the one hand, he would create the problem of accounting for those peculiar compounds with an over-all neustic, attached to no phrastic directly. On the other hand, he would incapacitate his view for accommodating other entailments. For example, in ordinary language the following inference is valid:

(*d*) It is not the case that you ought to graduate in June;
It is not the case that you ought to take the examination;

Hence,

(*b*) If it is not the case that you ought to take the examination, it is not the case that you ought to graduate in June.

In this inference nothing appears in the conclusion which does not appear in the premises, so that Poincaré's rule is not trivially violated. Yet, if Hare were to accept that (*b*) is imperative, in spite of its non-imperative components, Poincaré's rule would prevent Hare from recognizing that the two non-imperative premises in (*d*) together entail the imperative (*b*).

To sum up, the strict contradictories of assertions of the form "X ought to do A" are not evaluative in Hare's sense, so that Hare's view is incomplete. Since the word "ought" appears with the same meaning in both contradictories, Hare's view does not provide an adequate analysis of "ought" even in the unnegated assertion. Finally, the recognition that "It is not the case that X ought to do A" is not evaluative in Hare's sense leads to a distortion of the logic of ought-assertions. These distortions have to be traced back either to P1, to D3, part (1), or to P3, since P6 is correct. Hare's P1 ("A sentence is imperative if and only if it is used to tell someone to do something") is, however, essentially correct. Therefore, those distortions of the logic of ought-assertions must be relayed back to either D3, part (1) ("An ought-sentence is evaluative only if it entails an imperative"), or to P3 (i.e., Poincaré's rule: "A valid (relevant) imperative conclusion requires one imperative premise"). Poincaré's rule joined to P4* seems to me essentially correct. At any rate, since it is Hare's weapon against ethical naturalism (*LM*, pp. 29ff., 82ff., 171ff.), *only because* he has defined "evaluative" as in D3, whichever he chooses, his attack on naturalism collapses.

5
LIMITATIONS OF HARE'S VIEW: CONDITIONALS

It is a notorious fact of the logical grammar of ordinary imperatives that they cannot appear as subordinate clauses. This is a clue of great importance to the distinction between the function of imperatives and the role of ought-assertions. For the moment, however, let us consider the special case of the English particles which are used to form conditional assertions. It is clear upon examination that conditional imperatives are always mixed sentences. Compare, for example, "If he comes, tell him," "Only if he comes, tell him," "In case he comes, tell him," and "On his coming, tell him." Let us call the clause (or gerund phrase) following the conditional sign (apart from "then") the *conditioning sentence*, and the other clause (or gerund phrase) the *conditioned sentence*. (This distinction has nothing to do with the customary distinction between the antecedent or protasis and the consequent or apodosis of a conditional (or hypothetical). Note that (*a*), "If he comes, tell him," has as its converse (*b*), "Only if he comes, tell him," and as its contrapositive (*c*), "Only if he does not come, don't tell him." In all three the conditioned sentence is the imperative, and the conditioning sentence the indicative; nevertheless, in (*a*) the logical antecedent is the indicative "he comes," whereas in (*b*) it is the imperative "tell him," and in (*c*) "don't tell him.")

The fact is that *ordinary imperatives are never conditioning sentences*. This is not merely a great accident of grammar (common to at least all Indo-European languages, as far as I can tell); it relates to the function of the imperative sentence. A conditioning utterance cannot discharge the function of telling somebody what to do or to do something on a given occasion. Here we have another pre-philosophical datum, which can serve as a criterion for testing the adequacy of Hare's view. Since ought-assertions can be conditioned as well as conditioning, Hare's view fails the test. The same is true of the derived test that the ordinary language of action allows a conditional whose antecedent and consequent are both ought-sentences. Yet ordinary language does not allow both the antecedent and the consequent of a conditional to perform the job of telling somebody to do something.

Hare, of course, is not oblivious of the fact that a sentence in the imperative mood is never a subordinate clause. *Hare's contention* at this juncture is that the word "want" is, in one of its uses, a logical sign which expresses an "imperative inside a subordinate clause" (*LM*, p. 34). Hare argues for this, not to meet the above objection to his view, but to meet an apparent exception to Poincaré's rule, namely, what Kant called hypothetical imperatives. We shall not discuss Hare's defense of Poincaré's rule in detail. If Hare fails in his analysis of "want," that defense falls to pieces at the first step. Another line of defense which P7 opened for Hare we have closed in Section 2.

His own way of putting his contention (although the example is mine) is as follows. The inference below is valid:

(1) *Hamlet* is one of Shakespeare's plays;
Read all of Shakespeare's plays;
Hence, read *Hamlet*.

Because of that, the next inference is also valid:

(2) *Hamlet* is one of Shakespeare's plays,
Hence, if read all of Shakespeare's plays, read *Hamlet*.

However, in English it is nonsense to say "if read all of Shakespeare's plays." Hare suggests that that grammatical accident has no consequences because in English we write the conclusion of (2) as:

(*a*) If you want to read all of Shakespeare's plays, read *Hamlet*.

According to Hare (*LM*, p. 35), our knowledge of the meanings of "want" and the other terms suffices to justify our inferring that conclusion from "*Hamlet* is one of Shakespeare's plays." This declaration is (in a sense) true. That is precisely why the inference in question seems to be a clear-cut counterexample for Poincaré's rule. The central issue, nevertheless, remains unsupported, to wit, whether or not "If you want to read all of Shakespeare's plays, then read *Hamlet*" is a conditional with an imperative antecedent, namely, "Read all of Shakespeare's plays." To me the suggestion seems preposterous. Obviously, nobody is telling another person to read *all* of Shakespeare's plays categorically or on condition of something else if he says to him: "If you want to read all of Shakespeare's plays, read *Hamlet*." He may be said to be telling him to read *Hamlet* on the condition that the other person wants to read all of Shakespeare's plays, but he is clearly not telling him to bring about that condition.

Hare's contention is not that in English "You want to" is merely an alternative way of expressing what the imperative mood expresses. I take it that he is aware of the lack of self-contradiction in an assertion like "(I know that) you do not want to go home; nevertheless, go home—and the sooner the better," regardless of which ordinary, primary sense of "want" the speaker may choose. Hare alleges only that "You want to" completes the imperative mood: it is used inside subordinate clauses, where the imperative mood cannot be used. Hare's contention is, however, false. By Hare's thesis P1, his contention is that in normal speech the utterance of (*a*) is such that "(If) you want to read all of Shakespeare's plays" is used to tell the hearer to read Shakespeare's plays. This is clearly false. As is well known, the role of "if" is precisely to signal that the clause following it is left unasserted.

To belabor the point, Hare's contention involves serious distortions of the logical connections between ordinary imperatives. Let us illustrate with the same conditional

(*a*) If you want to read all of Shakespeare's plays, read *Hamlet*.

As any other conditional, (*a*) is logically equivalent to its contrapositive, which can be formed by either procedure (*b*) or procedure (*c*):

(*b*) Only if [Negation of "if" clause of (*a*)], [Negation of the other clause]

(*c*) [Negation of "if" clause of (*a*)], if [Negation of the other clause].

In ordinary language only procedure (*b*) is available, since conditioning imperatives are impossible. Thus, the ordinary contrapositive of (*a*) is

(*a*1) Only if you do not want to read all of Shakespeare's plays, do not read *Hamlet.*

Now, if Hare's contention were true, the phrase "you want to" in (*a*) would be the idiomatic formulation of the imperative mood in a conditioning clause. Hence, (*a*) would only be the grammatically correct version of the incorrect

(*d*) If read all of Shakespeare's plays, read *Hamlet.*

And (*d*) would have a contrapositive of form (*c*):

(*d*1) Do not read all of Shakespeare's plays, if do not read *Hamlet* (i.e., leave *Hamlet* unread).

Again, by Hare's contention, (*d*1) is the incorrect formulation of the idiomatically correct:

(*d*2) Do not read all of Shakespeare's plays, if you want to leave *Hamlet* unread.

Hence, if Hare's contention were true, (*d*2) would be logically equivalent to (*a*) and to (*a*1). Clearly, this equivalence does not hold. It can be made more apparent by constructing from (*d*2) the contrapositive of form (*b*); it should be either (*a*1) itself or something obviously equivalent to (*a*1). Such a contrapositive is:

(*d*3) Read all of Shakespeare's plays, only if you do not want to leave *Hamlet* unread.

It is evident that no equivalence holds between (*a*1) and (*d*3) taken in their ordinary meanings. Since (*a*) is equivalent to (*a*1), (*a*) is not equivalent to (*d*3), as Hare's contention would require. Therefore the contention is false: it cannot be the claim to have discovered that ordinary imperatives enter subordinate clauses disguised as sentences of the form "You want to. . . ." To nail down this conclusion let us note that if Hare's contention were true there would be tautologous imperatives of the form "If p, then p" to which it should be irrational not to assent. For instance, the grammatically incorrect imperative

(*e*) If torture him, then torture him,

would be correctly formulated as

(*e*1) If you want to torture him, then torture him.

It seems to me that there is no ordinary sense of "you want" in which (*e*1) is a trivial tautology like "If it rains, it rains." The assertion of the latter does not commit the speaker to claiming that there is rain; and its denial is self-contradictory. On the contrary, some of us hold to the denial of (*e*1) without contradiction and regardless of whom the hearer may be: "Even if you want to torture him, don't torture him."

I conclude, then, that ordinary imperatives, or sentences which serve to tell somebody what to do or to do something on a given occasion, are never conditioning sentences, or subordinate clauses. Hence the ought-sentences which appear as conditioning or as subordinate clauses are not evaluative in Hare's sense, i.e., in the sense of corollary C4 ("An ought-sentence is evaluative only if it is used to tell someone to do something or what to do").

6

LIMITATIONS OF HARE'S VIEW: REASONINGS

The preceding conclusion, that some ought-sentences are not evaluative in Hare's sense, is very important. It is not merely that Hare's view is too narrow to include certain ought-utterances of ordinary language. Hare's view produces, besides, a serious distortion of the logical relationships among ought-sentences, analogous to those encountered in Section 4. Consider, for instance, the case of Jones. He is discussing with his son Peter what Peter is to do during the next weekend. Jones is openly advising Peter what to do; so, in accordance with our pre-analytic datum (O*) mentioned in Section 3 ("An ought-utterance used essentially to guide choices of action, person, or thing is practical"). Jones's utterances are prima facie practical, or prima facie evaluative in Hare's sense. In the course of the discussion Jones offers the following argument:

(1) If you ought to graduate in June, you ought to take the comprehensive examination next Monday;
You ought to graduate in June;
So, you ought to take the (comprehensive) examination (next Monday).

Obviously, the argument is logically valid in the ordinary (English) language of action, and the sentences involved in it are practical in accordance with (O*). The minor premise ("You ought to graduate in June") and the conclusion ("You ought to take the examination") may certainly be said to be used by Jones with the purpose of telling Peter what to do in June and next Monday, respectively. Thus we may suppose that they are both evaluative in Hare's sense since they satisfy corollary C4 and since part (2) of D3 can be (or is) always satisfied. The major premise ("If you ought to graduate in June, you ought to take the comprehensive examination next Monday") may be said to entail the imperative "If you ought to graduate in June, take the comprehensive examination next Monday." Hence, it is perhaps also evaluative (in Hare's sense), in accordance with D3, part (1). So far, then, Hare's view seems to be an adequate elucidation of the practical role of ought.

Since no conditioning clause is imperative or can be used to tell somebody what to do, the antecedent of Jones's "*If you ought to graduate in June*, you ought to take the comprehensive examination next Monday" is not practical or evaluative in Hare's sense (of D3 or C4 or C5). Yet it seems very little different from Jones's second premise, his categorical "You ought to graduate in June." Indeed, Jones's argument (1) is regarded in ordinary language as valid only because it is assumed that both sentences have exactly the same meaning. The argument is taken to be an example of *modus ponens*, i.e., of the form:

F(1) If A, then B; A, hence B.

However, if Hare's view were correct, the argument could not have that form. On the one hand, since the second premise ("You ought to graduate in June") entails the imperative "Graduate in June," it may be evaluative; on the other hand, the antecedent of "If *you ought to graduate in June*, you ought to take the comprehensive examination," which looks identical, entails no imperative and cannot, therefore, be evaluative. So the argument is of the form:

F(2) If *a*, then B; A, hence B,

where the capital letters stand for imperatives or sentences that are used to tell somebody to do something, and the small letters for non-imperatives. (In the light of Hare's D1–D3 and P1–P4, it is an open question whether a non-imperative sentence is indicative, even though he always contrasts them with each other, only perhaps because it is not clear what is to be contrasted with both "telling to" and "telling that.")

If F(2) is the form of Jones's argument (1) addressed to his son Peter, it is difficult to see how on Hare's account it is valid. To be sure, Hare believes that the logic of imperatives is formally parallel to the logic of indicatives. He argues that the entailment relationships belong to the common core of an indicative and to its corresponding imperative, e.g., "Peter, tell him to go" and "Peter will tell him to go." Accordingly, we could (as Hare suggests in *LM*, Chaps. II and XII) discuss them with independence of the kind of sentence involved and then add the remark that some are imperative while others are indicative. Following this suggestion, with the limitations contained in Poincaré's rule, we might feel inclined to say that both forms F(1) and F(2) of argument are equally valid. Hence, we might say, it makes no significant difference whether we hold with Hare that Jones's argument (1) is really of the form F(2) ("If *a*, then B; A; so, B"), or whether we hold with a devotee of ordinary language that it is of the form F(1) ("If A, then B; A; so, B").

Nevertheless, the problem is not that of an inconsequential choice of description of logical form. In ordinary language arguments involving imperatives which are of form F(2) are normally invalid. Consider, for instance,

(2) If you are back before 3:00 P.M., call Peter up;
  Be back before 3:00 P.M.;
  So, call Peter up.

Reasoning (2) is of the form F(2), but it is clearly invalid. For the conclusion to follow, the truth of the condition is needed, not merely the command of, or the hope for, its truth. Thus, it is still difficult to see how on Hare's view Jones's argument (1) can be valid:

(1) If you ought to graduate in June, you ought to take the
  comprehensive examination;

You ought to graduate in June;
So, you ought to take the examination.

No doubt, Hare could add to his view some *ad hoc* rules to account for the validity of (1), without committing himself to the validity of (2). But it cannot be taken for granted that such rules will, as a matter of course, be consistent with the other parts of his view, or will solve the present difficulty. This difficulty continues to be the non-imperative character of (or the not serving to tell anybody to do some given act by) the conditioning sentence of the first premise of Jones's argument (1), namely, "(If) you ought to graduate in June." In ordinary language the validity of (1) depends on that sentence being the same as the second premise, the categorical "You ought to graduate in June." Thus, in ordinary language they entail each other (since every proposition entails itself), even though in one occurrence it is not imperative. But holding Poincaré's rule ("Only if a sentence is imperative can it entail an imperative"), Hare must, in all consistency, deny that one occurrence entails the other occurrence. Thus, once again we encounter a tension within Hare's view between his analysis, formulated in D3, part (1), of the practical role of ought and Poincaré's rule, which is so central to his whole theory, precisely because of that analysis of the role of ought.

Poincaré's rule is essentially sound, the only important exception to it being, as Hare pointed out, Kant's hypothetical imperatives. I will not establish either point here.[3] But if, as I think, Hare is on firm ground concerning Poincaré's rule, then his analysis of the practical role of ought is mistaken.

7

CONCLUSION

There are still further difficulties besetting that part of Hare's view constituted by definitions D1–D3 and propositions P1–P4. Some of them will be made apparent by our more detailed discussion (Secs. 18–19) of the role of ought in the language of action. It is sufficiently clear, however, from the preceding examination of Hare's view, that in spite of its great plausibility, it is incorrect to analyze the practical role of ought-sentences as a telling somebody what to do—alone or in conjunction with something else (universality, expression of feeling, etc.). The great plausibility of the view should not, nevertheless, be underestimated. It may be worthwhile to see why the view is plausible.

The examination of Jones's argument (1) in Section 6 points out very distinctly that an isolated ought-assertion (or its negation) can plausibly be treated as an imperative (in Hare's broad sense). To say "You ought to do A" is certainly to tell the interlocutor what action he is to perform. The utterance may be one of various sorts, but that feature seems to be always present; indeed, the difference may just consist of a stern pronouncement, as if it were a command, or of a moderate tone, as if it were a piece of advice, or of a persuasive inflection, as if it were a request or even, perhaps, an entreaty. The failure of the view appears when ought-sentences are brought together, not only as components of larger assertions, but also as parts of reasonings. I have indicated how the distortions of the view can grow with the logical contexts of which they are part, (not with the situations in which they are used). I want to regard these distortions as a reason for yielding to what I have called my Kantian prejudice. Here we have some evidence for the contention that the characteristic function and role of the practical ought is not to be described merely by pointing out one or more constant features which every ought-sentence will have to possess. It seems that there are several features, individually or jointly insufficient, all connected in some peculiar way, a way which depends on the language of oughts (rights, and wrongs) *as a whole*.

B. The Decision Approach

8

"I OUGHT TO DO A"

It is difficult to say with a clear conscience that the function of "ought" as a practical word is always to express a decision. When Jones tries to convince his son Peter that the latter ought to take a certain school examination, or that one of Peter's friends ought to do some act A, it is not easy to determine what decision is involved in Jones's utterance. No doubt, a resourceful philosopher can always devise a complex relation between Jones's utterance and some decision, either of Jones or of the person about whom Jones is speaking. Nevertheless, we shall suppose that a decision approach is combined with an imperative analysis of ought, or with something else. Only in that way can it be plausible enough. We may suppose that the view is like Nowell-Smith's, which includes as a central thesis the claim that the formula, "Peter ought to take the examination," when asserted by Peter "expresses a decision, but when spoken by Jones expresses an injunction." [4]

There are serious objections against the interpretation of isolated ought-utterances as expressions of decision. But, as in the case of the imperative approach, I am more interested in pointing out the difficulties which arise on account of the merely logical context, even if the circumstances of use remain the same. The great parallelism between imperatives and expressions of resolve produce parallel difficulties for both the imperative and the decision approaches.

To begin with, an expression of decision (hereafter called a *resolutive*) has one less distinct negation than its corresponding first-person ought-assertion. Suppose "I will take the examination" is a resolutive. Then "I will not take the examination" is its negation, since it is synonymous with "It is not the case that I will take the examination." The former might be said to be expressed by "I ought to take the examination," and the latter by "I ought not to take the examination"; but there is no resolutive left over for "It is not the case that I ought to take the examination." In the sense in which this third sentence is the contradictory of "I ought to take the examination" it must have the term "I ought" with precisely the same meaning it has in the latter. Hence, since in the third sentence "I ought" does not serve to express a decision, expressing a decision is not essential to the meaning of "I ought," let alone "ought."

In the second place, a resolutive (analogously to an imperative, as we saw in Section 5) cannot be a conditioning clause. Thus, all conditional expressions of decision are mixed utterances having only one resolutive component. On the contrary, an ought-assertion can be a conditioning as well as a conditioned clause, for example:

(*a*) If I ought to graduate in June, I ought to take the test. The sentence "I ought to graduate in June" cannot express a decision while it has the role of a conditioning clause as in (*a*). Yet it has exactly the same meaning it possesses when it is asserted categorically, or when it appears as a conditioned clause. Thus, expressing a decision is not essential to the meaning of "I ought."

In the third place, ought-assertions may combine as in:

(*b*) If I ought to do A, it is not the case that I ought to do B. While (*a*) as a whole might be said to express the conditional decision "I ought to graduate in June, I will take the test," (*b*) cannot be correlated to a decision in any normal similar way. Neither the antecedent nor the consequent of (*b*) expresses a decision. Yet the phrase "I ought" appears in both with exactly the same meaning it has in isolated assertions of the form "I ought to do A" and "I ought to do B."

Other difficulties parallel to those raised for Hare's view in Sections 4–5 can be raised for the decision approach.

The conclusion is similar to that formulated in Section 7. Clearly a combination of the two approaches just combines the difficulties of both.

C. *The Good-Reasons Approach*

9

THE ANALYSIS

Many philosophers have noticed both that often there are no reasons for commands and that there must always be reasons for a singular ought-assertion, like "You, Jones, ought to return that book to Smith" or "I ought to go to work now." They have rightly concluded that ought-statements are not commands, and some of them have proceeded to suggest that the meaning of utterances of the form "X ought to do A" can be analyzed in terms of the (good) reasons for X's doing of A.[5] Those philosophers have seen very clearly that the reasons for doing something can be varied and may conflict with one another. There may be reasons as well as counter-reasons, and the word "ought" may appear in a statement which formulates the final outcome of a deliberation. Thus, following Sir William David Ross,[6] we may distinguish two senses of "ought," which, on the good-reasons approach, may be defined as follows:

(1) "X ought prima facie (i.e., inasmuch as the situation is of a certain sort, that is, everything else being equal) to do A" means the same as "There are some good reasons for X's doing of A";

(2) "X ought *simpliciter* (i.e., everything being considered) to do A" means the same as (*a*) "There are conclusive, final reasons for X's doing of A" or (*b*) "The balance of reasons support X's doing of A."

On the assumption that the total system of reasons and counter-reasons is consistent, it may turn out that the two clauses (*a*) and (*b*) in (2) are logically equivalent. We shall assume that they are, unless something important hinges on the distinction.

The above double-analysis of ought is not beset by the troubles discussed in the preceding sections, which plague both the imperative and the resolutive views. The two "oughtish" negations of an ought-statement can be understood, and we can see why the conditioning clause of a conditional assertion can contain the word "ought." The view explains the lack of self-contradiction in an utterance like "You ought to do A; but I am not telling you to do it," which is a small difficulty for the imperative approach. In a way it also offers a direct explanation of why some ordinary ought-assertions are normally regarded as true while others are regarded as false.

The analysis is plausible. If (1) and (2) are weakened in order to combine a good-reasons approach with some other approach, the result is a powerful view. Hence, it is more profitable to discuss the weaker versions:

GR(1) The central part of the meaning of "X ought prima facie (i.e., inasmuch as the situation is of a certain sort) to do A" is the whole meaning of "There are some good reasons for X's doing of A";

GR(2) The central part of the meaning of "X ought *simpliciter* (i.e., everything being considered) to do A" is the whole meaning of "There are conclusive, final reasons for X's doing of A" or "The balance of reasons fully supports X's doing of A."

10

"REASON FOR DOING"

Neither GR(1) nor GR(2) are adequate partial definitions of the word "ought," unless the phrase "reason for doing" is furnished with a clear and adequate meaning. At first sight it looks as if the phrase is as difficult and obscure as the word "ought" (or "right" or "wrong") itself. It certainly will not do at all to take it simply as a mere synonym for "ought," a synonym which differs from "ought" by bearing its crystal-clear meaning on its face. No doubt, one can drop the ordinary expressions "ought," "right," and "wrong" and use in their stead variations of the phrase "there is a reason for doing," or "there is the balance of reasons supporting the doing." [7] But the mere substitution of words in no way adds to one's philosophical understanding of the meaning of an ought-assertion or of the sense in which an assertion of that kind is true (or false). (Nonphilosophical understanding, of course, is always assumed.)

In general there are two main types of uses (or senses) of the word "reason" which are relevant to our present inquiry:

R(1) reason as a sort of premise, and

R(2) reason as something like a motive.

II

REASON AS A PREMISE

R(1) seems to be in the back of the minds of writers who think of reasons for doing as facts which justify, which somehow imply the correctness of some action, as opposed to reasons which causally explain the act. Such writers have not stopped, however, to discuss the meaning of the phrase "justificatory reason for doing." Now, if, as it seems, they think of reasons as premises of a sort, certain important consequences follow.

Interpretation R(1) is very plausible. When we speak of reasons for believing, saying, supposing, etc., we are talking about premises which in a relevant mode of inference (perhaps together with some other assumptions) imply a certain conclusion, namely, the proposition believed, supposed, etc. For instance, to say that there are reasons to hold that the center of the earth is hot is often short for saying that there are true propositions which inductively imply, on the assumption of certain laws of nature, that the center of the earth is hot. Likewise, to assert that there is a conclusive reason for believing in the divisibility by 6 of the number 24,684 is to assert that there is a mathematical fact which entails that 24,684 is divisible by 6 without remainder. Furthermore, we normally say "There are reasons for believing that *p*" on those occasions on which either the reasons do not constitute a conclusive set of premises or, although they are conclusive, we are not able or willing to construct an argument for *p*. Thus, we have here a straightforward manner of making the distinction between the two senses of ought, as follows:

RP(1) The central part of the meaning of "X ought prima facie to do A" is the whole meaning of "There are facts (or true propositions) which, together with certain assumptions, imply S," where S is a specific utterance about X's doing of A.

RP(2) The central part of the meaning of "X ought *simpliciter* to do A" is the whole meaning of "There are facts (or true propositions) which imply S," where S is a specific utterance about X's doing of A.

The central issue reduces, then, on interpretation R(1), to determining the utterance S corresponding to each given ought-assertion. Obviously, the S corresponding to "X ought to do A" cannot be the latter assertion itself; for then we would be starting out on a vicious infinite regress. We would be defining "ought" in terms of reasons, where "reasons" can only be understood in terms of ought. It is also obvious that the utterance S corresponding to "X ought to do A," required by RP(2), cannot be the statement of fact that X performs A. In that case, to say "X ought to do A" would be to say that certain facts, or true propositions, imply that X performs A; thus, if the ought-assertion is true, the agent performs the action in question. But it is notorious that on some occasions some persons have failed to do what they ought, *simpliciter*, to have done.

We may try to get a clue to the identity of the utterance S corresponding to "X ought to do A" by focusing our philosophical microscope on statements like

(1) The fact that you have no tea is a good reason for your going to the store to buy some.

Such statements use the original expression "good reason for," they use it in the context of action, and they can be interpreted along the lines of R(1), i.e., as referring to some premises. Indeed, (1) can legitimately be regarded as a compact way of putting

(2) Since you have no tea, you ought to go to the store to buy some.

Now (2) is an invalid inference, but it may be taken as an enthymeme, whose unabbreviated version may run as follows:

(2*a*) Since you have no tea (and your going to the store is a necessary condition for your buying some tea, and you want to get some by buying it), you ought (prima facie) to go to the store; or

(2*b*) Since you have no tea (. . . , and you want above everything else to get some by buying it, and nothing else matters), you ought (*simpliciter*) to go to the store.

We may accept that (2*a*) and (2*b*) are both formally valid inferences. It is surely correct to suppose that the person who asserts (1) claims that either (2*a*) or (2*b*) is valid as well as that the implicit premises are true. Thus, if (1) is true, "You ought to go to the store" is also true, in one of the two senses of ought. This is very interesting. It shows that there is a close connection between oughts and reasons in the sense of premises, which enhances the plausibility of the good-reasons approach. But *that* connection is of no help to the view that ought-assertions are definable in terms of statements about the good reasons for doing something. The connection between (1) and (2*a*) or (2*b*) would lead us to regard "You ought to go to the store" itself as the utterance S in terms of which "You ought to go to the store" should be defined. We are exactly as before. If the good-reasons analysis is to escape circularity, it must explain how a statement about the good reasons for doing something can be understood to refer to an argument, whose conclusion is neither a statement about a person's performances nor one about oughts (or rights, or wrongs). Unfortunately, the proponents of this type of analysis have not discussed this issue.

If I were myself to develop a good-reasons analysis of "X ought to do A" along the lines of interpretation R(1), I would offer two ways of characterizing the utterances S, utterances which by the partial definitions RP(1) and RP(2) would be needed as conclusions of certain arguments. In some cases I would take the imperative "X, do A" as S, and in other cases the resolution expressed by "I (X) will do A." I am convinced that the resulting *partial* definitions are adequate. But I will not go into it at this stage. That the formulas produced by that identification of S cannot give *the* (full) meaning of "ought" is shown by the fact that "X ought to do A" is the form of an assertion ostensibly used to talk about agents and actions, not about arguments with imperative conclusions. Other reasons are given in Section 21.

12

REASON AS A MOTIVE

If we follow interpretation R(2) of the term "reason for doing," the problem of ascertaining what sort of utterance corresponding to "X ought to do A" comes as the conclusion of a certain argument vanishes. To say that you ought to go to the store is to say that there are good reasons for your going to the store, i.e., that the facts being what they are, you have a (strong) motive (or something like it) for going to the store. Clearly, a motive is a thought or belief, which moves, that is, which is causally involved in a person's doing something. Thus, to say that X ought to do A in the motivational sense would be to say that if X has certain beliefs, or if he thought of the facts as they are, he would be drawn toward doing A.[8] This is quite vague; there are several different ways in which the analysis could crystallize, depending on which of the following elements, among others, are selected:

A. *The reasons:*
 (1) all the facts of the situation;
 (2) some of the facts;
 (3) all the relevant facts.
B. *The human element:*
 (1) any man whatever;
 (2) a man of a certain type.
C. *The causal element:*
 (1) believing that the facts are . . . ;
 (2) knowing that . . . ;
 (3) reflecting on the facts.
D. *The motivational element:*
 (1) doing an act A;
 (2) trying to do A;
 (3) being inclined to do A;
 (4) wanting to do A.

We can refer to each view by the number obtained by putting the numbers of the elements in the order A, B, C, D. For instance, a view of type A(2)-B(2)-C(3)-D(1), i.e., (2231), is the following:

(2231) "X ought to do A" means the same as "There are facts about X's situation such that, X being a person of type T, if he were to reflect on them, he would do A."

I have formulated the analysis-schema with the help of a subjunctive conditional to stress the causal character of the view.

A little reflection suffices to grasp the inadequacy of those views including D(1), i.e., the doing of the act in question. Those views entail that a person cannot fail to perform an action which he knows why he ought to do, while thinking of (or knowing of) the relevant facts. That is clearly excessive. One may fail to bring about what one ought to do because of unexpected catastrophes. Hence, (2231) is not an adequate analysis of ordinary ought-assertions.

We can immediately disregard causal elements C(1) and C(2), since one can believe or know something without being aware of it, as, for instance, when one is sleeping. The causes of events are other events, so that it is proper to suppose that the motivational view, which is a causal view, explains rational action as action caused by thought or reflection.

Let us examine B(2). The pure motivational views including B(2) fall within two schemata, the first being

B(2)-a "X ought to do A" means the same as "(Some of) the (relevant) facts of X's situation are such that, *if X were a person of type T* who reflected on them, he would try (or be inclined, or want) to do A."

Views of this sort have a serious drawback. By tying "ought" too closely to action, they drain "ought" of its guiding role. It may be a well-established truth that any person of type T is such that his reflecting on some or all of the facts of his situation causes him to do some act A. On views of sort B(2)-a, that truth can be abbreviated to "Everybody ought to do A." It would follow that I, who am not of type T, ought also to do A; but this would only mean that if I were of type T, then, etc. But why should I worry about doing A? Whatever action I perform, even one incompatible with my doing A, leaves the causal truth that I ought to do A untouched: I never fail to do what I ought to do, whatever I do!

The second schema of the pure motivational views containing B(2) is:

B(2)-b "X ought to do A" means the same as "(Some of) the (relevant) facts of X's situation are such that because X is a person of type T, his reflection on them will cause him to try (or be inclined, or want) to do A."

Views of this sort are slightly better. But they entail that if a person is not of type T, then there is no act that he ought to do. Since any being who makes choices in the light of principles is in a position to use ought-language, type T cannot be less than the type of beings who deliberate and make choices from principles. This will exclude babies and complete idiots, which are normally excluded anyway. Thus we may continue to speak of all men, as if the view included B(1), on the understanding that it is a view B(2)-b, where type T is widely construed.

Let us discuss the facts of the situation. Views which include A(1), i.e., those which make reflection on all the facts of the situation the cause of the inclination to act, have difficulty in spelling out the meaning of "all the facts." Is the fact that one ought to do A one of the facts of the situation? Element A(3) is also difficult to analyze: what exactly is a relevant fact? A motivational analyst may use, however, A(2) and A(1) or A(2) to distinguish between a prima-facie ought and the ultimate ought. He may define, for instance:

(*d*1) "X *ought prima facie* to do A" means the same as "There are facts about X's situation such that if X reflects on them he will try (or be inclined, or want) to do A."

(*d*2) "X *ought ultimately* to do A" means the same as "X's situation is such that if he reflects on all the (relevant) facts he will try (or be inclined, or want) to do A."

Of course, the motivational philosopher need not follow this line. He may prefer to distinguish the two senses of "ought" in terms of, say, a weak and a strong—perhaps overriding—trying, inclination, or wanting to do A. But (*d*1) and (*d*2) are perhaps the best proposals.

Before we proceed further it is interesting to note that a pure motivational view is inadequate: it is weak precisely at the juncture where the imperative approach is strong. As the imperativists have emphasized, "You ought to do A" often involves the imperative "Do A"; at any rate, (*e*) below is self-contradictory or conceptually absurd:

(*e*) Everything being considered, you ought ultimately to do A; but don't do it.

In an unassuming way the contradiction can be explained by saying that the ought-assertion is the expression of the speaker's agreement that the hearer is to do A, while the imperative expresses at least the suggestion that the speaker believes that the hearer is not to do A. Now, on any of the pure motivational views that remain—those including the A elements and D(2) through D(4)—(*e*) involves no absurdity at all. For instance, if the view includes D(2), (*e*) is just short for:

(*f*) Everything being considered there are facts (or all the facts are) such that if you reflect on them you will (be caused to) try to do A, but don't do A.

Clearly, there is no trace of inconsistency in (*f*). Indeed, the very fact that you ultimately ought in the motivational sense, i.e., that you have a definite, perhaps overriding motive, or reason, if you reflect, may precisely be my reason for advising you not to do A, and even for advising you not to reflect on the facts. Hence, (*a*) and (*b*) are not equivalent, and any plausible motivational view has at least to supplement (*d*1) and (*d*2) with some imperative in order to make (*f*) self-contradictory in the way that (*a*) is.

The good-reasons analysts have always emphasized the fundamental role that ought-assertions play in deliberation. That has been, quite rightly, their starting point. That puts the analysis of ought within the larger context of practical reasoning. Nevertheless, the motivational view of ought fails precisely in that context. On that view, deliberation is a psychological experiment in which one tries out one's reflection on the facts of the case in order to discover what effects it has on one's inclinations. Only if one finds that the effect of one's reflection is that one tries, or is inclined to, or wants to, do A, has one found that one ought to do A. Thus, the central part of "I ought to do A" is, on the motivational analysis, a causal description of the effects of a person's deliberating thoughts, and not a conclusion logically related to those thoughts.

Suppose, for example, that Jones deliberates as follows:

(1) I promised to drive Jim to the airport; by not driving him I do not endanger his life;

(2) So, I ought prima facie (in one sense) to drive Jim.

(3) Paul cracked his skull and his life is in danger; somebody or other around here who can drive ought to drive him to an emergency hospital; I am the only one around here who can drive;

(4) So, I ought prima facie (in another sense) to drive Paul.

(5) If one has two prima-facie duties, and one duty involves saving a life but involves endangering another, one ought ultimately to do the first duty.

(6) Therefore, I ought to drive Paul to an emergency hospital.

In the ordinary senses of "ought" and "duty," (2) is entailed by (1), (4) by (3) and (6) by all propositions (1)–(5).

The motivational view, however, does not allow for the entailment of (2) by (1). In general, the fact that a person promised to do something would be, on the motivational view, beside the mark when it comes to ascertaining whether or not he ought to do it. Jones's promise to drive Jim to the airport may or may not give rise to a prima-facie ought, depending on whether or not, in accordance with (*d*1), Jones's reflection on it makes him try to drive Jim, or inclined or wanting to drive Jim. But suppose that Jones is wholly unmoved now by the thorough, careful reflection on the promise he made to Jim three days before. Then the motivational philosopher has to deny that Jones ought, even prima facie, to drive Jim. This is a serious defect, since one of the clearest entailments in the ordinary language of oughts is precisely the one running from (1) to (2). The motivational philosopher might try to patch up his view by saying that at the time Jones made his promise he was inclined to drive Jim. He might add that this is a necessary condition for the utterance "I promise you . . ." to count as a promise. Let us grant this. The point is, however, that "Jones promised *three days ago* to drive Jim today" does not entail "Jones ought prima facie to have driven Jim three days ago," but it entails "Jones ought prima facie to drive Jim *today*."

The motivational view has a serious difficulty in trying to provide room for the entailment of (4) by (3). In general, there are two similar, but different assertions which one can make with the words "Somebody ought to do A":

(*m*) "There is some person who ought, or has the obligation, to do A," and

(*n*) "It is obligatory, or it ought to be the case, that some person or other does A."

In ordinary language (*m*) entails (*n*), but (*n*) does not entail (*m*). If Jones meant his deliberating premise (3) in sense (*m*), the motivational view has no trouble with the entailment of (4) by (3). On the contrary, if Jones meant his premise (3) in sense (*n*), and it is likely that his expression "somebody or other" is a signal that he means (3) in sense (*n*), then the motivational view cannot accommodate the entailment. In fact, it faces a very serious difficulty: it cannot formulate Jones's premise (3) in sense (*n*). Sense (*m*) of "Somebody ought to do A" is easy: it can, on the motivational view, be paraphrased by "There is some person such that if he reflects on the facts of his situation he will be inclined (or will want) to do A." But sense (*n*) is troublesome: "It is obligatory that somebody do A" does not entail that there is somebody who ought or is obligated to do A; it only says that the obligation or the ought is assigned to a group of persons collectively, and not to anyone in particular, and it also says that anyone's doing of A will discharge the group's obligation. The last is the tricky part. The motivational analyst cannot analyze "It is obligatory that somebody do A" as: (i) "The facts are such that someone who reflects on them . . .";

or as (ii) "The facts are such that anyone who reflects . . ."; or as (iii) "The facts are such that if the group together reflects. . . ." Formula (i) corresponds to (*m*); formula (ii) corresponds to "Everybody ought to do A"; formula (iii) has no counterpart in ought-assertions. What the motivational analyst needs is a formula like "The facts are such that if the group delegates to someone the reflecting on the facts, he will. . . ." But there is no group thinking of the facts to be delegated by the group to one of its members.

The shift from "ought" to "obligatory" is not necessary. "Somebody or other ought to do A" in sense (*n*) is exactly equivalent to "It is not the case that it is right for all not to do A." Clearly, Jones could have replaced (3) with

(3*a*) Paul cracked his skull and his life is in danger; it is not the case that it is right for all of us around here who can drive not to drive him to an emergency hospital and. . . .

The replacement would have been incoherent for the motivational view. Since the replacement is perfectly legitimate in ordinary language, the motivational view is not an adequate analysis of the meaning of "ought."

The view does allow for the entailment of (6) by (1)–(5). But whether or not the entailment holds is of no significance, since Jones is deliberating to find out what to do immediately. In this case, at the end of deliberation, Jones will proceed to try to drive Paul to an emergency hospital, since, according to the view, his reflection on the facts inclines him to do so. Thus, Jones need not stop to think that he is being moved to drive Paul—let alone to think that he is moved to drive Paul if he reflects on the facts, i.e., let alone to think that he ought to drive Paul (in the sense the motivational allows for "ought"). In general, this view implies that none of the ought-assertions plays an important role in deliberation. All that is required for deliberation, if the view is correct, is that one savor the facts, so to speak, and let them work their influence on one. Jones's step (2), for instance, is true only if Jones's thought of (1) produces in him an inclination to drive Jim; but then (2), namely, "If I reflect on the facts I am caused to be inclined (or want) to drive Jim," is a weak *ex post facto* conditional description of the categorically describable inclination already brought about by the thought of the promise. It adds nothing to the tendencies to act to be elicited by the deliberation. The motivational analyst can deny this only by introducing a *psychological thesis:* that the making of those weak *ex post facto* descriptions of inclinations produced by thought facilitates the further working out of reflective thinking of the facts. This thesis may very well be true, but it contributes nothing to the claim that the motivational view gives an adequate analysis of the *meaning* of the word "ought." The fact remains that ought-assertions do play the role of conclusions in deliberation, and rather than being *ex post facto* descriptions of existing inclinations to act, they are conclusions of reasonings whose place is precisely in the middle between the thinking of reasons and the issuing of action. The singular ought-assertions may or may not precede a decision to act, but they at most overlap with the organization of tendencies to act without describing them.

The motivational view can explain how an ought-assertion can be a conclusion of deliberation only when there is a considerable temporal distance between the completion of the practical reasoning and the performance. Then deliberation might be viewed as an experimental process for the discovery of some recipe or formula that the agent could use to help himself to bring about a certain course of action. By deliberation, for instance, Jones may find out that while reflecting upon certain facts of his situation he is inclined to do an action A. Since the time for performing has not arrived yet, he may formulate his discovery (that if he reflects on certain facts he becomes disposed to do A) by saying, in accordance with the motivational view, "I (Jones) ought to do A." He can later on make use of his causal knowledge in forcing himself, if he feels somewhat disinclined, to do A; for, on the view, by thinking of the relevant facts he can stir up inside himself a causal process which may lead to the actualization of A.[9] This is obviously an exciting approach to the practical role of ought. Doubtless, there is an intimate relationship between oughts and motivation. But it does not seem to be exactly the one under discussion; to say that somebody ought to do some act is not to *say* precisely that his rehearsal of certain reasonings or descriptions will arouse in himself an inclination to do that act. For one thing, it is difficult to see how the person in question can be so sure that he has discovered a causal recipe to which he can resort when his time of action comes, just because on a certain rehearsal of the facts of the situation he became disposed to perform the given act. There is no guarantee that the inclination will arise the next time he thinks of the facts. He has only one instance. For another thing, "I ought to do A" can be the summary of a causal recipe for the agent to produce in himself at time *t* an inclination to do A, only if he already wants or is inclined at *t* to do A. But then there is not much point in his rehearsing the facts in order to want or become disposed to do A. (It may very well be true that saying to oneself "I ought to do A" is a means of strengthening one's inclination to do A, when one is the theater of conflicting tendencies. But this fact, if it is a fact, is not what the ought-assertion means. So it cannot be at issue in the discussion of the motivational view.)

On the current view, a singular ought-assertion would be more authoritatively made if it is about past action; then it would be fully confirmed, or disconfirmed. This is odd. In ordinary language, past ought-assertions not only lack any special authority, but are even less interesting, for the link between ought and action is oriented toward the future. It looks as if the motivational view, by stressing the connection between ought and motivation, has unduly weakened the role of ought in guiding conduct. Normally, for some of us to deliberate, i.e., to be concerned with determining what one ought to do, is to be concerned with finding what actions to *choose* to perform, not with discovering what actions one will perform, or will be inclined to perform, without choice, if he is reflecting on certain facts. And the conclusion "I ought to do A" embodies somehow the content of the choice one is interested in making. (Here lies the grain of truth of the resolutive approach.) And the question about the meaning of such conclusions, the sense in which they are (if at all) true, or false, is simply bypassed by the motivational view, which tells us that "I ought to do A" is a summary statement about the causal efficacy of my beliefs about the facts on my actions or inclinations.

13
CONCLUSION

The preceding remarks on the good-reasons approach are quite far from exhausting the topic. They are intended to show only that the approach fails to give an account of "ought" when this term is placed in the larger context of deliberation, or that it badly needs supplementation and development. I have hinted at its need for conflation with the resolutive and the imperative approaches, a conflation which may preserve and augment the insights inherent in each approach. What should such a conflation look like and how is it to be produced? Our selective and limited discussions of those important views suggest that an over-all examination of the structure of the language of action and the links among its different segments may be rewarding.

2 *Consolidation of Results*

14
APPROPRIATE ANSWERS

Before proceeding with our examination of the logical structure of the language of conduct, it is worthwhile to take stock of the results obtained thus far. We have been speaking of ought-assertions quite freely, without stopping to consider whether there are actually several different sorts of assertions involving the word "ought." We have assumed quite blandly that most of what applies to "ought" also applies to "right" or "wrong," with obvious changes. But this cannot go on. We should delimit the range of our inquiry with some precision. Now we can afford some preliminary definitions, whose purpose is merely to narrow down the subject matter of our inquiry. These definitions should embody results already established, but they are not definitions in the sense of philosophical analyses, definitions which must perforce appear at the end of the investigation.

By the language of action I have meant the type of discourse used for commanding, deciding, recommending, advising, etc. For the sake of clarity and uniformity I shall concentrate on the linguistic units in which commands, orders, rules, decisions, etc., are formulated. I shall speak of assertions as including commands, requests, petitions, pieces of advice, moral assertions, statements of empirical fact, mathematical and logical statements, assertions about oughts, rights, wrongs, permissions, obligations, interdictions, etc.

Our preliminary definitions are sets of instructions intended to give the reader some specimens of the assertions we are to study. Doubtless, there will be borderline cases, but that should not affect my main arguments, which concern the central functions of the assertions essentially connected with action.

To begin with, the answer to a given question is *appropriate* if and only if:

A(1) it provides a solution to the doubt, problem, perplexity, puzzle, or uncertainty expressed in the question;
A(2) it is unabbreviated; and
A(3) it is not excessive, i.e., at most A(1).[10]

For example, "I don't know" on account of A(1), "yes" on account of A(2), and "He came yesterday with his wife" on account of A(3), are all inappropriate answers to the question "Did he come yesterday?"

15

IMPERATIVES

For our present purposes, a three-part definition of an imperative will suffice.

(1) *An imperative is any assertion which is in fact used to formulate, or is used as if it were the formulation of, an appropriate answer to the question "Shall I (we) do that?" asked in interpersonal conversation.* In accordance with condition A(1), such an answer tells a person what to do in the given situation. Clearly, (1) is not a grammatical definition. On the one hand, in many languages such answers include a verb in the so-called imperative mood, but the converse is not always true. There may be rhetorical uses of sentences with an imperative inflection, in which the speaker tells nobody what to do. On the other hand, there are answers to those questions, or their translations, which do not contain a verb in the imperative mood. Clear examples are the Greek *mè toûto poiéseis* and the Spanish *No hagas eso,* whose verbs *poiéseis* and *hagas* are in the second person of the subjunctive mood.[11]

The (possible) answers to those questions are practical in the sense that they convey a command, or an order, or a piece of advice, or a suggestion, or a request, or a petition. But some of these can also be expressed by sentences which are not exactly appropriate responses to "What shall I do?" or "Tell me what to do." For example, "You ought to write him a letter" may give advice or convey an order, and thus contain an answer to such a possible question; however, it normally says a good deal more than the straight or appropriate answer "Write him a letter."[12] This will be clear from our discussion in Sections 16–22. (Of course, it is quite likely that on occasion some persons do use "You ought to write him a letter" to proffer a *mere* command or a *mere* piece of advice.)

Commanding, ordering, advising, requesting, entreating, etc., will be called *varieties of prescriptive discourse.* The elucidation of their nature will help our understanding of the insights of those philosophers who have assimilated moral judgments to commands, or to pieces of advice, etc. Here we shall not go into that, but will note that a *full imperative* (in our sense) always serves one variety of prescriptive discourse. Often there is an expression like "please"[13] or "that's an order" or "I command you" which clearly indicates the particular variety as well as the fact that the whole sentence is an imperative; but often it is the context or intonation which determines the former, while the latter is signaled by the imperative mood of the main verb.

Summing up, we may define a full simple imperative as an assertion made by a sentence containing:

(1*a*) a name or description of an agent or agents (often implicit),

(1*b*) a description of the act or acts to be performed,

(1*c*) an indicator of the imperative character of the assertion, and

(1*d*) an indicator of a variety of prescriptive discourse.

(2) An imperative is also an assertion which can be correctly translated into another language or correctly rephrased in the same language by means of an imperative in the sense of parts (1) or (3) of the definition. This, I take it, is the case of "I command you to . . . ," "I beg you to . . . ," and "I request you to . . . ," which are imperatives with an obvious indicator of a variety of prescriptive discourse.

Finally, (3) an imperative is the combination of an imperative (in the preceding senses) with other assertions, including those which convey statements of fact. Thus, "If he comes, tell him to wait" and "Write him, or don't write him" are imperatives. Part (3) allows us to speak of analytic imperatives, like the last one, even though it is artificial to say that they prescribe or recommend or command, etc.; their components would prescribe or recommend, etc., had they been uttered alone in the context in question.

16

RESOLUTIVES

The definition of a resolutive has three parts. (1) *Any sentence is a resolutive which is used in fact to formulate, or is used as if it were the formulation of, an appropriate answer to the question "What shall I do?" addressed to oneself.*[14] The most typical formulations of such answers include a verb in the future tense. But they are decisions or resolves, not predictions. (Of course, the same utterance can at the same time be both a formulation of the speaker's determination to perform some act and a means of informing the hearers that the act will be performed.) A decision is neither true nor false, even though it may be said to be reasonable (or justified, or right) or not. Resolutives are used (in public utterance or in private thinking) to *make* decisions.

(2) A resolutive is also a sentence which can be correctly translated into another language or correctly rephrased in the same language by means of resolutives. Thus, "I resolve to . . ." and "I have decided to . . ." are in many contexts versions of "I shall. . . ."

(3) A complex sentence, at least one of whose components is a resolutive, is also a resolutive.

17

NORMATIVES

Formulations of rules, whether permissive or prohibitive, form an important category within the language of action. Here they will be included in a larger class of sentences to be called normatives. Roughly, normatives are sentences which contain words like "right" and "ought," and which may be said to be used to prescribe or allow specified courses of action. For instance, "I ought to go now, for my class begins in five minutes" is a normative, and so are "You ought to go now, for your class . . ." and "He ought to go now, for his class. . . ." But not every sentence containing those words is a normative; e.g., "He is to the right of Jones" and "It ought to rain today, according to the weather man's report" are not normative, in the sense in which I want to use the word; in these cases we are not talking the language of action. An utterance of an ought-sentence may fail to be a normative because it is just the utterance of a command or an order. Indeed, in ordinary speech it seems sometimes that a person proffers "You *must* go home" or "You ought to go home" as an emphatic version of the command "Go home."

In order to preserve the main points of our preliminary discussion of imperatives in Sections 4–7, we have to introduce a rather complex semi-technical definition of normatives insofar as they belong to the language of action.

Definition 1. An imperative or resolutive I *can reinforce* an assertion S if and only if there is, or there had been, no absurdity of any kind in uttering one of the following: "Since S, I," "Because S, I," "I, for S," "S, hence I," "S, therefore I," "S, so I."

Definition 2. The *imperative corresponding* to the assertion expressed in a sentence or clause S containing one term of the following list: "ought to," "it is permissible," "it is obligatory," "may," "is right to (for)," "is wrong to (for)," "has a duty to," "is forbidden to (that)," "has to," or near-synonyms,[15] is the imperative expressed by the sentence which results from S by dropping the term of the above list and putting the remaining part of the affected clause in the imperative mood. For example: to "You ought to go home" corresponds "Go home"; to "You may go home" corresponds "Go home"; to "If Peter does not go home, it is wrong for you to call him up" corresponds "If Peter does not go home, don't call him up."

Definition 3. The *resolutive corresponding* to an assertion S as described in Definition 2 is obtained by dropping the term in question, putting the affected clause in the future tense, and bringing the subject to the first person. For example: to "Peter ought not to go" corresponds the resolutive "I (Peter) will not go"; and to "If Peter comes, you (Anthony) will have to stay here" corresponds the resolutive "If Peter comes, I (Anthony) will stay here."

Definition 4. A term N is *normative* if and only if (1) N is in the list given in Definition 2; (2) N appears in a sentence formulating an assertion (or assertion component) S such that either S or its negation not-S (i.e., "It is not the case that S") is in fact, or could in principle (had it been asserted alone in the circumstances in question) have been, correctly reinforced by its corresponding imperative or resolutive; and (3) the assertion "It is not the case that S" is different from the assertion obtained from S by negating the verb or clause following N.

Definition 5. A normative is (1) an assertion formulated by a single sentence or clause with a normative term; (2) an assertion which can be correctly translated into, or rephrased as, a normative; (3) a complex assertion which results from combining normatives with other normatives by means of "and," "or," "if," or their equivalents; and (4) a complex assertion which results from combining normatives with statements of fact by means of "and," "or," "if," or equivalent expressions. For example: it is clearly absurd to reinforce the statement "The tornado ought to be near downtown by 10:00 A.M." or its negation, by the corresponding imperative "Tornado, be near downtown by 10:00 A.M." Hence, neither the word "ought" nor the whole assertion is normative. Now, "You ought to shut the door" may very well be used to assert a command; in such a case either the two (possible) utterances, "It is not the case that you ought to shut the door" and "You ought not to shut the door," would have made one and the same imperative assertion, or the former utterance would have been meaningless.

Occasionally, for the sake of brevity, I shall refer to imperatives, resolutives, and normatives as *prescriptives*, or as *prescriptive assertions.*

3 *Functions of Prescriptive Thinking*

18

IMPERATIVES AND NORMATIVES: THEIR RELATION TO ACTION

The primary function of full imperatives of kind (1) (as defined in Sec. 15) is to guide behavior. In their primary use they are uttered on the expectation or hope that the person or persons to whom they are addressed will perform the acts mentioned in them. Their purpose is to move the agent to act. But they are not (complete) causes, since it is in the nature of an imperative presenting a course of action that it may remain unfulfilled or disobeyed.

The whole point of using imperatives, be it in commands, requests, pieces of advice, etc., is precisely to help the listener to act, to give him a "push" of some sort. The use of an imperative carries with it the idea or intention that the imperative is to participate, however small this participation may be, in a causal chain of events which will terminate with the agent's doing the action in question. We shall refer to this typical feature of imperatives as their *causal intention* or their *pushing aspect.* How strong the pushing aspect is in fact depends on the circumstances or context of utterance and on the sort of person the agent is, as well as on the variety of prescriptive discourse being discharged by the imperative, i.e., whether the latter is an imperative which formulates a command, a request, a piece of advice, etc. Regardless of the degree to which this pushing element is present, it is an essential part of imperative language that the use of an imperative may always, and must sometimes, be an efficient condition of the actualization of the event mentioned in the imperative.[16]

As pointed out in Section 16, it is in the nature of normative language that some normatives can be reinforced by imperatives. Moreover, a sentence like "You *ought* to do it" or "But it is *your duty*" is often tantamount to an order or an imperative with a strong pushing element; for one of the conventions governing its use is that it may be uttered with the intention of getting the person do the act in question, just as if it were its corresponding imperative. However, a similar pushing element can be found in sentences which seem to formulate statements of fact. For instance, if a person refuses to accept a given object, we may try to get him to take it by saying to him, "But she left it for *you.*" But clearly this quasi-prescriptive use of the statement belongs to it only *per accidens:* it has "borrowed" or taken on only the pushing aspect which essentially belongs to the imperative "Take it" by "contamination" with it in the given context: it contains no mention of the action to be performed. On the other hand, the normative "You *ought* to take it," having both the pushing aspect and the description of the action, can completely supplant the imperative.

Nevertheless, as we saw in Sections 4 and 6, not all normatives include a pushing aspect or can be reinforced by imperatives, such as those which formulate permissions, e.g., "Driving on the right is permitted." They are normatives because their negations, which formulate prohibitions (e.g., "Driving on the right is not permitted"), can in principle be reinforced by their corresponding imperatives (e.g., "Do not drive on the right"), and may very well take on the latter's causal intention.

Yet even the normatives of "prohibition" or of "injunction" (which are merely the two sides of one and the same normative coin) can be deprived of their pushing intention. Besides the cases discussed in Sections 4 and 6, there are others of even greater importance. In a somewhat complex discussion as to what course of action a person is to choose, one may say to him:

> "*Inasmuch as you made a promise,* you ought to wait for Peter; nevertheless, if you do that your mother and your wife will be greatly disappointed and you *must* refrain from disappointing them."

Here the linguistic context cancels the pushing aspect of the ought-statement; this cannot *in fact* be reinforced by an imperative, for it is not used to tell the hearer to wait for Peter. Some philosophers, e.g., Hare, would claim that we have here not a normative, but only an assertion containing the word "ought" in inverted commas; they would propose to translate that assertion into a statement to the effect either (*a*) that the hearer's waiting for Peter "is required in order to conform to a standard which people in general, or a certain kind of people not specified but well understood, accept,"[17] or (*b*) that the hearer has a feeling that he ought to wait for Peter.[18] But a moment's reflection shows that our assertion as it is often used in the actual exercise of the language of action cannot be correctly analyzed in either way. "Insofar as you promised, you ought to wait for him; but . . ." is not always the quotation of a principle which other people hold, or a description of our interlocutor's feelings, or both. There is no contradiction in saying, "Even though everybody I know (including you) holds that we ought not to keep promises, yet insofar as you promised, you ought to wait for Peter; nevertheless. . . ." The ought-statement *is* an instance of a general principle which is implied but *not* mentioned, yet is held by the speaker. The principle may be one which many people do not hold, including the agent himself, so that he may lack the feeling of being obligated to wait for Peter. On this account Hare might say that the "well-understood group" which holds the standard is made up of the speaker alone. This would be a great change of view, but it would not do either. For the speaker does not hold the principle "We ought (*simpliciter*) to keep our promises," where the "ought" is used with a pushing aspect. As his advice concerning his interlocutor's waiting for Peter shows, he holds "One ought (prima facie) to keep his promises," i.e., in a sense in which this principle tells one what to do *only if* no other, more stringent principles are also binding in the given situation.

Whenever we are confronted with genuine "conflicts of duties" there are at least two propositions about duties or obligations (not about the word "duty" or the word "obligation") which are true. We may say in such situations something of this form: "In one sense (or respect), I ought to do A; but in another I ought to do B." However, the expression "in a sense" does not make the assertion one about what other people believe ought to be done or about one's feelings of obligation—even if both are somehow related to the conflict. This is why the intuitionists quite correctly followed W. D. Ross in saying that moral principles like "One ought to keep one's promises," "One ought not to injure others," and "One ought to tell the truth" prescribe prima-facie duties or claims or responsibilities. When two of such principles apply, one can properly introduce a qualification to the "ought" and thus avoid the appearance of contradiction. But saying "Insofar as . . . , I ought to . . ." is to acknowledge both the legitimacy and the bindingness of the claim or prima-facie duty [19] through first-order (or object-linguistic) ought-assertions which are not actually reinforced by, and thus cannot properly be said to entail, an imperative. By the same token, the moral principles themselves fail to entail imperatives. The most we can say is that "One ought to keep his promises" *together with* "There is no other act that one ought to do" entail the imperative "If you made a promise, keep it." To indicate this by saying that the moral principle is really "One ought prima facie (or, in principle) to keep his promises" is to acknowledge that normatives containing the word "ought" and the qualifier "prima facie" or "in principle" may lack the pushing aspect of their corresponding imperatives.

In general, we must distinguish between the unqualified use of "ought," "duty," "must" or "obligation," which in fact always involves a pushing aspect, and the qualified uses of such words, in which certain qualifications *may* cancel or bracket the causal intention of the normatives containing them. This is not peculiar to the moral principles discussed by the intuitionists; it is a general feature of the rational choice of action, when the grounds for a decision or an order or a piece of advice are conflictive. Of course, often the expressions qualifying the normative word are to be gathered from the context, and the clue will be that the normative is not reinforced by an imperative.

Sometimes, however, we qualify the word "ought," or "duty," etc., not to bracket the causal intention of the normative, but to strengthen it. We may know that our interlocutor is a person who pays great attention to certain things. In that case to say simply "You ought . . ." or "You'll have to . . ." may slip past his notice; but if we say "But it is your *moral* duty . . ." or "It is your *legal* obligation . . ." or "You *promised* . . ." or "Considering that you *want to* . . . ," we are, so to speak, pressing on the buttons which turn on his action mechanisms. Thus, we must make two different distinctions in the use of normative words: (1) their qualified as opposed to their unqualified use; and (2) their use with a pushing aspect as opposed to their use without it. When a normative has a pushing aspect it is used to tell someone what to do, and we shall say that both it and its normative word are *used motivationally*. Now, from the preceding discussion it follows that, for example, the unqualified use of "ought" is also a motivational use; but the converse is not true.

To sum up, we can take as established that

(1) The causal intention, i.e., the behavior-influencing role

of prescriptive language, is essential to imperatives (and resolutives, as we shall see).

(2) The characteristic function of normatives as such does not consist in influencing behavior or telling somebody what to do, but in *somehow* relating actions to considerations or grounds for them.

(3) The fundamental function of normatives is intimately connected with the roles of their qualifiers.

These three points must be understood if we are to gain a deep insight into the nature of the language of action and the nature of the systematic organization of the different types of assertions (i.e., conceptual units) which enter into it. I shall refer to (1) and (2) together by saying that imperatives are more *basic* than normatives with respect to their behavior-influencing role.

19

IMPERATIVES AS BASIC PRESCRIPTIVES

Imperatives are more directly related to action than are normatives in three interconnected ways. To begin with, their pushing aspect cannot be cancelled. None of the qualifiers that can be attached to a normative word can be part of an imperative. This is a special case of the fact noted in Section 5, that imperatives are never dependent clauses. "Insofar as you promised, wait for Peter" is either a nonsense utterance or a queer way of putting "Wait for Peter, *since* you promised (to wait for him)." (It should be clear that the qualifying terms we are concerned with, e.g., "insofar as," differ *toto caelo* from expressions used to introduce conditionals, e.g., "if.")

Secondly, normatives as well as ordinary descriptive sentences are used in one of several possible *manners:* (*a*) to make assertions about actions or objects: (*b*) to formulate presuppositions or assumptions; or (*c*) to present something for consideration, etc. In deliberation we examine both possible consequences, without asserting that they will in fact happen, and possible duties or courses of action which are proper to undertake, without asserting that they are unqualifiedly obligatory (or proper). On the contrary, *imperatives can be used in one manner only, namely, that corresponding to assertions of fact.* They are not the proper means to formulate tentative results in a reasoned commanding, advising, requesting, etc. They can only formulate final results. In the reasoning prior to telling somebody what to do we may certainly say "In relation to . . . , if nothing else mattered, I'd say 'Do A,' " but obviously to proffer this is precisely to *refuse* to use the imperative, even though it is to mention it.

Thirdly, imperatives, as we saw in Section 5, can never function as antecedents of conditionals; and they cannot reinforce those normatives which so function. The normative "If one ought to do A and B, one ought to do B" entails, or is reinforceable by, no (synthetic) imperative because it is analytic. But even if synthetic, the antecedent "One sought to do A and B" is not asserted and, therefore, it is not to be reinforced by "Do both A and B"; a fortiori, it cannot entail the imperative.[20] We shall summarize the preceding three points by saying that *imperatives can only be used assertively*.

20

NORMATIVE WORDS

It may be argued that our distinction between the qualified and the unqualified uses of a normative word actually shows that these words are ambiguous, and that it is a mistake to think that the same concept is expressed by "ought" in "You *ought* to do it," "You morally ought to do it," "Inasmuch as you promised you ought to do it," and "Legally speaking, you ought to do it." Indeed, people often contrast obligation or a legal ought with a moral ought.

Normative words seem particularly ambiguous when they appear without accompanying qualifiers because the context allows the latter to remain unsaid. But a legal ought is then simply an ought with an implicit qualifier like "legally" or "in accordance with the law," whereas a moral ought is one with an implicit "morally," etc. This ambiguity presupposes a basic common meaning;[21] it is, therefore, quite different from, say, the ambiguity of the word "is" in the senses of existence and identity. In contrasting "One morally ought to (or, must) . . ." and "One legally ought to (or, must) . . . ," it is quite natural to say that the word "ought" has the same meaning, and that the differences between the two assertions are to be traced down to the contrast between "morally" and "legally."

The fact that the normative words "ought," "duty," "obligatory," "must," do have a basic common meaning is compatible with their not being synonymous. As lexicographers and the followers of J. L. Austin may tell us, "duty" is more often used in moral contexts than "ought," and "ought" much more than "must" or "obligatory," etc. Since the existence of two absolutely synonymous words is a waste, whenever a language develops synonyms, differences soon begin to creep in. Thus, many of our normative words tend to be restricted to certain contexts, i.e., to be preferred for certain qualifiers, which they may end up by "devouring."

In English, for instance, the words "obligatory" and "forbidden" are more commonly used to formulate conventional rules, often with a complex system of punishments for the several ways in which they can be violated. These words embody a general qualifier pointing to some context in which conventions of some sort have been established. These conventions prescribe sanctions for certain kinds of acts. But from this it does not follow that "A is obligatory" *just* means "If A is not performed, punishment will ensue."[22] The normative does *not* function as a description of (any part of) the context, but includes, as it were, the surname of a family of contexts, which surname in the given circumstances of utterance will pick up the specific context.

Similarly, "must" is preferred to "ought" in connection with Kant's hypothetical imperatives (i.e., normatives in my terminology), like "If you want to kill him quickly, you must give him a stronger dose." This has lent ground to the view that these are not really normatives, but statements of fact.[23] Further ground comes from the fact that hypothetical normatives or rules of skill (as Kant also called them) are not reinforced by imperatives (in my definitional sense [1]) unless the agent is actually in a position to make use of them.

It is quite possible for a language to have what we may call an *absolute normative term,* i.e., one which (1) when used unqualifiedly, either it or its negation would be reinforceable by imperatives, (2) could be completely neutral with respect to all possible contexts or qualifications, and (3) would never be used motivationally without some special word. In such a language every other normative word would be defined by means of that term, a qualifier, and perhaps the word with the motivational force. Probably no language has such an absolute term; but in English the word "ought" is almost absolute. Aside from its slight preference for moral contexts (which moral philosophers ought to explain), it is used in connection with all sorts of considerations brought to bear in the choice of action for either one's own performance or for recommendation to others. But it also has a preference for motivational uses; often "should" replaces it when the normative is deprived of its pushing aspect, i.e., when "ought" is not motivational. Yet, for the sake of simplicity, we may regard all normatives as formed with a fundamental neutral normative term, which we may take to be "ought." [24]

Summing up, we may define a *full single normative* as an assertion made by a sentence containing

(1*a*) a name or description of some agent or agents,

(1*b*) a description of the act or acts to be performed,

(1*c*) the word "ought" (or its equivalent), which merely indicates the normative character of the assertion.

A full single normative will often contain also

(1*d*) a qualifier which indicates relevant considerations and acts as a name of the context to which those considerations belong.

We could also suppose that some normatives have (even if only implicitly in the proper context)

(1*e*) an indicator of their pushing aspect, when this aspect is present.

21

NORMATIVES AND REASONS FOR ACTION

As shown in Sections 4–7 and 20, we must not look for the fundamental role of normatives in their motivational use. Their main function seems to be in deliberation or in reasoning leading to an imperative, where the qualifiers express or point to relevant considerations. This involvement of normatives with reasons or considerations is so strong that it prevents them from mixing well with formulations of threats. We may tell a person what to do and at the same time threaten him with some harm, as, e.g., in "Give it to me or I'll cut your throat" or "Help Peter or you'll suffer the consequences." But there is some oddness in saying to that person:

> "You ought to (must, have the obligation to) give it to me or I'll cut your throat," or
>
> "You ought to (must, have a duty to) help Peter or you'll suffer the consequences."

To be sure, the fact that some harm will fall upon the person if he fails to do the act in question is often a weighty reason which will justify his doing it. The normative "*Inasmuch as* X will kill me I should give it to him" may very well be a true qualified normative. Proper normatives seem to be rational means of guiding conduct (as opposed to simply influencing behavior) in a deeper sense than, and in addition to, that in which imperatives are rational (Sec. 18); namely, normatives (1) point through the normative word to the existence of reasons for or against the performance of the action mentioned in them [25] and (2) even formulate such reasons through the qualifier.

I have said that the normative word *points to* the reasons because "X ought to do A" cannot be synonymous with "There are reasons for X's doing of A" if a reason is a fact or true proposition which will justify X's doing of A. Of course, it is quite possible to use the latter sentence as a mere synonym of the former—just as one can use "You ought to do A" as a mere substitute for "Do A," and this could become the only use of "ought." But in such a case, "reason" does not mean something which can be adduced to *justify* the doing of A. A reason in the latter sense is a premise, or something formulated in a sentence which functions as a premise. Thus, if "X ought to do A" and "There are reasons for doing A" are synonymous, and "reason" means a premise, the two statements assert that "There are (true) premises which imply in some manner X's doing A or that X is to do A." As discussed in Section 11, "X's doing A" and "X is to do A" cannot be assertions of fact, nor can they be proxies for statements of fact. For to say that X ought to do A is not to predict that X will do A if certain facts obtain. It seems that "X's doing A" and "X is to do A" have to be abbreviations for sentences like the normative "X ought to do A" or the imperative "X, do A." The former cannot do, for then we are involved in a vicious circle: we are explaining the meaning of "ought" in terms of the meaning of "reason," and the latter in terms of the former. Hence, the imperative is more promising. As shown above (Sec. 15), imperatives are the appropriate means to tell somebody what to do; thus, it is not surprising that the analysis of "ought" (and, so, of all normative words) should take us back to imperatives. Indeed, here we have another important reason for saying that they are basic prescriptive sentences.

However, it does not seem correct to analyze the meaning of "X ought to do A" as a statement to the effect that certain facts imply in some manner the imperative "X, do A." First, such a statement belongs to a different context, namely, that context in which we discuss the logical relationships between assertions or sentences and evaluate inferences; whereas "X ought to do A" belongs to the context in which we talk about actions and give commands, advice, etc. Second, the first-person normative "I ought to do A" should on this view be a statement about a first-person imperative; but this is a *rara avis in terra* (see note 13). Third, on this view imperatives must function as conclusions of arguments, and this is denied by almost everybody. Fourth, the view (as outlined) fails to distinguish between the motivational and the non-motivational uses of "ought" (see Sec. 18).

Of those points the first and the fourth seem to be insurmountable. The second might be taken care of by saying that "X ought to do A" means that there are facts which imply both the imperative "X, do A" and the resolutive "I (X) shall do A." The third can be met by acknowledging that imperatives have logical properties just as much as statements of fact, that is, that imperatives can be analytic, inconsistent, or synthetic, that they can function as premises or conclusions.[26] There are indeed two good reasons for holding that imperatives have the same logical properties that statements of fact have. As Hare has pointed out,[27] the logical words ("all," "some," "and," "or," etc.) *on which* the validity of inferences involving statements of fact depend are properly and freely present in imperatives. And we may add that every inferential word which announces a premise (like "since," "for," "as") or a conclusion (like "hence," "so," "therefore") can be used correctly as a link between imperatives, or between imperatives and statements of fact, or between imperatives and normatives; e.g., "Open the window, *for* it is too hot," "*Since* he is too busy, please sit down and wait," "That's the best thing for you to do, *so* (*therefore, hence*) do it, and don't hesitate."

The difficulty logicians have found in the idea of a logic of imperatives lies in the latter's lack of truth-values. Every book in logic treats the validity of an argument as the impossibility of considering both all premises as true and the conclusion as false. Clearly a logic of imperatives requires a revision of that traditional view of validity. All published attempts at formulating the imperative semantical values involved in inferences have failed.[28] This is certainly the most important step in the elucidation of imperative logic, and if the preceding discussion about the meaning of "ought" is correct, it is also an essential step in the analysis of normatives, which *somehow* say that imperatives can be conclusions. This is too large an issue to be discussed here. I beg the reader to grant me, for the sake of argument,

(1) that imperatives can appear in inferences and have all the logical properties mentioned in logic textbooks, and (2) that they have some values analogous to truth and falsity which can be used in testing imperative arguments for validity.[29]

It seems to me that the semantical values involved in imperative inferences are complex and multiple. They pertain to the justification of the commands, orders, requests, pieces of advice, or petitions they formulate. These prescriptions must be distinguished from the *acts* of ordering, requesting, begging, etc. The former are *justified* or *appropriate* in relation to some specific end or purpose and on account of the facts of the situation, and often in regard to procedural conventions and decisions to which the speaker and the agent subscribe. Each set of ends, facts, conventional procedures, and decisions determines a context for justification-values of certain imperatives and resolutives. Thus, an imperative has as many justification-values as one cares to parcel out contexts. An imperative may be justified in one context and non-justified in another in view of the possible conflicts of ends as well as of procedures. But the *justifiedness* or *non-justifiedness* of an imperative relative to a certain context constituted by facts, ends, procedural conventions and decisions would be useless unless the conflict were resolved in a larger context. In cases of conflict, life itself forces us to make choices and produce a balance, so that we may speak of a total or *absolute context*, in which we regard the ends and procedural conventions as hierarchically organized, even if that organization is rough and revisable and if its structure and outline are only dimly conceived (as it may well be, especially in the case of a conflict). This cannot be elaborated here [30]; but, obviously, the distinction between the relative and absolute contexts of justification (or justifiedness) of an imperative is connected with that between the qualified and unqualified uses of ought as well as with the fact that proper imperatives are always used assertively. I take it that imperatives are used against the total background of ends, facts, and decisions, i.e., with a claim that they are justified in the absolute context; I also take it that asserting a sentence with an unqualified ought involves, too, the claim that the assertion is true with respect to the absolute context; and finally, I take it that assertions with qualified oughts indicate through their qualifiers in what context they are staking a claim. Thus, it seems that a complete elucidation of the nature and structure of normatives requires an understanding of the logic of imperatives.[31]

22

NORMATIVES AND THE JUSTIFICATION OF IMPERATIVES

Here I will just dogmatically say that, as I view it, one of the fundamental links between "X ought (unqualifiedly) to do A" and "X, do A" is that the former *expresses, points to*, or *obliquely talks about*, the justifiedness of the latter in the absolute or total context of ends, facts, conventions, and decisions; but it does not assert what these are. Indeed, it does not even assert that the imperative is justified, much less talk about the justification directly. It merely says in the object-language, i.e., in the material mode of speech (to use Carnap's helpful term, but without its old sting) what the second-order statement, "The imperative 'X, do A' is necessarily justified in the absolute context of ends, etc.," says in the metalanguage of the language of action. The two statements belong to different conceptual contexts: the normative, to that in which we are directly engaged in guiding behavior; the metalinguistic statement, to that in which we discuss propositions and evaluate inferences. Since to think or talk about language presupposes that language be used to talk about objects or actions, the latter context presupposes the former and may in a sense be said to include it; thus the two statements entail one another in the latter context but *not* in the former. This makes it incorrect to regard the metalinguistic statement as the analysis of the meaning of, or as synonymous with, the normative. Since imperatives are only used assertively (Sec. 19), the manner in which we can talk about actions and their reasons without stepping into the metalanguage in which imperatives are mentioned but not used, is to use normatives. Thus, the division of functions between normatives and imperatives allows each greater efficacy.

There is an analogous relationship between the normative "X ought (in the unqualified use) not to do A" or "It is wrong (in the unqualified use) for X to do A," the imperative "X, don't do A," and the metalinguistic statement "The imperative 'X, don't do A' is necessarily justified in the absolute context of facts, ends, conventions, and decisions." On the other hand, "X may (in the unqualified use) do A" is, in one of its senses, the image in the material mode of speech of the metalinguistic statement "The imperative 'X, don't do A' is not necessarily justified in the absolute context." The word "image" includes here the mathematical sense of "object onto which another is mapped."

A qualified use of "ought," "obligation," "duty," etc., on the other hand, *points to* the necessary justification of the corresponding imperative in the context indicated by the qualifier. The same holds, mutatis mutandis, for the other normative words: "forbidden," "permissible," "wrong," etc. Thus, if a normative word with a qualifier is not used motivationally, (1) the normative indicates that the whole hierarchical complex of ends, conventions, and decisions is not necessarily considered in ascribing a relative justifiedness-value to its corresponding imperative; so that (2) a different value may be ascribed to the imperative in a final examination; (3) it picks out the part of such a complex of ends which has been selected for the current discussion; and (4) its pushing aspect is cancelled.

Now, if the qualified normative word is used motivationally, (1) the normative does express, but does not assert, that the whole complex of ends, etc., either has been considered or may be taken as having been considered, since the action described in it "fits" well with such a complex; thus, (2) it involves the claim that the justifiedness-value ascribed to the imperative is that corresponding to the absolute context; (3) it picks out the relevant part of the total complex; and (4) this relevant part is claimed to be dominant, in conformity with (2).

23

RESOLUTIVES AND NORMATIVES

Decisions can also be justified or reasonable or proper; they are sometimes required of the agent if he is to achieve some previously chosen end, given that he is to follow certain procedures and that the facts of the case are such and such. Finding this out is the task of deliberation. Now resolutives, like imperatives, are only used assertively, i.e., to formulate the results of deliberation, not the actions merely under consideration. When I say to myself "Let's see; suppose I do A, or I decide to do A . . . ," I am not making a decision, even a tentative one, but only starting to examine the consequences of a possible *event*, namely, my doing A. The same is true of conditional utterances; in "If I (shall) do A, I'll have to face him," the antecedent does not formulate a decision, it merely describes a possible act qua happening. Resolutives also have a sort of causal intention, in the sense that they are used as part and parcel of a process which is essentially oriented toward, and must at least sometimes culminate in, the person's doing the act mentioned in it. To say "I shall do A" in all sincerity is a lot more than simply evincing readiness to do A, it is actually to put oneself in the process of doing A, to have started to do A; if A is an act that can only be performed immediately, tokening the resolutive and performing are all in one piece. On the other hand, when in deliberation we consider the act and the reasonableness of doing it we must resort to normatives, which will often include a qualifier, perhaps to be supplied by the context. In short,

(1) like imperatives, resolutives are more *basic* than normatives with respect to their behavior-influencing role, and
(2) normatives are rational means of guiding conduct in a deeper sense than that in which resolutives are. This is so because normatives point to the existence of reasons for or against performing the action mentioned in them; they even formulate such reasons through their qualifiers; and they say in the material mode of speech what meta-

linguistic statements say about the justification of resolutives.

Just as in the case of imperatives, "I ought (in the unqualified use) to do A" is just an image of, not a synonym for, "The resolutive 'I shall do A' is necessarily justified in the absolute context of facts and ends, conventions, and decisions I already subscribe to." The same holds for the other unqualified normatives as well as for all qualified ones, mutatis mutandis.

24

NORMATIVES IN GENERAL

So far we have discussed normatives in their first- and second-person uses; but they are also used in the third-person. When I say "He ought to do A," regardless of how much unqualified the ought is, my utterance cannot contain or be reinforced by my resolutive "I shall do A." It may in principle be reinforced by the imperative "Do A," and in practice it sometimes is; but it does not normally contain the latter. Now, since logical relations (as is well known) depend on the logical words or features of a sentence, *whatever makes an imperative "X, do A" necessarily justified in a given context C will also justify the resolutive "I (X) shall do A" in C.* Thus, "X ought to do A" stands in essentially the same relationship to all imperatives "X, do A," whether they formulate commands, or pieces of advice, or requests, etc., as well as to the resolutive "I (X) shall do A." This logical point is the substance of the universality of ought-assertions, emphasized by Kant, which ought not to be confused with a universal quantifier like "all," "every," etc. The third-person normative is like a formal summary of its first- and second-person counterparts. Once normatives are formulated in all grammatical persons, we "come" to look upon the third-person as a reservoir from which we can get the other persons. The relations between "I (X) ought to do A" and "You (X) ought to do A" are also homogenized through their conflation in "X ought to do A." The first-person assertion "comes" to point to the necessary justification of the imperative "X, do A," which others and one can occasionally use, as well as to the necessary justification of the resolutive "I (X) shall do A," which one alone can use.[32] Deciding is, in this manner, *almost* reduced to another variety of prescriptive discourse. On the other hand, we see how a normative *cannot* be synonymous with, or fully analyzed in terms of, the metalinguistic statement about the justifiedness-value of its corresponding imperative, not only because of the difference in conceptual level or context already emphasized, but also because of the connection between the normative and a metalinguistic statement about its corresponding resolutive.

4 *Metaphysics of the Language of Action*

25

INTUITIONISM AND THE NORMATIVE NON-NATURAL CHARACTERISTICS

From the preceding discussion it follows that whatever a normative says about an action is nothing more than a reflection of the semantical value of the corresponding imperative and resolutive. To say that A is obligatory (or due), or right, or wrong, or that A is the right, or wrong, object to do some action to, looks like the attribution of a characteristic to A. But when one tries to identify that characteristic, one becomes involved in great perplexities. Yet the attribution cannot be denied.

It is too well known that on account of both the attribution and the perplexities deontological intuitionists have asserted that (1) "ought" or "right" or some other normative word is indefinable; (2) it designates a characteristic, which (3) is (metaphysically) simple, and (4) non-natural; and (5) we know what objects or actions possess such normative characteristics by means of a non-sensory operation called "intuition." It seems to me that the deontological intuitionists were essentially correct in all but (3); by not going farther they were bound to be misleading.

From the preceding discussion of normatives it follows that

at least one normative word is indefinable or unanalyzable in the sense that we cannot provide a formula which can always be replaced by it in the first-level (or object-) language of action. Given the sort of language of action that we now have, it is impossible fully to translate all normatives into non-normative sentences (in the senses defined in Secs. 14–17). As we have seen (Secs. 11, 21–24) some of the functions of normatives can only be described, and in these descriptions we have to mention some normative word.

There is a point in saying that rightness, wrongness, and obligatoriness are characteristics. It is not merely that "right," "wrong," and "obligatory" are adjectives.[33] To say that an action A is right or that A is the right object to do an action to (with, for, . . .) is to say something about A which holds for all people; it is to claim that any normal person in similar circumstances could in principle agree that A is right. It is to say something about which we can argue and have contradictory beliefs. It is to utter a sentence which can function as a premise or conclusion in deductive inferences, governed (though not exclusively) by the rules of ordinary logic—regardless of whatever emotive or contextual implications it may have. It is also to classify A. To be sure, this classifying is done through complex criteria. But legions of descriptive classificatory predicates involve complex criteria: "angry," "envious"; "deficient in vitamin C," "having a predisposition to cancer"; "150 light-years away," "being an isotope," "emitting alpha particles"; "being a Christian," "being a politician"; etc. As discussed above, the attribution of wrongness to an object or an action is as objective and intersubjective as anything can be, even if it is a complex attribution which relates to ends, decisions, conventions, and states of affairs, and one which presupposes the existence of a prescriptive language.

From (1) that some normative word is indefinable, and (2) that it designates a characteristic, one may be tempted to conclude that the universe contains that characteristic independently of human or rational beings. This metaphysical view may come from believing that since normatives cannot, according to

(1), be translated away, they are absolutely unavoidable once we start talking about our environment. If we follow the intuitionists' assumption that a characteristic is simple if no word expressing it is definable, we seem to be stuck with at least one ultimate characteristic of a very peculiar kind. True, *within our ordinary way of thinking about actions* we cannot fail to encounter those indefinable, yet somehow complex, characteristics rightness, wrongness, etc.—at least insofar as we use attributive normative words rather than auxiliary verbs, as in "X ought to do A." But this necessity of talking about such characteristics would be absolute if and only if the normative form of prescriptive language were unavoidable for a practical being. On reflection, however, such unavoidability is found to be missing. The whole category of normative assertions may be discarded without our life suffering a bit, save for some linguistic complications.

The primary functions of practical thinking consist of bringing about rational action through one's own decisions and of helping others to bring about rational action. As we saw in Sections 19 and 23, those fundamental practical functions are discharged fully by the imperative and the resolutive segments of the language of action, particularly if they are supplemented to the hilt by the metalanguage of the language of action. Thus, the complex metalinguistic assertions about resolutives and imperatives formulated in Sections 22–24 could replace the corresponding normatives; in the case of motivational normatives we could also use imperatives or resolutives which would furnish their causal intention. Our deliberations could move from the facts, ends, and conventions to the justifiedness-value of a resolutive, or imperative, and from the metalinguistic statement about the resolutive, or imperative, to this.[34] Or, alternately, we could enrich our present imperative and resolutive discourse by developing unasserted imperatives and resolutives (Secs. 18–19, 23), which could be used in deliberation or in reasoned commanding, requesting, advising, etc., without a causal intention.

In Sections 4–7 we saw that normatives are not reducible to imperatives, but we also noted in Sections 11 and 21 that normatives presuppose imperatives. These are the results of the logical investigation, embodied in the analysis outlined in Sections 22–24, which make it impossible to eliminate the imperative segment of the language of action in favor of the normative segment. In general, part of the view developed in this essay is, then, that normatives are supernumerary, and that, although more cumbersomely, the language of action can discharge all its practical roles with the resolutive, the imperative, and the metalinguistic segments.

Now, if a rational and practical being can get on just as well in the world without the language of normatives, the deontic properties rightness, wrongness, etc., will not be part of his world. But their absence would leave no hole; their disappearance would leave behind logically equivalent remainders: the semantical properties, justifiedness and unjustifiedness of imperatives and resolutives. That being can plan and act as always, recognize his circumstances, make decisions, and guide other persons' actions.

On the contrary, by way of example, a being's world devoid of colors would be limited. Perhaps the cognition of colors is dependent on a color terminology, so that he who has no color language at all may be unable to have colors in his world. Be this as it may. The point is that if the colors of one's world go away with the color terminology, on losing the terminology, one would lose both the enjoyment of colors and the identification of objects by color. The color properties are, thus, not eliminable with logically equivalent remainders that can do duty for them.

The deontic properties are eliminable with logically equivalent remainders. They are like the shadows or mirroring images of those remainders. This is the metaphysical thesis suggested by the preceding arguments and discussions, and it deserves a precise formulation.

Definition 1. L(S) is a *sublanguage* = S is a set of terms, L(S) is a set of assertions involving at least one term of S, each term of S is involved in some assertion of L(S), and L(S) is closed under all the logical operations present in its assertions.

For example: if S is the set of color terms, L(S) may be the totality of all propositions ascribing a color to some object, and the negations, conjunctions, disjunctions, and conditionals formed with such propositions.

Definition 2. A sublanguage L(S) is *truth-functional* = The only logical operations involved in the assertions of L(S) are negation, conjunction, disjunction, and quantification, or their equivalents (that is, the operations customarily denoted by "not," "and," "or," "all," "some," and their equivalents).

A truth-functional sublanguage of the terms "blue" and "yellow" can contain "This is both blue and yellow" and "Either this is blue or it is yellow," but not assertions of the form "X believes that Y is blue" or "X sees (hears, feels) that something is yellow."

Definition 3. A sublanguage L(S) *presupposes* sublanguage L(S′) = It is logically necessary that whoever has a full understanding of L(S) must have some understanding of L(S′).

I take it that to understand a defined expression like 'bachelor' it is necessary to understand the terms which enter into its definition: "unmarried," "adult," "male," etc.

Definition 4. Sublanguage L(S) is *dispensable for* L(S′) = Every assertion of L(S) is logically equivalent to some assertion of L(S′), and L(S) presupposes L(S′).

A trivial example of a dispensable sublanguage is one made up of assertions involving some defined terms.

Definition 5. A set P of properties is *partially language-dependent* = Every truth-functional sublanguage L(S), where S is a set of terms designating those properties of P, is dispensable for some sublanguage L(S′), such that no term of S′ designates a property of P, but no L(S′) is dispensable for some L(S).

It follows from this definition that defined properties cannot be language-dependent, unless some defining property is.

Definition 6. A set of properties is *fully language-dependent* = Every truth-functional sublanguage L(S), where S is a set of terms designating those properties, is dispensable for some sublanguage L(S′), but no L(S′) is dispensable for some L(S), where S′ is a set of terms designating properties of assertions.

Now, in Sections 5–8 we saw that normatives are not reducible to imperatives or resolutives, or a combination of both, by itself or further combined with something else. In Sections 20–24 we saw that normatives are logically equivalent to some complex metalinguistic assertions which ascribe to imperatives or resolutives some semantical properties, which in the absence of better names I called justifiedness, non-justifiedness and unjustifiedness. We also saw that those metalinguistic assertions neither are synonymous with normatives nor contain any description of the deontic properties that normatives assert. Furthermore, in Sections 11 and 19 we saw that a full understanding of normatives involves some understanding of imperatives and resolutives. Hence, any truth-functional sublanguage L(S), where S is the set of normative terms, is dispensable for a sublanguage of the metalanguage of imperatives, resolutives and statements of fact, in accordance with Definition 4 above. As noted in Sections 11 and 19, imperatives or resolutives do not presuppose any understanding of normatives; clearly, statements of facts do not presuppose normatives. Hence the metalanguage of imperatives, resolutives, and statements of fact does not presuppose the language of normatives. Thus, the former is not dispensable for the latter. Therefore, the deontic properties form, by Definition 5, a partially language-dependent, and, by Definition 6, a fully language-dependent set of properties.

By contrast, the color properties are not language-dependent. No assertion to the effect that an object has a certain color is equivalent to an assertion to the effect that the object has some property other than color. "X is red," for instance, is equivalent to " 'X is red' is true"; but the latter presupposes the former. Suppose that the color orange were logically identical with the color between red and yellow, or that there were a complete list of colors. Then "X is orange" would be logically equivalent to "X is between red and yellow" or to "X is neither red nor yellow . . . nor purple." But "Between yellow and red" and "neither red . . . nor purple" are also terms which designate the same property of being orange, so that they cannot be members of the set S′ mentioned in Definitions 5 and 6.

Now, if it is assumed that there are no assertions in the absence of a language or a system of concepts, the full language-dependence of the deontic properties requires that they exist if and only if there is a normative language or system of normative concepts. Thus, on that assumption, the deontic properties do not exist *in rerum natura*, so to speak, regardless of whether that *rerum natura* is physical or supra-physical. Those properties are, then, a creation of the conceptual machinery of oughts, rights, and wrongs; but they are not merely subjective properties, as some philosophers have thought, because they are, though reflections, the reflections of non-subjective properties of imperatives and resolutives.

The intuitionists were right in holding that, given our ordinary framework for thinking about actions, in it we do recognize non-natural properties. And there is no mystery: such characteristics are only the product of our having divided the language of action into two segments: the basic sentences whose function is to present actions to some possible agent(s) with a causal intention (imperatives and resolutives) and the sentences which bring the reasons for the former *into* the material mode of speech. Clearly, what we attribute to an act or to an object affected by such an act on account of a logical property of the imperative or resolutive mentioning it, cannot be a natural characteristic of anything. The characteristic so attributed is independent of the existence of the act or the object, for it reflects something about the imperatives and resolutives which has nothing to do with whether they are fulfilled (obeyed) or not. Hence, such a normative characteristic is not primarily attributed to a particular act or event *simpliciter*, but to the members of a class of acts or objects satisfying certain conditions, namely, those whose names or descriptions appear in an imperative or resolutive entailed by a set of sentences formulating certain facts, ends, etc.

We can charge the intuitionists with having been arrested by Moore's sense of "unanalyzable," i.e., "not synonymous with a longer expression several of whose words have an independent meaning." [35] In this sense "ought" is unanalyzable; however, there is a good sense of "analysis" in which Sections 18–24 offer an analysis of the several basic elements in the meaning of "ought," "right," etc. We can see how this analysis (*not* definition) provides an account of the non-natural character of rightness, as well as of its universality and its dependence on natural properties. Hence, even though indefinable, the normative characteristics are far from being simple. From our analysis it follows that the relations between the natural characteristics of an object and the rightness (or wrongness) of an action to be done to (on, with) it are logical. However, there is no formal contradiction, in the first-order language or object-language of action, in both enumerating *all* the properties of an object and denying that an action done to (on, with) it is right. On the contrary, there is a contradiction in saying something like, "The object has certain properties such that if and only if an action A is performed on (with, to) it, a certain result will obtain which is desired above everything else by all of us," and denying that "A is the right action to do." But this contradiction comes about *via* what the two assertions entail about imperatives or resolutives, even though the latter is not definable in terms of the former. The intuitionists seized upon this undefinability, but their view that rightness is simple made it impossible for them to see the contradiction; for being simple (in their sense), it cannot entail anything about ends or events.

The opposition of inference to intuition or intellectual seeing was more misleading. Yet that was the intuitionists' way of emphasizing both that the causal intention present in unqualified first-person ought-statements cannot be the conclusion of an argument and that there is no special power for making moral inferences, i.e., that there is a unity of reason.[36] And this is correct. However, reason's seeing of rightness is akin to an immediate inference, like "the apprehension that this three-sided figure, by virtue of its being three-sided, *must* have three angles." [37]

Clearly, when we reflect on our situation and examine the probable consequences of the acts open to us in it as well as the possible bearing of previous commitments, etc., we may have in fact considered everything that enters into the justifiedness-value of the resolutive "I shall do." We do not have to tell ourselves that this resolutive is justified, just as we do not tell ourselves that the conclusion of our inference is true; we *see* that it follows from the premises and assert it without further ado. Likewise, we see that our resolutive or imperative follows from the premises formulating the relevant facts, ends, conventions, etc., and this seeing transforms itself into a decision—or the issuing of a command, or a piece of advice, or a request. Indeed, often we do not trouble ourselves to use a resolutive or imperative sentence to express our resolutions or commands; instead, we use a normative sentence with an unqualified "ought," which has both with it a causal intention and behind it the authority of the balance of reasons from the absolute context of facts, ends, conventions, and previous decisions.[38]

There is, therefore, in a manner of speaking, a "sort of fact" to which a normative may "correspond." Normatives are true or false essentially in the same way in which a statement about entailment or consistency is true or false. They have truth-values in a legitimate and direct sense, not by an act of courtesy. Hence, those views are mistaken which (*a*) reduce normatives to ejaculations and then concede that they may be true in the secondary sense that two persons who disagree in attitude cannot both properly evince their attitudes by using the same word, or (*b*) assimilate normatives to resolutives or imperatives and then accept that the former can be true only insofar as they contextually imply certain facts.[39]

The "non-natural properties" oughtness, wrongness, etc., as characterized above, do not fall under the charge that "if, for example, there were such a property as 'rightness,' it would make sense for a man to say 'Yes, I know it would be the right thing to do; but shall I do it?' "[40] The "non-natural property" rightness (in the unqualified use of the word "right") entails the justifiedness of the resolutive in the absolute context, so that the first-person normative carries the causal intention of "I shall do it." The question does not make sense *on account of* the very constitution of such a property, not simply because of contextual implications of the word "right," which may well be absent without contradiction, or because "This is the right thing to do," as uttered by me, is, leaving the contextual features aside, merely another way of saying "I shall do it"; for, as discussed above, normally it is not; and, as we have seen, it is a good deal more.

To sum up, as the intuitionists correctly emphasized, the normative segment of the language of action is patterned on the language of (natural) facts. It brings, so to speak, onto a par with the language of the imperatives and resolutives, the language of the justification of imperatives and resolutives, *as* the language of the grounds or reasons for actions, a language carved out as an imitation of the language of objects and properties. It provides a "picture" or "transcendental schema" (to use Kant's term) of the justification values of imperatives and resolutives. A schema is, Kant tells us, "a general procedure of the imagination to furnish a concept with images." [41] And normatives provide the users of the language of action with the model of empirical facts so that they can imagine the non-natural properties rightness, wrongness, obligatoriness as inhering in objects or in actions. We may suppose that the empirical "picture" inherent in the language of normatives is of some use to the human animal, that it is a product of that metaphysical nature of man in which Kant was greatly interested. But this is a question to be dealt with on another occasion.

NOTES

1. The basic schema of the systematic account of the language of action here outlined was conceived betwen 1952 and 1954, while I was writing an M.A. thesis and a doctoral dissertation under the guidance of Professor Wilfrid Sellars. His criticisms of those manuscripts led to many serious changes. I have learned so much more from him and Kant, and from Kant partly through him, than from any other philosopher, that this acknowledgment cannot even begin to discharge either my gratitude or my debt. I am also grateful to Mr. Richard M. Hare, who was kind enough to discuss several chapters of the doctoral dissertation in 1955–56 while I was at Oxford. In April 1959, my colleagues at Wayne State University, particularly Alvin Plantinga and Edmund Gettier, kindly criticized an earlier version of this paper, and Dr. Plantinga also corrected many grammatical and stylistic errors.
2. R. M. Hare, *The Language of Morals* (Oxford: Clarendon Press, 1952).
3. They are discussed in my "Are Hypothetical Imperatives Analytic?," *Proceedings of the Twelfth International Congress of Philosophy* (Firenze: Sansoni, 1960), Vol. VII, pp. 85–93.
4. P. H. Nowell-Smith, *Ethics* (London: Penguin Books Ltd., 1954), p. 195. See also notes 32 and 39.
5. This analysis has been suggested by S. Toulmin in *An Examination of the Place of Reason in Ethics* (Cambridge: Cambridge University Press, 1950), pp. 28, 43, 57, *et passim.* It is expressly asserted by Kurt Baier in *The Moral Point of View* (Ithaca: Cornell University Press, 1958). A most penetrating critique of Toulmin's contributions to moral philosophy is found in George Nakhnikian's "An Examination of Toulmin's Analytical Ethics," *Philosophical Quarterly* IX (1959), 59–79.
6. W. D. Ross, *The Right and the Good* (Oxford: Clarendon Press, 1930), pp. 19ff.
7. Kurt Baier seems to be doing precisely that in his book, mentioned in note 5. He emphasizes that "reason" appears in deliberation in the sense of "justificatory reason" (*op. cit.*, pp. 150ff.), and he insists that reasons are facts. Since he allows us to conceive of the reasons as facts which, in accordance with special rules of inference, imply the conclusions of deliberation (pp. 94–95), he might be supposed to offer

an analysis of "reason for doing." But no analysis is really given. For one thing, the conclusions obtained in deliberation are of the form "I ought prima facie to do A" or "I ought in balance to do A," which Baier prefers to formulate as "There are reasons for my doing A" and "There is the balance of reasons for my doing A," without any clarification of "ought" or of "reason for doing" coming out of the mere substitution. For another thing, the meaning of "reason for doing" is not clarified until the special rules of inference (or major premises of practical reasonings) are analyzed.

It is true that Baier tries (*op. cit.*, Chap. XII) at great length to prove that some of those special rules are true. From his argument emerges the principle that those rules are true if and only if they increase satisfactions and/or diminish frustrations more than their contraries or contradictories. But it would be a serious mistake to infer from that that on Baier's view "reason for doing" just means "increases satisfactions and/or diminishes frustrations, etc." Now, when all of Baier's discussions of "reason" are considered, it seems that he replaces "ought" by "reason for doing," and trusts his luck to the clarity of the latter phrase. My "Baier's Justification of the Rules of Reason" (forthcoming in *Philosophy and Phenomenological Research*) presents a long argument on this point.

8. A motivational analysis of "ought" was proposed by W. D. Falk in his essay "'Ought' and Motivation" (1947), in *Readings in Ethical Theory*, ed. W. S. Sellars and J. Hospers (Appleton-Century-Crofts, 1952), pp. 492–510. He states that there is a motivational sense of the word "ought," in which an ought-assertion is "about the person who ought having dispositionally, though not concurrently, a compelling motive for doing an act" (pp. 504–505). But Falk emphasizes that "ought" is ambiguous, that its ambiguity is crucial to the language of action, and that the motivational sense is just *one* sense of the word "ought." Hence, my discussion of the motivational interpretation of "reason for doing" cannot apply to Falk's view without qualifications and careful exegesis of his paper, which is beyond the scope of my present inquiry. My purpose is to examine the type of view his remarks suggest.
9. This possible defense has been suggested by some remarks in Falk's essay. He says, e.g., that a man "in the very thought that he ought to do the act, had dispositionally a motive for doing it, so that if he tried he would induce himself to do it" (*op. cit.*, p. 497). But, once again, my discussion may not be what Falk had in mind.
10. I am adopting here a definition of "appropriate answer" proposed for the case of statements by Gerold Stahl in his illuminating paper "La lógica de las preguntas," *Anales de la Universidad de Chile*, No. 102 (July 1956), pp. 71–75.

11. In many languages the future tense is often used instead of the imperative mood to formulate commands and orders. This had led some philosophers to suggest that the category of imperatives is somehow dispensable; see, e.g., P. T. Geach, "Imperative and Deontic Logic," *Analysis*, XVIII (1957–58), 49–56. For a refutation of Geach's claim, see my "Imperatives and Deontic Logic," *Analysis*, XIX (1958–59), 42–48.
12. Kurt Baier (*op. cit.*) holds that when the question "What shall I do?" means "Tell me what to do," it is identical with "What would you do in my place?" (p. 57) as well as with "What is *the best* thing I can do?" (p. 85) and "What ought I to do?" (p. 86). He assimilates moral judgments and ought-assertions to pieces of advice. This assimilation is vulnerable to four criticisms. (1) Even if on many occasions those questions conflate, a sentence containing the word "ought" is not always the appropriate answer to "What shall I do?" Baier is not *altogether* wrong in writing "There is, therefore, no difference between saying 'One ought to . . .' and 'There is reason for . . .'" (*op. cit.*, p. 280; see also p. 103); however, "There is a reason for . . ." is not an appropriate answer to "What shall I do?" One may correctly add: "But don't do it, because . . ." (see Secs. 7–10 for my discussion of the importance of this point). (2) To "What ought I to do?" we can appropriately answer "There's nothing that you ought to do," which is not appropriate to "What shall I do?" (3) In general, Baier's view distorts the formal logic of ought (a logic which he just ignores). For example, "X ought to do A" is inconsistent with two "negations": (a) "It is not true that X ought to do A," and (b) "X ought not to do A." On the contrary, "I shall do A" is inconsistent with only one, "I shall not do A"; similarly, "Do A" has only one negation, "Don't do A." (4) As Baier says, ought-statements are true or false (*op. cit.*, pp. 85ff., 58ff., *et passim;* see also Sec. 25 for my analysis of the truth of ought-statements); but neither imperatives nor resolutions (expressed by "I shall . . .") are true or false—at least Baier cannot deny that the latter are answers to "What shall I do?" asked in deliberation.

    For these reasons and others given, I conclude that we must distinguish (1) from each other the several questions which Baier identifies, (2) straight pieces of advice which simply tell a person what to do from *normal* ought-statements, and (3) both pieces of advice and ought-statements from formulations of resolution or decision. We must also avoid distorting the relationships of advising to the other varieties of prescriptive discourse: commanding, requesting, entreating, etc.
13. The ordinary use of "please" to indicate the requestive variety of prescriptive discourse has little to do with Hare's technical use of it

as a sign of the imperative character of a sentence (*op. cit.*, pp. 17ff., 187ff.).

14. Hare's definition of "imperative sentence" (see D2 in Sec. 3) excludes resolutives. But his noticing that (some) answers to the question "What shall I do?" come in the imperative mood (*op. cit.*, p. 15) leads him to identify resolutives with imperatives; yet his "Decisions on Principle" (*op. cit.*, Chap. IV) is one of the best philosophical essays on the topic. Decisions are for him commands to oneself (*op. cit.*, pp. 19–20, 44, 168–169 *et passim*). However, self-commands are very rare (as R. B. Braithwaite has pointed out in "Review of *The Language of Morals*," *Mind*, n.s. LXIII [1954], 249–262). Besides, they require a splitting of personality not present in decisions. More importantly, they presuppose decisions, since for a person to command himself to do an act A, it is necessary that he had previously decided to do A. The same is true of suggestions, pieces of advice, etc. Thus resolutives cannot be reduced to imperatives, whatever the variety of prescriptive discourse the latter may be serving.
15. The paradigmatic list of normative words may actually be curtailed, for normally, e.g., sentences containing the word "right" are synonymous with sentences containing the word "wrong," and both may be rephrased as ought-sentences. However, there are, or may be, idiomatic uses of the normative words such that "right" and "wrong," for instance, may not be fully interchangeable. Although I believe that this has no philosophical significance (see Sec. 20), at this stage we ought not to prejudge the logical importance of the linguistic facts.
16. Hare (*op. cit.*, pp. 13ff.) denies that imperatives have a causal intention; he argues that the function of imperatives is to tell someone to do something and that this "and getting him to do it, are quite distinct, logically, from each other." His reason is that we must distinguish between telling someone that . . . and getting him to believe it. But even though he is right in assuming that the logic of imperatives is parallel (*op. cit.* Chap. II) to the logic of statements of fact, he has no reason to assume that their functions are also parallel. It is difficult to see what "telling to" means as contrasted with "telling that" if the former is deprived of its pushing aspect.
17. Hare, *op. cit.*, pp. 164, 167ff.
18. *Ibid.*, pp. 166ff.
19. Since Hare's definition of evaluative ought-sentences makes it impossible to talk of a genuine conflict of duties, here we have another objection (in addition to those I have outlined in Secs. 3–4) to his view on the relation of imperatives to normatives.
20. According to Hare's definition, we should say that every "ought" appearing in an antecedent is in inverted commas, or at least that it does not appear in an evaluative or normative sentence; but both

descriptions are inadequate. The difficulties discussed in Section 6 would become more pressing.

21. The fact that essentially the same "ambiguities" are present in the translations of those words into other languages strongly suggests that this "ambiguity" is of a special sort, and not merely an idiomatic feature of English.
22. For a view of this type, see Alan Ross Anderson, "The Formal Analysis of Normative Systems" (monograph, Sociology Department, Yale University, 1956), and "The Logic of Norms," *Logique et analyse*, I (1958), 84–91. For a critical examination of Anderson's views, see my "Obligation and Modal Logic," *Logique et analyse*, III (1960), 40–48, as well as P. H. Nowell-Smith and E. J. Lemmon, "The Logical Basis of Escapism," *Mind*, n.s. LXIX (1960), 289–300.
23. Kurt Baier is the latest defender of this thesis (see Baier, *op. cit.*, pp. 283–284).
24. This philosophically innocent practice was implicit in Kant and has been adopted by many philosophers whose philosophizing is concerned with the functions and logic of types of sentences, not with the typical nuances of English words. The words "right" and "wrong" are a bit more general than "ought," but perhaps often the motivational force of an unqualified "ought" is stronger.
25. This point has always been made by intuitionists to attack the assimilation of ought-statements to commands. See, e.g., H. Sidgwick, *The Methods of Logic* (7th ed.; London: Macmillan & Co., 1907), Chap. III, Sec. 4; E. F. Carritt, *The Theory of Morals* (New York: Oxford University Press, 1928), A. C. Ewing, *The Definition of Good* (New York: The Macmillan Co., 1947), pp. 15ff. More recently it has been greatly emphasized by S. Toulmin, *op. cit.*, Chaps. II and III, and Kurt Baier, *op. cit.*, Chaps. III, IV, and XI.
26. This important matter is simply ignored by most philosophers, except the logical empiricists, most of whom assumed that imperatives only relate to their reasons psychologically. See, e.g., C. L. Stevenson, *Ethics and Language* (New Haven: Yale University Press, 1944), pp. 27–28, 113, *et passim.* This is a serious deficiency in his very penetrating account of the interpersonal functions of normative language. One of the greatest merits of Hare's work has been to face the problem of the existence and nature of imperative logic most seriously (*op. cit.*, Chaps. II and III).
27. Hare, *op. cit.*, p. 25.
28. A very incisive criticism of such attempts is found in A. Ross, "Imperatives and Logic," *Philosophy of Science*, XI (1944), 30–46. In particular, he shows how it will never do to define truth-values for an imperative "X, do A" in terms of the truth-values of its corresponding statement "X does A." See also note 30.

29. See the essays mentioned in note 30.
30. I have discussed in detail the nature of the imperative semantical values in "Imperative Reasonings," *Philosophy and Phenomenological Research*, XXI (1960), 21–49. See also my "Imperatives and Deontic Logic," *Analysis*, XIX (1958–59), 42–48.
31. For a systematic discussion of the fundamental formal relationships between imperatives (as well as resolutives) and normatives, see my "Lógica de las normas y la ética," Parte I, *Universidad de San Carlos* (Guatemala), XXX (1954), 129–196; "Un sistema general de lógica normativa," *Diánoia* (Mexico), II (1957), 303–333. A summary with improvements appears in "The Logic of Obligation," *Philosophical Studies*, X (1959), 17–23, and a more extended outline appears in "Outline of a Theory about the Logical Structure of the Language of Action," *Theoria*, XXVI (1960), 151–182.
32. The preceding discussion runs counter to Nowell-Smith's contention that "disaster has followed" because philosophers have talked of a sentence of the form "X ought to do A," which is neutral in respect of grammatical person and "if true when spoken by one man, must also be true when spoken by another" (*op. cit.*, p. 195). He is led to this accusation by (1) his concern with the circumstances in which a word is used, which allows him to offer a more detailed account than Stevenson's of the different attitudes and beliefs "contextually implied" by uttered ought-sentences (pp. 152, 158, 192, 198) but prevents him from seeing the purely logical relationships between them and imperatives, resolutives, finitives, etc.; (2) his treating the connection between the ought-statement and the reasons for the action as a loose matter of contextual implication, and not as a purely formal relationship, as it is on our analysis; (3) his unbridgeable separation of commands, pieces of advice, etc., from decisions; (4) his neglect of the logical properties of imperatives. In fact, Nowell-Smith provides so little room for third-person normatives that the relevant part in the two pages devoted to them reads: "If Jones says 'You ought' (*giving advice*) and Smith says 'No, I ought not' (*deciding to reject it*), we should naturally say that one of them must be wrong or mistaken or even that what one of them says is false . . ." because one "cannot side with both of them" (pp. 195f.; my italics). Understandably, this rupture of the unity of normative language is the outcome of assimilating first-person normatives to resolutives and second-person normatives to a species of imperatives, namely, advice (as I show in Sec. 8). See also note 39.
33. As Nowell-Smith claims in *op. cit.*, pp. 63–64.
34. For an illuminating discussion of the application to experience of object-languages and metalanguages, descriptive and normative, see

Wilfrid Sellars, "Some Reflections on Language Games," *Philosophy of Science*, XXI (1954), 204–228.

35. George E. Moore, *Principia Ethica* (Cambridge: Cambridge University Press, 1903), Chap. I, Sec. 10.
36. See, e.g., H. A. Prichard, "Does Moral Philosophy Rest on a Mistake?" (1912), in Sellars and Hospers (eds.), *op. cit.*, pp. 149–162. Perhaps the best discussion of the intuitionists' view of intuition is that of A. C. Ewing, "Subjectivism and Naturalism in Ethics" (1944), in Sellars and Hospers (eds.), *op. cit.*, pp. 131ff.
37. Prichard, in Sellars and Hospers (eds.), *op. cit.*, p. 155.
38. Generally speaking, the intuitionists failed essentially in the same way in which their heirs, the good-reasons philosophers like Toulmin and Baier, have failed; e.g., (1) in overdrawing the differences between commands and ought-assertions and thus losing the systematic unity of all prescriptive language; (2) in not analyzing the nature of rightness and wrongness (or "reason for doing"); and (3) in ignoring the logic of normative and imperative inference.
39. Nowell-Smith combines these views, as I discuss in Section 8. Here is his list of the elements contained in Jones's "You ought to see the film": (1) injunction to see the film (*op. cit.*, pp. 192ff.); (2) contextual implication that he has reasons for it (pp. 190ff.), viz., a command or rule (p. 192) and some causal propositions (p. 152); (3) contextual implication that he has a pro-attitude toward his hearer's going to see the film (pp. 189, 194); (4) contextual implication that the hearer has a pro-attitude toward seeing the film (pp. 158, 192); (5) contextual implication that he believes that there is a considerable chance of his advice being taken (p. 199); (6) contextual implication that he believes that his hearer will be entertained by the film (p. 152); (7) contextual implication that "the consensus of reputable opinion is on his side" (p. 189). All of this is interesting and probably true, but (3)–(7) are rather peripheral to the basic functions of normatives. Since (2) is, according to Nowell-Smith's Rule 2 of contextual implication (pp. 81–82), true of *every* statement and presumably of imperatives as well, it adds nothing to the characterization of ought-assertions; (2) mentions the reasons for the normative *itself*, not for the action (pp. 81–82, 189, 192). Here "reasons" means premises or something very much like premises, and this would be a good place for a discussion of the logic of inference involving sentences which are neither true nor false in the fundamental sense. But for Nowell-Smith the *full logic* of "You ought" is summarized and illustrated by (1)–(7).
40. Nowell-Smith, *op. cit.*, p. 152.
41. I. Kant, *Critique of Pure Reason*, A, 139.

8

THE DESIRE TO DO ONE'S DUTY FOR ITS OWN SAKE

John Ladd *Brown University*

INTRODUCTION

It is often supposed that in addition to mundane desires like the desire to eat and the desire to be loved, there is also a desire to do one's duty for its own sake. The question that I want to discuss here is whether or not there really is such a desire, and if there is, whether it is a desire in the same sense that other, more garden-variety types of desires are desires.

The supposition that there is a desire to do one's duty for its own sake is generally based on the widely accepted view that a person can be moved to do an action by the mere thought that it is his duty. The belief that men can be moved by the thought that an action is a duty prevails not only among laymen, but also among philosophers; indeed, it is shared by philosophers of the most divergent schools. Among moral philosophers there are some who maintain that as a matter of fact men sometimes actually do do their duty merely because they think it is their duty, while others are content to assume that it must at least be possible that men are able to do their duty for its own sake.

In this paper, I shall not question the proposition that the thought that an act is a duty can, as such, function as a motive for doing that act.[1] The issue with which I shall be concerned is whether or not it follows from this proposition that there is a desire to do one's duty for its own sake. Must we assume that, if the thought that an act is a duty can be a motive for conduct, there must also be a desire to do one's duty for its own sake which is a desire like the desire for food, for money, for fame, or for friends? Although at first glance it might seem that the question of the existence of a desire to do one's duty is an empirical problem, after further exploration it will become clear, I think, that the issues involved are logical (or conceptual) rather than empirical.

It is obviously impossible in this paper to examine all the facets of the relationship between motivation and morality. In this paper I shall deal with only one aspect of this subject. In particular, as opposed to the problem of *akrasia*, with which Hare, Ewing, and others have recently been concerned, i.e., the problem of how a person ever could fail to do what he thinks he ought to do, I am asking why a person ever would do what he thinks he ought to do just because he thinks that he ought to do it.

My main contention will be that, although the thought that an act is a duty can be a motive for doing that act, there is no special desire to do one's duty for its own sake. More precisely, there is no such desire in the sense of an empirically observable desire like the desire to eat. Instead, the desire to do one's duty, in the sense in which there is such a desire, is a peculiar kind of a priori desire that, for want of a better name, we may call a "transcendental" desire.

The main points of my argument are as follows. First, desires must be distinguished from motives. Desires are empirically observable phenomena that are invoked to explain actions and feelings; motives, on the other hand, are not observable in the same way and are invoked to justify actions. I shall argue that motives, in contradistinction to desires, are reasons, and as such are always used to justify actions. Second, there is and can be no empirical evidence for the existence of a desire to do one's duty for its own sake. There is, indeed, empirical evidence for the existence of a "sense of duty," but, I shall argue, the desire to do one's duty for its own sake cannot be identified with any of the empirical phenomena collected under the name of the "sense of duty." Third, the peculiar character of this proposed desire to do one's duty can best be understood after we have analyzed the various kinds of motives and the respective ways in which they involve desires. There are, I shall argue, two kinds of motives: (1) material motives, which, to be efficacious, require the existence of a corresponding empirical desire; and (2) formal motives, which, as such, do not imply the existence of any specific empirically observable desire, but which could be said to imply an a priori desire, a transcendental desire. My conclusion is that the desire to do one's duty is the formal transcendental desire that corresponds to a formal motive, namely, the motive to do one's duty, by which, as was assumed at the outset, men can, indeed, be moved to action. It follows that instead of being one distinct kind of desire among others, the desire to do one's duty can sometimes, if not always, be identified with one or more specific empirical desires, e.g., the love of fellow men.

I

ARGUMENTS FOR THE EXISTENCE OF A DESIRE TO DO ONE'S DUTY FOR ITS OWN SAKE

There are three main arguments to be considered. The first argument is based on the apparent fact that people actually do act dutifully; the second maintains that the existence of this kind of desire is a necessary presupposition of moral discourse; and the third cites as evidence for the existence of this desire the fact that we take a practical interest in the solution of moral problems. In addition to these three arguments there is another argument that adduces introspective evidence of a sense of duty. Inasmuch as I shall argue later that the sense of duty is not the same as the proposed desire to do one's duty, I shall defer discussion of this argument until later. Accordingly, I shall regard the present three arguments as arguments for the existence of a desire to do one's duty rather than as arguments for the existence of a sense of duty.

The first argument is stated most clearly by H. A. Prichard. He writes as follows:

> For it seems mere wild paradox to maintain that in no case in which we do what we think of as right, do we ever in any degree do it *because* we think it right; and to say that we do some action *because* we think it right seems to imply that the thought that it is right is our motive. . . . Again, if we face the purely general question "Can we really do anything whatever unless in some respect or other we desire to do it?" we have to answer "No." But if we allow this, then we have . . . to maintain the existence of a desire to do what is right. And it does not seem difficult to do so with success. For we obviously are referring to a fact when we speak of someone as possessing a sense of duty and, again, a strong sense of duty. And if we consider what we are thinking of in these individuals whom we think of as possessing it, we find we cannot exclude from it a desire to do what is a duty, as such, or for its own sake, or, more simply, a desire to do what is a duty.[2]

A. C. Ewing, who shares Prichard's view on this subject, writes:

> To think that I ought to do A is already to think that there is good reason why I ought to do A, and as long as I think this the desire to do what I ought will be an adequate motive to explain why I do A.[3]

The conclusion of this argument is that there is a desire to do one's duty for its own sake that is just one desire among others, like, as Ross says, the desire to eat. Indeed, it is held to be a desire that competes with other desires, sometimes winning and sometimes losing. Thus, Ewing, for instance, maintains that only if we regard the desire to do our duty in this light will it be possible to account for the "fact of sin," and Ross believes that "the familiar conflict between the sense of duty and other motives could not take place unless both were operating in the same field. . . ."[4]

The second argument for the existence of a desire to do one's duty for its own sake is an argument that would be advanced by a contemporary linguistic analyst who holds a theory like that of Hare or Nowell-Smith. It starts from the fact that one of the ways we have of persuading a person to do something is to convince him that it is his duty to do it—although, of course, there are many other ways of persuading him. This fact implies that in some cases at least, if a person accepts A as being his duty, then he will have a motive for doing A, and that, in turn, means that he will be inclined to do it. Accordingly, the possibility that a person can be moved to act by moral considerations is implied whenever we attempt moral persuasion, exhortation, or counselling. Indeed, this possibility appears to be a presupposition of moral discourse in general. If this presupposition were false and no one ever could be moved to action by moral considerations alone, we would have to abandon moral discourse as inevitably futile and hence as completely pointless. In order to save moral discourse, therefore, we must admit the possibility that A's being a duty can function as a motive for doing A; and, the argument continues, it can operate as a motive only if there is a desire to do one's duty for its own sake.[5]

The third argument is based on the fact that we deliberate about moral problems. It is a fact that we often seriously ask ourselves the question: What is my duty? That is, human beings can be genuinely perplexed about what they should do under certain circumstances and even about what moral principles they should adopt and follow. It is also clear, I think, that in many such cases the perplexity is not a purely theoretical curiosity, that is, it is not like the kind of curiosity that impels us to try to solve a scientific or metaphysical problem. The moral perplexity is felt to be of a totally different character, in some ways more serious and important. On the other hand, the interest in the solution of a moral problem is not the same kind of interest that impels us to seek the solution of a practical (or technological) problem, such as that of finding the most effective means to a certain desired end. The discovery of what is one's duty is not, as such, the discovery of a means to an end. A moral perplexity appears to resemble more closely another typical kind of interest that arises from having a general desire, namely, an interest in discovering suitable objects to satisfy the desire. For instance, the desire to hear good music may make a person try to find out what musical compositions there are in order that he may properly satisfy that desire. Similarly, it could be argued, the desire to do one's duty makes people try to find out what is their duty.

2

DESIRES AND MOTIVES

Many different meanings can and have been given to the words "desire" and "motive"; indeed, these words are frequently used interchangeably. It is obvious, however, that if we want to make sense out of the arguments just presented, we must differentiate between desires and motives. For unless we assign different and independent meanings to "desire" and "motive," the thesis that there is a desire to do one's duty will become an uninteresting truism, inasmuch as it has already been admitted that the thought that an act is a duty can be a motive for doing it. Again, for our present purpose, we cannot define a "desire of a certain kind" merely as the capacity to be moved to act by a thought of a certain kind, for this would again make the thesis under consideration a truism, since it would make the proposition that there is a desire to do one's duty follow automatically from the proposition that the thought that an act is a duty can be a motive to do it—by the general principle that if X actually is A then it has the capacity to be A (*ab esse ad posse*). It is clear therefore that we have to treat "desire" and "motive" as logically independent concepts, and that the only analysis of them that we can accept is one that keeps them distinct.

Neither psychology nor ordinary language provide us with a standard meaning for "desire" that will help us to understand the notion of a desire to do one's duty for its own sake. We find that the word "desire" is no longer used by psychologists, and that in ordinary language "desire" has special connotations which make it difficult to combine with the concept of duty. In fact, in ordinary discourse, desire and duty are usually conceived as opposites; that is, desire and duty are thought to represent competing and incompatible demands on a person's choices. The word "desire," in its ordinary use, has other connotations that make the expression "desire to do one's duty" seem incongruous. Thus, according to the dictionary, "desire" connotes "yearning, hankering, pining, hungering, thirsting, aspiring, and panting." [6] Accordingly, a desire seems to be more often something that is felt, a certain kind of feeling, rather than the source of action. Of course, none of these connotations of the English word "desire" is intended when we speak of "a desire to do one's duty for its own sake." Rather, this desire is likened to desires like the desire to eat, to sleep, for fame, or for knowledge. The clue to what is meant here by "desire" is contained in Prichard's statement that we cannot "do anything whatever unless in some respect or other we desire to do it." Perhaps there is some other term in ordinary English that will convey the meaning that we want more satisfactorily than does "desire." We might try some of the following: "inclination" (Ryle), "interest" (Perry), "pro-attitude" (Nowell-Smith), "affection" (Richard Price), or "passion" (Hume). However, each of these words also has its own special connotations. For our purposes, it is probably easier to adopt the old-fashioned term, "spring of action." This term is more neutral than the others and yet seems to convey the meaning that we want. Thus, it would be quite proper to call any of the desires in the above list "springs of action," and it makes perfectly good sense to say that there is a spring of action for everything that we do.

If we decide that "desire" in the present context means spring of action, we have, of course, merely shifted the problem to that of explaining the concept of a "spring of action." It is clear, however, that "spring of action" and "desire" in the sense of spring of action can no longer be considered to be concepts belonging to ordinary language. They have become technical or at least semi-technical concepts. They are concepts that are employed to explain certain psychological phenomena. (Indeed, as

I shall explain presently, "spring of action" will be given the meaning that contemporary psychologists attach to "motive" or "need.")

Let us now examine the term "motive." To begin with, if we wish to make sense out of the three arguments being examined, we cannot appeal to psychologists for a definition of the word "motive," for, in the first place, "motive" is used by psychologists to stand for something rather like what I have called a "spring of action," and using their definition would again tend to obliterate the distinction between desire and motive. In the second place, in these three arguments the term "motive" is used as it is used in ordinary language, and consequently we will miss the point of the arguments if we assume that "motive" is used in a technical psychological sense. It is quite clear that the psychologists' use of "motive" differs quite markedly from its ordinary use, for in ordinary speech we would not use "motive" in such a way that we could attribute motives to animals, nor would we speak of hunger, thirst, or sex as motives.[7]

"Motive," in its ordinary use and as it is used in our arguments, means the thought that moves us to act, the purpose that we have in mind, our end-in-view, or more generally our *reason* for doing something. Anscombe has called attention to at least three kinds of motive, which she calls "forward-looking motives" (intentions), "backward-looking motives" (e.g., revenge), and "motives-in-general" or "interpretative motives" (e.g., admiration).[8] It is clear that forward-looking motives, intentions or purposes, are the only kinds of motives that are relevant when we speak of the thought of an act's being a duty as a motive for doing it. Hence I shall confine my discussions of motives to motives in this sense.

Instead of continuing our search for a standard meaning of "desire" and of "motive" in psychology or in ordinary language to help us understand the arguments being considered, I suggest that we examine the types of questions for which desires and motives are considered to provide answers. Clearly they are both used to provide answers of one sort or another to the question: Why? Let us begin by considering the following two kinds of question: (1) Why did he (or I) do so and so? and (2) Why should he (or I) do so and so? The first question asks for an explanation of an action, while the second asks for a justification of an action.

Clearly there are many different kinds of answer to the question: Why did he do so and so? Some of these kinds of answer can easily be excluded as irrelevant to the present issue. For example, we can exclude answers that merely give a cause (e.g., "He went through the door because somebody shoved him" or "He sneezed because he whiffed some pepper"). We may also exclude explanations in terms of habit (e.g., "He scolds his wife out of habit"), in terms of temperament (e.g., "He slapped her because he has a violent temper"), and in terms of moods (e.g., "She is biting her fingernails because she is nervous").[9] The kind of answer that interests us is the kind in which we naturally tend to use the word "wants" (e.g., "He is studying hard because he wants to pass the examinations"; "He went to Oxford because he wanted to study philosophy"; "He wrote all that trash because he wanted to become famous"; "He sacrificed his life because he wanted to do his duty"). In some cases, we can substitute the word "desire" for the word "wants," e.g., "He wrote because he had a desire to become famous" (or "because he desired to become famous"). Perhaps in other cases this substitution cannot be made. In any case, both the concept of desire and that of motive seem to be tied up with the concept of wanting.

Let us now turn to the second kind of question, namely, why should he (or I) do so and so? Here we are asking for a reason or motive for doing the action in question, that is, a justification for doing it. It should be noted that here again it is quite natural to use the word "want." He should go to Oxford because he wants to study philosophy. This suggests that sometimes the explanation of an action and the justification of it are the same. For example, wanting to study philosophy both explains and justifies going to Oxford. But, on the other hand, some explanations cannot also be justifications. For example, it seems odd to say that a person should do something because he has a desire of a certain sort or because of a certain spring of action. We would not say that Jones should go to Oxford because he desires to do so or because he desires to study philosophy. Ordinarily, when we use "desire" and "spring of action" we are, I submit, explaining but not justifying.

We have now discovered one way of distinguishing between motives (reasons) and desires (springs of action). Motives can be used to justify actions as well as to explain them, whereas desires can be used only to explain them. (I shall call these two types of explanation *justifying explanations* and *descriptive explanations* respectively. My reasons for doing so should become clearer presently.)

3

DESIRE AS A SPRING OF ACTION

The concept of desire considered as a spring of action that explains a person's actions is, I submit, quite similar to, if not identical with, what is often also called a "motive," particularly by psychologists. For example, Woodworth and Marquis define a "motive" as "a set which predisposes the individual for certain activities and for seeking certain goals." [10] Ryle, also, gives a somewhat similar definition of "motive": "To say, then, that a certain motive is a trait in someone's character is to say that he is inclined to do certain sorts of things, make certain sorts of plans, indulge in certain sorts of daydreams and also, of course, in certain situations to feel certain sorts of feelings." [11] For the purposes of the present discussion, I shall consider these definitions to be definitions of "desire," as a spring of action, rather than of "motive."

The first thing to be noted about a desire thus defined is that it is a complex kind of readiness or disposition. It is a disposition not only to perform certain acts, but also to try or to set oneself to perform them, to have certain feelings, to think certain thoughts, to attend to certain kinds of things, etc. The distinctive characteristic of the kind of readiness that constitutes a desire is that it has an objective, that is, there is a state of affairs (or type of state of affairs) that fulfills or satisfies the desire. In other words, a desire is always a desire *for* something or *that* something be the case. All the multifarious activities just mentioned are considered to belong to a single desire if they are related in some way or other to one single objective. There are certain characteristic activities that are associated with the various stages of fulfillment or non-fulfillment of a desire. Thus the attainment of the objective is usually accompanied by feelings of satisfaction, quiescence of activity, satiation, etc. On the other hand, before the attainment of the objective the desire is manifested in continued striving, thinking about ways and means, etc. Finally, if the objective is not attained, there are feelings of disappointment or of frustration.

Now, the existence or non-existence of a desire thus defined can be determined by empirical observation. Inasmuch as it is a readiness for any or all of these various kinds of activities, the observation of any one of them provides us with some empirical evidence of the existence of the desire. However, in order to establish the existence of a desire conclusively, we must have observed more than one of these types of activity. For example, although a reflex is a readiness (or disposition) for certain acts, we cannot call it a desire since other characteristic desiderative activities are absent.

Another feature of desires, in the sense of spring of action, is that their existence calls for a causal explanation. Thus, the existence of a particular desire may be explained by organic needs, innate drives, inherited temperamental factors, conditioning of various sorts (including social conditioning), etc.

A final feature of desires is that they have relative strengths with respect to each other, and the strength of a particular desire varies at different times and under different conditions. In fact, some quite powerful desires (e.g., thirst) may at times be entirely latent. This variation in strength of particular desires also calls for causal explanation. It is noteworthy that questions concerning both the existence and the strength of a particular desire are answered by referring to subjective facts, that is, facts about the present or past condition of the individual who has the desire.

From this brief sketch of the concept of desire we can now see some important differences between motives and desires. In the first place, the kind of evidence that we have for a person's motives (reasons) for acting comes directly or indirectly from what he says (or from what people are likely to say in similar situations). Concerning a person's desires, on the other hand, we have additional evidence over and above what he says he desires—for example, evidence from various kinds of behavior or from his reports of his feelings. This is because all the multifarious kinds of activities that are attributed to a desire cannot be attributed to a motive; for instance, the occurrence of some kinds of feeling is neither necessary nor sufficient to establish the existence of a motive, although it may be so for a desire. In the second place, when questions concerning the "why" of a motive are raised, the answers take quite a different form from the answers to questions about desires. For instance, if I ask you why you want X (in the sense of motive-reason), your answer will consist of statements describing X, whereas if I ask you why you desire X (in the sense of spring of action), the answer will consist of statements about yourself. This is because motives, as reasons, are justified by appeal to characteristics of the object, whereas desires, as springs of action, are causally explained by reference to conditions of the subject. Thirdly, it does not make sense to speak of strong or weak motives; at least, if one does so, he is comparing the soundness of the reasons being examined rather than their operative efficacy; a strong motive would, in this sense, merely be a particularly compelling reason. Here again, questions concerning the strength of a motive refer to characteristics of the object, while questions concerning the strength of desires refer to conditions of the subject. These differences will be explained in greater detail later.

Now it may be asked: what is the relation between desires (springs of action) and motives (reasons)? The relation is an ambiguous one. The ambiguity, I submit, is due to the fact that motive-explanations and desire-explanations are designed to perform different functions—do different jobs—in discourse. One way to bring this out is to consider the use of the word "want."

In ordinary speech, the word "want" is often used to make the transition from motive to desire, and so tie them together. It can do this because it is itself, in the current jargon, a Janus-word, that is, it has two uses: it can be used to refer either to a motive or to a desire. That is, the statement "P wants X" can be used either to justify his action by giving a motive or to explain it by invoking a desire.

In the first use, for giving motives, there is no distinction between "thinking that one wants X" and "really wanting X." To make this distinction implies that it is possible to challenge a person's statements about his own motives. But this is absurd. For example, if you tell me that you went to New York because you wanted to hear the opera, it would be absurd for me to ask: "Did you really want to hear the opera or did you just think that you wanted to hear it?" This would be like asking: "Did you really feel pain or did you just think you felt pain?" and admittedly this is nonsense.[12] In other words, when I say that I am doing A because I want X, the fact of my wanting X is not and cannot be brought into question.

Now, I submit, the use of "want" that does not admit of the distinction between "thinking" and "really wanting" is the use of "want" as a motive, that is, when it performs the function of a reason offered to justify the action; for, when wanting is used as a reason, there is no distinction between thinking that one wants and really wanting. This can be seen by comparing the following two statements. On the one hand, it makes perfectly good sense to say: (1) "Although he thought that he went to New York because he wanted to see the opera, he really went because he wanted to get away from home." On the other hand, it does not make any sense to say: (2) "Although he went to New York because he thought he wanted to see the opera, he went to New York because he really wanted to get away from home." In the second statement the grammar makes it clear that "wants" is intended to serve as a reason, but the use of the distinction between "thinking that one wants" and "really wanting" has no use here. In the first statement the distinction between "thinking" and "really" does, indeed, have a use; but it is with reference to the explanation of his going rather than to the fact of his wanting. In other words, when it is a question of motives (reasons) we cannot question the fact of wanting as such, although we can, indeed, raise the question whether or not the wanting performed the function of a motive. As a matter of fact, exactly the same point can be made with respect to reasons for belief; for reasons for belief cannot be divided into facts that are thought to be so and those that really are so. Thus, I can sensibly say: (1) "Although he thought that he believed *p* because of *q*, he really believed *p* because of *r*," but one cannot sensibly say: (2) "Although he believed *p* because he thought *q* was so, he believed *p* because *r* really was so."

There is, however, another use of "wants" where there is a perfectly valid distinction between "thinking that one wants X" and "really wanting X." Suppose, for example, that I tell you that I want to hear the opera. You might start arguing with me: "You don't really want to hear the opera. They are playing *Die Walküre*, and I remember that the last time you heard a Wagner opera you walked out in disgust." Note that here you are making use of kinds of evidence about what I like other than what I myself say, namely, my previous behavior in like situations. Indeed, we can argue about whether or not I really want to hear *Die Walküre*, and many sorts of empirical evidence are relevant to the dispute. In this sense of "want" we are concerned with "desires" or springs of action, rather than motives.[13]

Let us now return to our main question and ask whether or not there is a desire to do one's duty for its own sake in the sense of desire in which it is a spring of action having the features that have been described. Is there an empirically observable desire to do one's duty? Should a list of typically human desires include this particular desire in addition to the desire to eat, to sleep, for sex, for human affection, for social acceptance, etc.? The answer to this question appears to be simple and easy: yes, there is such an empirically observable desire, and it is usually called the "sense of duty." Let us now turn to an examination of this empirically known sense of duty and inquire whether it can be identified with the hypothesized desire to do one's duty for its own sake. We shall find, I believe, that the sense of duty cannot be the kind of desire whose existence is at issue.

4

THE SENSE OF DUTY

When we speak of the sense of duty as an empirically observable phenomenon, we generally have in mind a variety of phenomena, mostly feelings. For example, we usually include under the concept of the sense of duty the feeling of obligation, the feeling of making an effort of will when confronted with obstacles and temptations, the feelings of remorse and guilt—indeed, all the feelings that are associated with the term "conscience." We also use the sense of duty to explain why men sometimes act conscientiously, why they do not always neglect their duty, why they sometimes prefer to do their duty rather than to follow their inclinations, etc.

There are two questions that we must answer concerning the phenomena that are commonly thought to be empirical manifestations of a sense of duty: first, what kind of a desire does each of these phenomena really reflect, and, second, can any of these desires be identified with the desire to do one's duty for its own sake?

I shall first examine some of the general problems that are involved in defining the concept of the sense of duty. I shall begin by considering McDougall's definition of the sense of duty:

> Our "sense of duty" is, in short, at the lower moral level, our sense of what is demanded of us by our fellows; and, at the higher level, it is our sense of what we demand of ourselves in virtue of the ideal of character that we have formed.[14]

If the sense of duty is the kind of desire described by McDougall, then it obviously cannot be identified with the desire to do one's duty for its own sake, for the objectives of the two desires are different. In McDougall's sense, the objective of the sense of duty at the lower level is the fulfillment of the ideal set to us by our fellows, and at the higher level is the fulfillment of the ideal we set to ourselves. In both cases, the objective is the fulfillment of an ideal, that is, a condition of the self, which we may call the "condition of being moral"; and the performance of duties is desired not for their own sake but as a means to the attainment of this condition. In contrast, the objective of the desire to do one's duty for its own sake is merely the performance of duties.

To this objection the reply might be that the objectives of the sense of duty and of the desire to do one's duty are actually the same—that is, that there is no essential difference between being in the condition of being moral and doing one's duty for its own sake. Whether or not there actually is a difference cannot be determined until we have settled on a more precise definition of the "condition of being moral." It is quite worthwhile for our purposes, however, to survey briefly some of the possible meanings that could be attached to this expression, for this will show us what might be meant by the term "sense of duty." I shall begin with those meanings that interpret the condition of being moral as a state of the self.

The "condition of being moral" might mean any of the following: being in the state of always having done one's duty, of usually having done so, of always having done one's most important duties, etc. Then again, it might mean being the kind of person who is in one of these states. Each one of these objectives defines a different kind of desire and as a consequence would be manifested in different kinds of activities. For example, one would expect the desire always to have done one's duty to be manifested in an over-ardent attention to detail and to a multitude of minor duties and an absence of discrimination between major and minor duties.

It is interesting to note the special and peculiar function of the term "always" and "usually" in the definitions just given of the "condition of being moral." These terms occur rarely, if ever, in the definition of the objectives of ordinary mundane desires, like the desire to play music or the desire for good food. The function of the "always" and the "usually" in these definitions is to relate the doing of one's duty to the self; in this context "always *x*" and "usually *y*" are part of the descriptions of the self rather than of the doing of one's duty, for they mean "always for the self P" or "usually for the self P." If all of these objectives do contain an essential reference to the self, then none of the desires they define can be identified with the desire to do one's duty for its own sake. For, if they relate to the self, then the associated activities will be different; for example, in failing to do one's duty one will be disappointed not only at not having done certain particular acts, but also at having the kind of character that one has. If we eliminate the words "always" or "usually," then the condition of being moral will, of course, become identical with the desire to do one's duty for its own sake. If we do so, however, we shall have to find some other term to use for those empirically observable desires whose objectives relate the performance of duties to the self.

A further complication arises when we have to decide what kind of acts are demanded by the sense of duty. Does the "condition of being moral" mean (*a*) being in the state of doing what actually is one's duty or of having done what actually is one's duty, or does it mean (*b*) being in the state of having done what one now thinks is his duty, what one thought at the time was one's duty, or what is generally thought by one's society to be one's duty ("duty" in the inverted-commas sense)? It is clear that each of these states constitutes a different objective, and the conditions of fulfillment and frustration of the respective desires differ for each one. Here again, if we simply identify the sense of duty with a desire for objective (*a*), then it will become identical with the desire to do one's duty for its own sake. The objection to making this identification is that most, if not all, of the empirical accounts of a sense of duty that are given by psychologists, psychoanalysts, and anthropologists relate to desires with objective (*b*).

The purpose of this brief survey of possible meanings of "sense of duty" has been to call attention to the fact that although we can find empirical evidence to support the thesis that there is a sense of duty, the simple identification of this sense of duty with the desire to do one's duty for its own sake is quite unwarranted and, what is worse, misleading.

Let us now try a new approach and apply our questions about the sense of duty to some of the specific introspectively observable phenomena (feelings) that are generally associated with the notion of a sense of duty. Before proceeding to a discussion of these introspectable phenomena, I should like to stress that reports of feelings based on introspection are bound to be imprecise and inexact, and so, by the very nature of the kind of evidence involved, what I have to say will be impressionistic and inevitably dogmatic. With this proviso, my conclusion after examining the introspectively observable phenomena will be that it is unnecessary to postulate the existence of a desire to do one's duty for its own sake in order to explain these phenomena. I shall begin by considering the feeling of obligation.

Is the feeling of obligation evidence for the existence of a desire to do one's duty for its own sake? Granted that feelings of obligation do occur, we must ask if they are a kind of feeling that can be explained only by supposing that there is a desire to do one's duty, or if they are feelings that might arise from other desires of a more mundane sort? Consider the following example. An amateur gardener desires to have a nice flourishing garden throughout the summer. On a certain evening he thinks that his flowers need to be watered if they are to stay alive, but he is exhausted and would rather relax on the sofa and look at television. In this situation, to go out requires an effort of will. Although, of course, he does not think that he has a moral duty to water his flowers, still he has the feeling that he must do so—a feeling that arises from the demands that his objective makes upon him. Now, it may be asked: does the gardener's feeling of "mustness" differ in quality from the feeling of obligation? It seems to me that it does not; indeed, it seems to me that one of the most characteristic manifestations of a really dominant and persistent desire is the feeling of having to set oneself to fulfill it when one is faced with obstacles and the demands of other desires. If the feeling of obligation can occur with other kinds of desires, then it follows that by itself the existence of this feeling cannot be considered to be evidence for the existence of a desire to do one's duty.

The reply to this objection might be that the uniqueness of the feeling of obligation can still be preserved if it is considered to be the kind of feeling that is always associated with the thought that a particular act is a duty. It might be contended that when so qualified, the feeling of obligation can be taken as evidence for the existence of a desire to do one's duty. Nevertheless, even after this qualification has been added, the question still remains whether the feeling of obligation arises from a desire to do one's duty or from some other desire. To show this, let us consider a new example.

Suppose that you believe that you have a duty to make a sick friend happy by calling on him. Then, as a consequence of thinking it your duty, you will have a desire the objective of which is to make the friend happy. If there is a desire to do one's duty, then you would have two desires, the desire to make him happy and the desire to do your duty. (In this case, *ex hypothesi*, the desires coincide in their immediate objectives, although the former is derivative from the latter.) Let us also suppose that an effort of will is required to make the call, and you have the feeling that you must make the call. Now, is there any way of establishing that the feeling of obligation (of "mustness") comes from a desire to do one's duty for its own sake rather than from the desire to make the friend happy? There is, I submit, none.[15] We must conclude that the feeling of obligation cannot be used as evidence for the existence of an independent desire to do one's duty, inasmuch as the same feeling characterizes other acknowledged kinds of desires and could always be attributed to these other desires even when considerations of duty are involved.

The next kind of feeling to be considered is the feeling of guilt or remorse that is felt after the failure to have done one's duty. It is difficult to consider this feeling to be of the same kind as the feeling of disappointment or frustration that accompanies the non-attainment of the objective of ordinary desires (like, for example, the feeling of disappointment or frustration you have when you fail to solve correctly a mathematical problem which you want very much to solve). The very fact that these feelings of guilt and remorse are not feelings of disappointment or frustration may in itself be significant. The feeling of guilt or remorse is much more like kicking oneself for the failure. It is unnecessary to appeal to psychoanalytic theory to see that guilt and remorse involve an essential reference to the self and assume the form of self-reproach, self-disapproval, or self-punishment. They may perhaps present psychological mechanisms related to fear and anxiety, but they could hardly be said to be manifestations of a desire. To bring out this point more clearly let us return to our gardener. Suppose that he succumbs to temptation and does not water his flowers, and they die. Of course, he might merely feel disappointed at not attaining his objective; but on the other hand, he might reproach himself. If he reproaches himself it would be for being lazy, weak-willed, a poor gardener, etc.; in other words, for having a certain kind of character. Thus, the feelings would be related more closely to his ego than to the flowers in the garden; for the gardener is likely to reproach himself regardless of whether or not the flowers actually die. (Furthermore, the gardener might well reproach himself for bringing upon himself the contempt of other amateur gardeners. In some cases, undoubtedly, people have guilt feelings, or feelings of shame, that are due to fear of the contempt of others.) As in the case of self-reproach, a person who feels guilt or remorse has feelings that relate to the self, the ego-ideal or the superego, rather than to a supposed desire to do one's duty. In sum, the existence of a supposed desire to do one's duty for its own sake is neither necessary nor sufficient to explain the occurrence of remorse and of guilt feelings—as an examination of both phenomenological and psychoanalytical descriptions of those feelings adequately attests.

My conclusion is that the various kinds of feelings that come under the heading of a "sense of duty" provide no substantial evidence for the existence of an independent desire to do one's duty for its own sake. They provide evidence either of the operation of psychological mechanisms other than desires, or else of the operation of some kind of desire or other, but not necessarily of the kind of desire in question. All this, of course, would be conclusively demonstrated only after a much more detailed analysis and evaluation of the empirical data.

5

THE EXTRAORDINARY CHARACTER OF THE SUPPOSED DESIRE TO DO ONE'S DUTY

So far I have argued that there is no incontrovertible empirical evidence for the existence of a desire to do one's duty for its own sake. I shall now try to show that there are positive grounds for believing that if there is such a desire, it cannot be a desire in the sense of a spring of action, that is, an empirically observable desire. There are a number of paradoxes that arise if we regard this "desire" as a desire of the same kind as, say, the desire for money or fame, and as a desire competing with such desires.

The first paradox concerns the relationship of this supposed desire to do one's duty for its own sake to other desires. The relationship would have to be most curious. Consider, for example, the following. If there is such a desire, then we would have to say that when a person thinks that A is a duty, he will have a desire to do A by virtue of the fact that he has a desire to do his duty. But if he has a desire to do A, then this desire explains his doing A and there is no need for a desire to do one's duty in order to explain his doing it. Here we might be tempted to say that the desire to do A can be distinguished from the desire to do one's duty (= A) by virtue of the fact that if A were not thought to be a duty, there would be no desire to do A. Sometimes this appears to be the case. For example, I might want to mail a book solely because I think that it is my duty to do so, and if I did not think that it was my duty, I would not want to mail it. But I think that it is my duty to mail the book because I have promised to return the book, and I think I have a duty to keep my promises. Now again we may ask: if I mail the book will I do so because I have a desire to keep my promises or because I have a desire to do my duty as such? The question of whether the motivation is due to the desire to do one's duty or to some other desire keeps cropping up each time. In sum, the general issue is whether a genuine empirical distinction can be made between desiring to do X's (= duties) and desiring to do one's duties (= X's).[16] I believe that no such distinction can be made and shall try to show later why this is so.

Secondly, if the desire to do one's duty is regarded as a desire that can compete with other desires, then we are confronted with a strange problem that has sometimes puzzled moral philosophers, namely, whether it is morally more praiseworthy to do one's duty from a sense of duty or to do it from some other "virtuous motive," such as love of one's fellow men. On the one hand, we can take the position commonly (though mistakenly) attributed to Kant that moral worth is to be assigned only to actions done from a sense of duty rather than to actions done from what other philosophers, e.g., Aristotle and Hume, would call "virtuous" (or natural) desires. The paradoxical consequence of taking this position is, in Ross's words, ". . . that (if, as Kant holds, sense of duty is the only good, or even if it is the best motive) to form a good habit [of dutiful action] is to become a person who acts less well, and therefore a less good person."[17] It is obvious, however, that we would like to be able to assign greater moral worth to a man who has good habits and whose actions are done out of good will (in the ordinary, non-Kantian sense) than to a man who acts only from a sense of duty. We usually detest the man who never does anything he ought to do except from a sense of duty, and rightfully so. On the other hand, if we take the position that greater moral worth is to be assigned to men whose acts are done from desires other than a sense of duty, then we encounter another paradox, namely, that for an ideally good man the sense of duty is of no significance whatsoever. In other words, the desire to do one's duty for its own sake would, as such, never motivate a good man to do his duty, and, in effect, it is there only as a kind of moral policeman for people who otherwise would not do their duty. But all of this is surely highly paradoxical, for, even though we might not want to say that the good man acts from a *sense of duty*, we still want to say that he does what is his duty because it is a duty. All of this shows us that there is something very strange in the conception of a desire to do one's duty for its own sake if this desire is thought to be a spring of action alongside other springs of action like benevolence, love, the desire for food, etc. The example just given also shows that there is something odd in the identification of the desire to do one's duty with the sense of duty.

There is a third difficulty that we encounter in the conception of the desire to do one's duty for its own sake as an empirically observable desire, namely, that this desire—unlike ordinary empirically observable desires, which are contingent—would appear to be, in some sense, necessary. This necessity makes it impossible for us to establish its existence or nonexistence empirically, as we do other desires, but makes it seem logically absurd to deny that it exists. Thus, for example, suppose that a moralist has persuaded his pupil that it is his duty to do A, then there would be something rather strange in the following sort of response: "Of course, I have a duty to do A—I admit that freely—but I never have any desire to do anything that I think is my duty (i.e., what I ought to do) just because it is my duty. So don't ever expect me to do my duty just because it is my duty." Or suppose that you knew that the moralist was going to advise that person, it would be odd for you to say: "He never has any desire to do duties for their own sake, so you are wasting your time." [18] In contrast to this, there is nothing absurd in denying that a person has one of the garden-variety desires. For example, if you try to persuade me to come to a concert by telling me who is conducting, etc., I could quite naturally reply: "Of course, I'm sure that he is a good conductor, etc.,—but I never have any desire to go to a concert simply to listen to music. So you are wasting your time." (We can make this last statement empirical by adding: "Whenever I've tried to listen to music in the past I was just bored." And, of course, a third person's statement to the same effect would presumably be founded on empirical observation.) Accordingly, there seems to be something necessary about the existence of a desire to do one's duty that makes it absurd for us to deny it either of ourselves or of others. Of course, there are situations in which it is perfectly sensible to say that I do not want to do my duty; but it is significant that we allow such statements only where the performance of a particular act is concerned, and not for the general case. There is an analogue here to the oddness of a person's denial that he has any desire to believe what is true; he may have no desire to believe a particular truth, but we would not allow his denial to be general. (Perhaps in both cases, that involving duties and that involving beliefs, the word "desire" is inappropriate. We are inclined to use words like "compelled.")

Because of this aspect of necessity, it has often been held that having a desire to do one's duty is one of the essential properties of a moral agent or moral person, that is, that such a desire is necessarily contained within the conception of a moral being. The conception of a moral being, however, cannot itself be an empirical conception, and hence the proposition attributing a desire to do one's duty to moral beings cannot be empirical. Such considerations suggest that we might call this rather peculiar kind of desire a "transcendental desire." (Indeed, this is what I believe Kant's conception of the free will amounts to.) Such a desire is transcendental only in the sense that the ability to be moved by the thought that certain acts are duties is a necessary presupposition of all moral discourse, and that having this ability is part of what it means to be able to understand and participate in moral discourse. If, and whenever, this ability is absent, then moral discourse is pointless, as is the case when we are talking to children, idiots, and moral imbeciles.[19] Another way of saying the same thing is to say that the possession of this ability is a necessary prerequisite for anyone who wishes to play the language game of morals, just as the acceptance of the rules of relevant evidence and of the rules of logic are necessary before one can play the language game of science.

In sum, there are many objections to the proposition that there is a desire to do one's duty in the sense of an empirically observable desire, that is, a spring of action. First, I have argued that although there is empirical evidence for the existence of a sense of duty (perhaps it would be better to call them "senses of duty"), the desire in question cannot be identified with the sense of duty. Second, I have argued further that the peculiar character of the proposed desire to do one's duty means that it cannot be an empirical desire in the ordinary sense. In general, if there is an ability to be moved by moral considerations, and we have assumed that there is, it cannot simply be explained by postulating the existence of a particular empirically observable desire, namely, the desire to do one's duty for its own sake. Consequently, we must seek an explanation of this fact elsewhere. We shall, I suggest, discover a clue if we examine the nature of motives and reasons.

6

MOTIVES AND REASONS

As I have already indicated, for our purposes it is best to use "motive" in the sense in which it stands for a reason for action, or, more loosely, for the thought that moves us to act. If we use "motive" in this way we can preserve a distinction between motive and desire, and thus make the arguments for the existence of a desire to do one's duty for its own sake nontrivial. Furthermore, these arguments will make sense if we interpret "motive" as a reason for action; for it is clear that in them the word "motive" functions in one of its ordinary uses, and one of its most typical ordinary uses is to stand for a reason for action. That this is a typical ordinary use of "motive" is evident from the fact that when we say: "His motive for robbing the bank was to get enough money to buy his wife a fur coat," we might equally well have said: "The reason why he robbed the bank, etc." or "His reason for robbing the bank was, etc." Similarly, when we say that the thought that a particular act was his duty was his motive for doing it, we can just as well say that its being a duty was his reason for doing it. If need be, motives can be distinguished from reasons for action in general by specifying that a motive be someone's reason, that is, a reason that actually moves or might be expected to move a particular person to perform a particular action. Accordingly, a reason would become a motive by the addition of a possessive to it: a reason is a motive for my doing something if it is *my* reason for doing it, a motive for him if it is *his* reason, etc.

Motives in the sense of reasons are often used to give one kind of answer to the question, "Why?" When we are asked to explain why a person did something, we often answer by stating his motives, that is, his reason for doing it. As we have already seen, motives in this sense can be used not only to explain actions but also to justify actions, that is, they can function as reasons that justify the action in question, whether it be in the past, present, or future. The point to be remembered is that the identical motive can be used in answering the question: "Why should he do so and so?" as is used in answering the question: "Why did he do so and so?" ("In order to study philosophy" is both a reason why Jones went to Oxford and a reason why Smith should go.) I have already called attention to this double function of motives, namely, to explain and to justify, and have contrasted them in this respect with desires, which can never as such be used to justify. I shall now try to show that even though motives are sometimes used to explain they are always used to justify; that is, whenever we use motives to explain we are always giving a justifying explanation. As such, an explanation in terms of motives is to be distinguished from a non-justifying explanation, a descriptive explanation, which is purely empirical and is usually based upon observed uniformities of one sort or another, for example, desires, dispositions, and causes.

Before explaining what is meant by calling a motive a reason, I shall recapitulate the differences between motives and desires to which I have already called attention. I contend that these differences arise from the fact that motives are used to give justifying explanations, while desires are not. First, our ways of knowing about motives and desires are different; second, desires, in contrast to motives, are manifested in many different kinds of activity; third, we can give a causal explanation of the existence and strength of desires, but not of motives. In order to bring out the differences between motive-explanations and desire-explanations I should like to dwell for a moment on two characteristic differences.

The first way in which explanation by desires differs from explanation by motives is this: the identical desire can be invoked to explain many kinds of phenomena besides particular overt actions. In addition to explaining actions, the same desire can also be used to explain certain feelings, certain thoughts, certain tryings, etc. For example, the desire to eat not only explains why I have come down to dinner, but also explains why I enjoy eating, why I thought and talked about food beforehand, why I kept coming downstairs to see if dinner was ready, why my mouth was watery, etc. The same motive or reason, on the other hand, cannot be used to explain such a variety of phenomena. I may come down to dinner "in order to eat," but I do not enjoy eating "in order to eat," nor do I think and talk about food "in order to eat." We can understand the difference just noted as soon as we see that the motive explanation is also a justification, for, by the very nature of the case, each of the various phenomena mentioned requires a different justification. For example, the act of coming to dinner would be justified in one way, enjoying eating in another way, thinking and talking about food in yet another way.

A second noteworthy difference between motive-explanations and desire-explanations is this: when we describe and explain motives, we do so by mentioning the characteristics of the object (e.g., its causal properties), whereas when we describe and explain desires we mention characteristics of the subject (e.g., his organic condition). Consider the difference between the ways in which a prosecuting attorney would show that the accused had a motive for murdering his grandmother and that he had a desire to murder her. In showing his motive, facts about the grandmother's wealth, etc., would be relevant, that is, objective characteristics of the situation that might be a reason for anybody's murdering his grandmother. Indeed, we often attribute motives to a person without knowing anything about him as an individual. In showing his desire, on the other hand, statements about the accused's character, e.g., his inclination to aggression and violence, his announced intentions, would be relevant. (The final scene of *The Brothers Karamazov* provides a striking illustration of this in its description of the way in which prosecuting and defense attorneys argue over whether Dmitri had a desire to kill his father.) The fact that explanations of motives characteristically refer to the objective situation whereas explanations of desires characteristically refer to subjective conditions of the agent explains why motives can be used to justify while desires cannot be so used; for by their very nature, justifying reasons are "objective" and hold, in some sense, independently of the idiosyncrasies of the subject whose reasons they are.

The same difference between motives and desires, that is, the objective-subjective difference, can be seen when we compare the concept of a strong desire with that of a strong motive. When we speak of a strong desire we are comparing the desire in question with the rest of the person's desires and suggesting that he is likely to act on that desire—or at least that his feelings in relation to it are more intense, more salient, etc., than other feelings. On the other hand, when we speak of a strong motive we usually mean only that there is a very good reason for the person to do the act in question—quite independently of whether or not there is any likelihood of his acting in accordance with that motive or of his having any associated feelings. The previous example also illustrates this point: there may be a strong motive for Jones to murder his wealthy grandmother, namely, his being her only heir, and impecunious; but this is different from his having a strong desire to murder her.

At this point, in order to forestall certain objections to the thesis that motives are reasons for action, a few necessary distinctions must be introduced. A reason is either an *adequate* or an *inadequate* reason. An inadequate reason is a reason that is overridden by other reasons, although if such other reasons did not exist, it would be an adequate reason. For example, eating roast pork is normally an adequate reason for lighting up the oven, but not, as in Lamb's tale, for burning down the house. Whether or not a reason is adequate obviously depends upon the circumstances, which determine whether or not there are reasons on the other side that override it. (To be entirely precise, I should say, "ought to override it.") Nevertheless, even though a reason may be inadequate, I wish to emphasize that it still is a reason; for under different circumstances it would become adequate to justify an action. In other words, an inadequate reason is inadequate only because there is a better reason competing with it. (For example, getting rid of a man could be a reason for killing him. It would be an adequate reason if it were necessary for self-defense, but an inadequate reason if it were necessary only to exclude him from a dinner-party.)

Reasons may also be either *decisive* or *indecisive*, that is, a reason may be acted upon or not. For example, although two students may have the same motive or reason for studying, for one of them the motive will be decisive and he will remain in his room studying, while for the other, if he also likes to enjoy life, it will be indecisive and he will leave his room in search of better things. It is obvious that decisive reasons are not always adequate reasons, although they ought to be, and, of course, adequate reasons are not always decisive.

The contention that motives are reasons is certain to provoke a storm of protest from those who share Hume's view that reason cannot of itself move to action. There is no doubt that the theory I am advocating runs counter to many traditional views of the nature of reasons, which limit their jurisdiction radically. All that I can say in reply is that in ordinary, everyday discourse the plain man feels as much at ease in speaking of reasons for actions and attitudes as he does in speaking of reasons for beliefs and statements. One explanation of why philosophers tend to avoid talking about reasons for actions and for attitudes is that in these spheres we do not have established standards (rules, criteria) for determining what is and what is not to count as a reason as we do when we use deductive or inductive logic. Be that as it may. The point I want to stress is that even if there are no established *criteria* of the use of the concept of "reason" in relation to actions and attitudes, the use of this concept still has a distinctive *force*, that is, there is a point to using the term "reason." [20] It is this force or point that is a common characteristic shared by "reason" in all of its uses, including when it is used to mean a premise in a syllogism.

Let us now see what the force or point of the concept "reason" is. What are we trying to do when we say that R is a reason for A? What is a reason? There are two characteristic and generic features of reasons in general to which I wish to call attention. First, any reason qua reason provides a justification for anyone if it does so for one person, that is, qua reason a reason is universally valid. For example, if passing the examinations is a reason for one student studying, then, if the relevant circumstances are the same, it is equally a reason for any other student. (And whether or not they do study, it is equally a reason why they ought to do so.) The universality of reasons explains why motives direct our attention to the objective characteristics of a situation rather than towards the subjective condition of the subject; because reasons can be universal only if there is some way of objectifying the characteristics that form the basis of reasons.[21] It may be noted in passing that "because he wants X" is always a reason for any action for anybody. That is, the kind of universality that characterizes all reasons is built into the very concept of wanting.

A second feature of reasons in general, hence also of motives, is their capacity to oblige people to accept that for which they are reasons. In other words, reasons are said to "compel," "necessitate," "bind," or "oblige." It is impossible to explore in detail the notion involved here, but what it amounts to is this: one way of getting a person to accept something is to show him the reason for it, to justify it to him; for if a person accepts the reasons, he is, as it were, compelled to accept the conclusion. Of course, this does not mean that everyone always does as a matter of fact accept the conclusion once he has accepted the reasons for it. But if he does not, then we say that he ought to accept the conclusion, that the conclusion is worthy of acceptance, etc.[22] In other words, we say that a person is *bound* to accept the conclusion if he accepts the reasons for it—and by this we mean not only that he ought to accept the conclusion, that it would be desirable for him to do so, but also that he may be expected to do so. Closely related to this is the fact that reasons are used to make and support claims of one sort or another; in particular, as I have just pointed out, they are used to procure an acceptance.

There are, therefore, two basic characteristics of reasons qua reasons that account for special use of the concept of reason in discourse, namely, their universality and their capacity to oblige an acceptance. Together they constitute what is referred to when a reason qua reason is said to be universally binding. The force—although not the criterion—of R's being a reason consists in its being universally binding.

What I have said about reasons in general applies to motives as one species of reason. For our purposes, the most important thing to see is that when we introduce motives we are, in one way or another, trying to oblige others or oneself to accept the action in question. The kind of acceptance involved obviously varies with the individual circumstances; in one case the acceptance might consist of an action, in other cases it might be approval, etc. The easiest, although perhaps somewhat misleading, illustration of the thesis that one mentions motives in order to procure acceptance is provided by the psychoanalytical phenomenon known as "rationalization." When someone gives rationalizations for his actions he is using reasons to try to get others and himself to accept those actions. Rationalization makes use of the capacity of reasons to oblige acceptance in order to secure and safeguard the acceptance of an abnormal pattern of action by the ego and by others.

Although rationalizations are abnormal, they do bring out one of the principal purposes of talking about motives, namely, the procurement of acceptance. Let us see how in more normal cases the same kind of purpose operates. Consider some of the situations in which we ask a person for his motives. Sometimes we are asking him to defend his action, as, for instance, when a judge asks a driver who has been arrested for speeding why he was in such a hurry. In this situation the speeder naturally feels that he has been called on to justify his speeding, and he may even hope that the reasons he gives will induce the judge to let him go.[23] Suppose, for example, that he says that he was trying to get a sick man to the hospital. That is a reason that might successfully procure his acquittal by the judge. If it is, then his motive becomes an adequate reason for the acceptance of his action by the judge and *mutatis mutandis* it also becomes a decisive reason for the judge—as it was for the speeder.

On the other hand, if the speeder's reason for driving fast was that he was in a hurry to meet his girl-friend, he might secure the judge's sympathy and the girl-friend's approval, but not an acquittal. In most cases, even where the defense of an action is weak, by giving his motive (reason) the individual generally succeeds in justifying the action to himself, and usually secures its acceptance in some way by others. (The effect of stating one's motives in these examples should be contrasted with a person's statement about his desires. If the speeder were merely to mention his desires, he could expect nothing from the judge, certainly not his acquittal. The statement of desires, as such, does not make or support any kind of claim, as the statement of motives does.)

The characteristic effect of mentioning one's motives can be seen in a completely different type of situation, namely, one in which someone directly or indirectly gets others to do something by mentioning his motives. Suppose that you suddenly see me start running and ask me why I am running, and I reply: "In order to catch the bus." The effect upon you would, of course, vary with the circumstances: it might make you start running, too, if you also wanted to catch the bus, or it might make you feel better about the sudden loss of my company. In one way or another, the reason has the capacity to oblige you as well as me to the acceptance of something or other, and by virtue of this capacity it often has the effect of getting you to do something. (An obvious illustration of this effect occurs when someone is asked for advice; e.g., when I am thinking of buying a car. I ask you: "Why did you buy a Ford?" Your reply will not only give *your* reason for buying a Ford, but will also give *me* a reason for buying one.)

Of course, the most usual situation in which we ask for a person's motives is when we want to understand why he did something. "Why did he marry that girl?" "Because he wanted her money." "Why did he murder that woman?" "Because he wanted her money." "Why did he take that job?" "Because he wanted the money." Of course, we should not consider all of these reasons as adequate to justify the particular actions referred to, and so for us they would not be decisive, as they were for the agent. Nevertheless, they still are reasons; for in the absence of conflicting reasons they would, as such, be adequate to oblige us either to the particular action or to the approval thereof. This is evident because under most circumstances the reason given in all three examples, "in order to get money," is a perfectly good and adequate reason for doing something. If it is a reason in one case, then it is also a reason in other cases, although in these other cases it may be neither an adequate nor a decisive reason.

When we are given a reason that is neither adequate nor decisive for us (e.g., an immoral reason), our acceptance of the action is a qualified acceptance, that is, it is an acceptance that falls short of action, and perhaps even of approval. Some kind of acceptance, qualified or unqualified, is at issue whenever there is talk about a person's motives.

There are many different ways in which an action can be "accepted." We have already seen that the acceptance can take the form of imitating the action (e.g., running for the bus), or of condoning it (e.g., the judge and the speeder), or of approving it (e.g., taking a job). If none of these is possible, our acceptance is qualified. This minimum form of acceptance is what we mean when we speak of "understanding" or "seeing" why the agent did the action even though we condemn it. This is another way of saying that we feel the force of the agent's reasons for doing the act. It is somewhat like admitting to ourselves that if we were in the agent's shoes we would be tempted to do the same thing, or, if this is too strong, it is like admitting that we could imagine ourselves acting as the agent did under certain circumstances. What I mean by "qualified acceptance" may become clearer if we think of the difference between *understanding* and *knowing* why a person acted as he did. (By "knowing why" I mean being able to explain.) We can, I think, understand why someone might murder a policeman (e.g., in order to escape from him), but we cannot understand why a kleptomaniac keeps stealing women's underwear (unless, perhaps, we are his psychoanalyst). We can know why the kleptomaniac steals in the sense that we can subsume his behavior under a principle of abnormal psychology, but we cannot understand it, for we could never feel or even imagine feeling the kleptomaniac's temptations—we do not feel the force of the kleptomaniac's motives. For us, it is impossible to "see" the reason for his stealing. It is impossible for us to say anything that might conceivably justify the action. The action can, indeed, be excused, but not justified. (Perhaps these statements need some qualification if we interpret the psychoanalyst's role to be that of uncovering hidden motives, that is, hidden reasons.)

It is important to note that the kind of qualified acceptance to which an inadequate (e.g., immoral) reason obliges cannot be a merely hypothetical acceptance, that is, an acceptance to which we would be obliged if the reasons were adequate. An inadequate reason is still a reason, and as such obliges us to an acceptance, even if it is a partial or incomplete acceptance; it obliges unconditionally rather than conditionally upon the reason's becoming an adequate reason. This is so for the following reason. If the acceptance of A that is required were merely hypothetical, then when the reason R is inadequate, no acceptance of A whatsoever will be required. But if we do not accept A, then we will be obliged to repudiate either R or R's being a reason for A in accordance with the principle of *modus tollens*. We can, however, repudiate neither. We have already accepted R (e.g., getting money) as a reason in some cases, so we cannot repudiate R as such, and we cannot repudiate R's being a reason for A because the connection between R and A is a causal connection established empirically (see my earlier examples). Hence we must actually accept A in some way or other, and so our acceptance cannot be merely hypothetical. But this conclusion need not disturb us, because our reason for not fully accepting A has nothing to do with the acceptability of R as such or of R's being a reason for A; instead, it is that the existence of A is incompatible with other things that we want or think desirable. For example, committing murder is unacceptable not because getting money is an unacceptable reason for doing things, but because it conflicts, it interferes, with other things. The reasons against murdering do not disprove those for it, they merely override them.

To summarize the argument thus far, motives, in contradistinction to desires, have the effect of justifying an action, and this effect determines their use. "To justify A" means to secure its acceptance by means of the capacity of reasons qua reasons to oblige everyone to accept that for which they are reasons. When we are justifying actions by giving motives for them, the acceptance intended may take diverse forms: it may be the performance of a particular action, e.g., trying to get what the motive prescribes, cooperative action, imitative action, or acquittal, or else it may be the adoption of an attitude, e.g., approval, sympathy, forgiveness, or understanding. Inasmuch as motives are always used to justify, an explanation of a person's actions in terms of his motives may, as I suggested earlier, be called a "justifying explanation."

At this point the following objection might be raised. All the arguments that I have presented to support the thesis that motives are used to justify actions ignore the fact that in explaining a person's action we often say that he did it because he *thought* that such and such was a reason for doing it. A distinction, it might be contended, must be made between "R's being a reason for P's doing A" and "P's thinking that R is a reason for his doing A," and if this distinction is made, then my arguments collapse; for, in general, "thinking *p*" cannot be a reason for *q*, even though *p* is a reason for *q*. For example, Jones may go to the station at 6:30 because he thinks that he has to do so in order to catch his train. But if he is mistaken in believing that the train leaves at 6:30, then "to catch the train" is not truly a reason that justifies having gone to the station at 6:30. By putting all of my arguments in the first-person form, I have, the objection continues, begged the question, inasmuch as the first-person form fails to make the distinction just mentioned.[24] If we examine accounts of motives in the third-person form, then we shall see that a motive for a person's action could only be what he *thinks* is a reason and not what actually is a reason, and inasmuch as what he thinks is a reason may not be a reason at all, motives cannot always be used to justify.

The difficulty here arises from an ambiguity in the notion of "reason for." The two senses of "reason for" are evident when we see that there are two ways of showing that R is *not* a reason for A. We can show that R is not a reason by showing that it is false or mistaken. On the other hand, we can show that it is not a reason by showing that the relationship "reason for" does not hold between R and A, that is, that R is not the kind of consideration that would be a reason for A even if it were true. Just as in deductive logic a distinction is made between the truth of the premises and the validity of the argument, so we must also make an analogous distinction here between the truth and the "validity" of the reasons. In the present context, we are interested only in the question of the validity of the reasons and not their truth. To return to our example, when we say that Jones thinks that the train leaves at 6:30, we, as reporters, do not commit ourselves concerning the truth or falsity of Jones's belief. So, in the first sense of "reason for," Jones's motive is not a reason. (Perhaps we should call it a bad reason or a mistaken reason.) Nevertheless, his motive still is a reason in the second sense, namely, in the sense in which, if the beliefs upon which it is founded were true, we would be compelled to accept A. In the present discussion, we are concerned with reasons for something only in this second sense. Therefore it is unnecessary for our purposes to distinguish between R's being Jones's reason for doing something and Jones's thinking that R is a reason for doing it.

It is worthwhile to note that the analysis that I have just offered of "R being a reason for X" is consistent with the way in which we talk about reasons for belief. We would, for example, say that Ivan believes the Russians invented Coca Cola because he believes that the Russians have invented everything worthwhile, that is, his reason for believing is his belief that the Russians have invented everything worthwhile; if the latter were true, then the belief about Coca Cola would be true. Contrast this with a belief founded upon invalid reasoning: Smith believes that all patriotic Americans are Republicans because he believes that all Republicans are patriotic Americans; here we should feel disinclined to use the word "reason." In sum, in ordinary speech we can use the word "reason" if in fact the premise involved is false, but not if it does not entail the conclusion.

Before proceeding, I should point out that although it is always legitimate to ask for the motive of an action, not every action has a motive. Sometimes we have no reason at all for having done something. As far as actions are concerned, the situation is in this respect the same as it is for beliefs. Of a belief we can always ask: "Why do you believe that? i.e., what reason do you have for believing it?" even though the believer may not be able to give any reason at all and even though there may be none. As a matter of fact, the reply: "For no reason," is itself an answer to the question.[25] When no reason can be given for an action or a belief, the only other kind of answer to the question "Why?" is a descriptive explanation, e.g., a causal explanation or an explanation in terms of an empirically observable uniformity of some kind. Such an answer might be, for example: "Because I do (or think) that sort of thing when I'm tired and nervous."

As I have already pointed out, when any question regarding motives for an action is raised, a logically complete answer is always provided when we use the term "want." "I did A because I wanted X." Other expressions serve the same function, for example, "for the sake of," "in order to," "for the purpose of." Nowell-Smith calls answers of this type to the question "Why?" "logically good reasons . . . , that is to say, a reason which leaves no further room either for the question 'What shall I do?' or for the question 'Why did you (he) do that?' "[26]

We must now pursue our examination of reasons one step

further. Although we reach the end of one series of questions when we are told that Jones's motive for doing A is that he wants X, our questions concerning the reasons for his action need not stop here. We can continue by starting a new series: "Why does (or did) Jones want X?" When we examine the kinds of answers that can be given to questions about wanting, we find all the same distinctions that were made earlier with respect to actions. The question may call for either a descriptive explanation or a justifying explanation. If it calls for a justifying explanation, then when we ask why a person wants X, we will be asking for an explanation justifying anyone's wanting X. Again, a distinction must be made between adequate and inadequate reasons, and between decisive and indecisive reasons, for wanting something.

Of course, the commonest reason for wanting one thing is that it is a means to something else that one wants. "Jones wants X because he wants Y." Let us skip over those reasons that involve wanting something for the sake of something else and turn immediately to the ultimate ones, namely, those which involve something that is wanted for its own sake. Let us begin with an example. "Why are you driving up to New Hampshire?" "Because I want to go climbing." "Why do you want to go climbing?" "Because I like climbing, I enjoy climbing, I want to go climbing just for the sake of climbing." It appears that here again we have reached a logically good reason that it would be odd to question. It is obvious that we have come to the end of another series of questions, namely, those that ask "For the sake of what?" Once more, however, we are able to shift to a new series of questions, namely, to those that ask for reasons for liking or wanting something for its own sake.

Although it is often difficult, it is by no means impossible to give reasons for liking or wanting something for its own sake. No lover of mountain-climbing would admit that there is nothing more to be said in favor of mountain-climbing. Similarly, music-lovers and art-lovers may find it difficult, but not impossible, to give reasons for liking a certain piece of music or a painting. Even philosophers may feel that they are able to give reasons for wanting to do philosophy for its own sake.[27]

Whenever we give reasons for liking or wanting something for its own sake, we are still giving reasons, that is, considerations that are universally binding and that will therefore oblige the questioner to an acceptance of some sort. For example, when someone asks why you like climbing, his question has the same effect as: "Why should *I* like climbing? What reasons are there for *my* liking climbing?" In other words, in his question he is implying that whatever is a reason for your liking climbing will also, *mutatis mutandis*, be a reason for his liking it, although in his case it might be a reason that is either inadequate or indecisive, or both. This point becomes obvious when we reflect on our own experience of trying to provide acceptable answers to questions like: "Why do you like X (e.g., mountain-climbing, doing philosophy, M's Quartet in D, T's Still-Life)?" The questioner never seems to be satisfied until you have convinced him that he ought to like it, or would like it.

Finally, as with other sorts of reasons, the reasons involved here refer to features of the object itself. For example, in giving your reasons for liking the Quartet in D you would describe the form, development, harmonies, etc., of each movement.

7

FORMAL REASONS

There is, however, an entirely different sort of answer that can be given to the question: "Why do you want X for its own sake?" or "Why do you like (enjoy) X?" Instead of pointing out particular features of X, you can reply: "Because X is desirable (nice, beautiful)." For example, you might tell me that you like the Quartet in D because it is beautiful or moving.

When this type of reason is introduced we are forced to adopt a completely new line of questioning. It makes no sense to ask: "Why do you want what is desirable?" or "Why do you like what is nice?" or "Why do you enjoy what is beautiful?"

Instead, if we wish to proceed with our questioning, we must ask: "Why do you think that X is desirable (nice, beautiful)?"

For convenience I shall call the former type of reason *material reasons*, and the latter type *formal reasons*. A formal reason rules out as senseless any further question concerning the appropriateness of the corresponding attitude (e.g., why do you want what is desirable?). Instead, it permits questions concerning the ascription to the thing in question of a formal characteristic which, by definition, belongs to the appropriate object of that attitude (e.g., why do you think that X is desirable?). There are many concepts that are used to state formal reasons: for example, X's being frightening is a formal reason for being frightened, Y's being funny is a formal reason for laughing at or being amused by Y, Z's being interesting is a formal reason for being interested in Z. In fact, most of the -able and -ible words in English can be used to give formal reasons: being adorable, agreeable, horrible, detestable, admirable, and so on. In general, wherever there is a formal reason there is a corresponding kind of attitude which it justifies, that is, is a reason for. A formal reason is, by definition, the kind of reason that always justifies the attitude in question; hence, if the formal reason is invoked it is absurd to ask why a person does or should have that attitude. Nevertheless, as will become evident presently, formal reasons are empty, that is, they act like schemata that borrow their substantial content from elsewhere.

It may help if, before continuing, I show how the concept of formal reasons that has been introduced here differs from certain other concepts that appear in contemporary philosophical discussions. To begin with, formal reasons cannot be given an expressivist or emotivist interpretation. When a person gives a formal reason, it is neither necessary nor sufficient that he be expressing an attitude or attempting to evoke an attitude in others; it is quite possible for him to accept the formal reason and not have the corresponding attitude at all, and for him to have the attitude towards an object without applying the formal reason to it. For example, a person could admit that Bach is nice even though he does not himself like Bach, and he could like

Elvis Presley without thinking that he is nice. What is impossible is this: for him to admit that X is nice and at the same time deny that there is any reason for liking X. In other words, to say that X is nice means that there is a reason for liking X, or, what amounts to the same thing, that one ought to like X. (The same considerations apply, of course, *mutatis mutandis* to all the other concepts embodying formal reasons.)

There is some similarity between the adjectives that are used to express formal reasons and Nowell-Smith's A-words (aptness-words) and G-words (gerundive-words). According to Nowell-Smith A-words (like "nice" and "terrifying") are "used to give explanations and to make predictions. . . . They are also used to express reactions." [28] Thus, in his view, when we say that X is nice we are explaining our reaction of enjoying X, or predicting that we or others will enjoy X, or expressing our enjoyment of X, etc. In giving formal reasons, as I conceive them, a person can, of course, be indirectly explaining, predicting, or expressing the appropriate attitude, but, if my analysis is correct, he can use formal reasons for these purposes only by virtue of the fact that they state that there are reasons for the attitude in question and because, as a matter of fact, there is some degree of correlation between the attitudes people generally have and those that they think they have reasons for having.[29]

Formal reasons bear a much closer resemblance to Nowell-Smith's G-words, inasmuch as "G-words are those that imply not merely that the relevant person is likely to have a certain reaction, but that he ought to have it." [30] Formal reasons do, indeed, have a gerundive force, since to say that there is a reason for, e.g., liking X, is equivalent to saying that one ought to like X. My analysis, however, in contrast to Nowell-Smith's, emphasizes the role of reasons in the concepts he lists under A-words and G-words and regards their predictive and expressive force as secondary and derivative.

Let us return to the relationship between material and formal reasons. We saw that when asked for a justification for liking X, we can give material reasons which point out various features of the object (*a,b,c,d*). On the other hand, we can give a formal reason. When we invoke a formal reason there is no longer any need to justify the attitude of liking; instead, we may be required to justify the use of a formal reason. The question then becomes, "Why do you think that X is nice?" rather than, "Why do you like X?" Now, it will be recalled that to say that X is nice is the same as saying that there are reasons for liking X. Therefore, in order to say why we think that X is nice, we must give reasons for liking X. But in doing so, we would only be able to give the same reasons (*a,b,c,d*) that we would give for liking X in the first place. The conclusion is obvious: the material reasons (*a,b,c,d*) that are given for liking X are identical with the reasons that are given for thinking that X is nice. From this it follows that whenever we are able to justify our liking something, we are *eo ipso* able to justify the assertion that it is nice. (The converse, however, does not hold, because we can think that something is nice, that is, that there are reasons for liking it, and still not in fact like it.)

Everything that has been said of "nice" holds also of other, similar concepts like "desirable," "funny," "frightening," etc. For example, reasons for desiring Y are also reasons for thinking that Y is desirable. If we want to state the point succinctly and in general terms, we can say that formal reasons state that the object in question is an object of a reasonable attitude, that is, an attitude for which there are (material) reasons (e.g., X is desirable means X is an object of reasonable desiring).

We are now ready to apply our analysis to the main question of this paper, namely, whether or not the fact that the thought that A is a duty can function as a motive for doing A implies the existence of a desire to do one's duty for its own sake. According to our analysis, when we say that the thought that A is a duty can be a motive, all that we mean is that A's being a duty is a reason for doing it, and therefore also a reason for wanting to do it. Is A's being a duty a material or a formal reason? If it were a material reason, then there would have to be a desire to do one's duty that is a desire like other desires that are empirically known, e.g. the desire to eat. We saw in Sections

5–6 the objections to asserting the existence of such a desire. If A's being a duty is not a material reason, then it must be a formal reason. Indeed, as soon as we see that "being a duty" is a formal reason, the need to postulate a desire to do one's duty for its own sake disappears. In particular, the three arguments presented in Section 1 are seen to rest on a false premise, namely, that every motive for action implies the existence of a corresponding desire. We can therefore admit the "facts" upon which these arguments are based, namely, that we can do an action because we think it right, that by convincing a person that an act is a duty we are providing him with a motive for doing the act, and that one can have an interest in discovering what acts are duties—we can admit all of these "facts," for they are merely different ways of stating that "being a duty" can be a motive; but in doing so we need assume only that this motive is a formal reason for wanting to do certain actions.

Furthermore, when we take the thought of an act as being a duty to be only a formal reason for wanting to do it, then the various paradoxes that puzzled us earlier, notably in Section 5, also disappear. To begin with, our analysis shows why it is odd to ask: "Why do you want to do your duty for its own sake?" Such a question is analogous to the question: "Why do you like nice things?" This question is not absurd because one always wants to do his duty or because one always likes what is nice; for it is obvious that as a matter of fact one often does not want to do one's duty or like what is nice. The question is absurd because when formal reasons are involved, the question "Why?" already contains a kind of answer within itself; the formal reason itself says that there is a reason. The question therefore amounts to asking: "What is your reason for doing (liking) that for which there is a reason for doing (liking)?" The answer is: "Just because there is a reason," or "My reason is simply that there is a reason." It reminds us of the child's answer, "Just because." Of course, we feel that we are asking for something, and indeed we are, namely, a specific reason. But as soon as we ask for a specific reason we have stopped asking the general question; for the usual way of asking for a specific reason is to ask: "Why do you think that A is a duty (nice)?" Thus the nature of the question defeats its own purpose.

Hence the question, "Why do I want to do my duty?" is superseded by the question, "Why do I think that A is a duty?" The reasons that are given in answer to questions concerning the application of formal reasons (e.g., "being a duty" or "being nice") are, as we have seen, identical with the material reasons for the corresponding attitude; the features *a,b,c,d* that are reasons for liking X are also reasons for thinking that X is nice, etc. Similarly, with certain necessary qualifications, the features *p, q,r* that are reasons for wanting to do A are identical with reasons for thinking that A is a duty. Of course, inasmuch as not everything that we have a reason for wanting to do is a duty, some limitations on the kind of wanting-to-do involved here must be made so that there will be a correspondence of this desire with duty. Just how and on what basis this limitation is to be formulated presents a difficult problem that cannot be discussed here. It is a problem which is not, in my opinion, insoluble.[31]

Once we see that material reasons for wanting to do A can at the same time also be reasons for thinking that A is a duty, we have found a solution to the problem of whether or not a thoroughly good man can act for the sake of duty. In a nutshell, his reasons for wanting to do things are identical with his reasons for thinking that they are duties. He does not want to do two different kinds of things, namely, what he has reasons to want to do and his duty; rather, there is only one kind of thing that he wants to do and this can be described equally well as what he has reasons to want to do or as his duty. The situation is strictly analogous to liking what is nice; in addition to liking all those things which he has reasons to like, a man does not also like nice things; in liking those things that he has reasons to like he *eo ipso* likes what is nice. It follows, likewise, that if a man were always to want to do what he had reasons to want to do, he would always want to do his duty; and in that case it would be impossible to say whether he was doing his duty for its own sake or was doing what he wanted to do, for this would be like asking whether a man likes certain things because he has reasons for liking them or because they are nice.

Unhappily, for us poor sinners, there is no such strict correlation as there is for the good man between what we want to do and what it is our duty to do. But this is because in many cases we do not want to do what there is reason to want to do, and not because we do not want to do our duty as such. To deny that one would ever want to do his duty just because it is a duty would be the same as denying that he would ever want to do what there is a reason to want to do. And although most people are not reasonable most of the time, no one is ready to deny that he ever can be moved to act by a reason. In that sense, we can say, if we wish, that men have a desire to do their duty for its own sake; for all that we would be saying is that men are sometimes reasonable creatures. Instead of saying that we all have a desire to be reasonable, or to do our duty as such, it would be better to say that sometimes reason can arouse and give direction to our ordinary mundane desires.[32]

NOTES

1. Philosophers are not entirely unanimous concerning this proposition, and hence its truth should not be assumed dogmatically. For a general statement of the view that value as such does not function as a motive, see R. B. Perry, "Value and Its Moving Appeal," *Philosophical Review*, XLI (1932), 337–350. The view that duty can, but perhaps never does in fact, function as a motive is, of course, Kant's.
2. H. A. Prichard, *Duty and Interest* (Oxford: Clarendon Press, 1928), pp. 27–28. Also to be found in "Duty and Interest (Excerpt)," in *Readings in Ethical Theory*, ed. W. S. Sellars and J. Hospers (New York: Appleton-Century-Crofts, 1952), p. 485.
3. A. C. Ewing, *Second Thoughts in Moral Philosophy* (London: Routledge and Kegan Paul, 1959), p. 17. See also W. D. Ross, *The Right and the Good* (Oxford: Clarendon Press, 1930), pp. 157–160.
4. *Op. cit.*, p. 157.
5. Nowell-Smith's actual argument is very similar to Prichard's. See P. H. Nowell-Smith, *Ethics* (London: Penguin Books Ltd., 1954), p. 245.
6. *Webster's Dictionary of Synonyms* (Springfield, Mass.: G. & C. Merriam Co., 1951), p. 242.
7. When we speak of duty as a motive we could hardly mean that it is a "tension gradient in a tissue" (Gardner Murphy's definition of "motive").
8. G. E. M. Anscombe, *Intention* (Oxford: Basil Blackwell, 1957), pp. 18–24.
9. For further distinctions of this order, see G. Ryle, *The Concept of Mind* (London: Hutchinson's University Library, 1949), Chap. IV.
10. R. S. Woodworth and D. G. Marquis, *Psychology* (20th ed.; New York: Henry Holt & Co., 1947), p. 332.
11. Ryle, *op. cit.*, p. 92.
12. See L. Wittgenstein, *Philosophical Investigations*, trans. G. E. M. Anscombe (Oxford: Basil Blackwell, 1953), No. 246.
13. The analysis offered here throws light on the nature of psychoanalytic therapy. The whole process of psychoanalytic therapy consists, I submit, of a constant shifting back and forth between want in the sense of motive and want in the sense of desire.
14. W. McDougall, *Introduction to Social Psychology* (30th ed.; London: Methuen Co., 1950), p. 328.
15. Note that if there is an independent desire to make your friend happy,

it becomes even more difficult to attribute the feeling of obligation to the desire to do one's duty. In this case it becomes like the gardener example given before.

16. The problem involved here arises from the fact that moral characteristics are supervenient. (See R. M. Hare, *The Language of Morals* (Oxford: Clarendon Press, 1952), pp. 80ff.) A characteristic G is supervenient if it is logically impossible for two things to be identical in all of their properties except G (and their location in space and time) and for one of them to possess G and the other not to possess G; conversely, if one of them possesses G and the other does not, then there must be a difference between the two in some other property. Hence, if we had a list of things that had G, it would be logically possible to give a completely unequivocal and determinate description of all the things on the list without mentioning G. Similarly, if we had a list of all those acts that are duties, we could give a completely unequivocal and determinate description of the acts on the list without mentioning that they are duties. If we call those acts X's, Y's, and Z's, a description of the desire to do one's duties would be identical with a desire to do X's, Y's, and Z's, and we would not need to mention that these acts are duties in our description of the desire.
17. Ross, *op. cit.*, p. 159. See also Nowell-Smith, *op. cit.*, pp. 245–248. If this were a correct interpretation of Kant's teaching, it would make an absurdity out of many of his doctrines, e.g., that we should cultivate moral qualities in our character, that benevolence and fellow-feeling are duties of a kind. See *Tugendlehre, passim.* The misunderstanding arises from the failure to distinguish, as Kant does, between *Triebfedern* (springs of actions) and *Bestimmungsgründe* (grounds or motives). Benevolence and the sense of duty (respect) are *Triebfedern*, but when one does one's duty for its own sake, duty is a *Bestimmungsgrund.*
18. It would be more natural to say: "Talking to him would be pointless because he doesn't understand the difference between right and wrong. He doesn't know what duty *means.*"
19. Elsewhere I have called this capacity "ethical competence." See my *The Structure of a Moral Code* (Cambridge, Mass.: Harvard University Press, 1957), pp. 181–187.
20. The distinction I have in mind is set forth by Hare in his *The Language of Morals*, Chap. VI, "Meaning and Criteria."
21. The universality of a reason qua reason is explained by the fact that "being a reason for" is a supervenient characteristic. See note 16.
22. For a gerundive analysis of reasons, see S. Toulmin, *The Place of Reason in Ethics* (Cambridge: Cambridge University Press, 1953), pp. 70–72 *et passim.*

23. Defending an action by justifying it is quite different from defending it by providing excuses for it. See J. L. Austin, "A Plea for Excuses," *Proceedings of the Aristotelian Society*, Vol. LVII (1956–57), pp. 1–30. As Austin points out, one makes excuses in order to evade responsibility or full responsibility for the action. When one attempts to justify an action, one is taking full responsibility for it.
24. If Jones thinks that the train is leaving at 6:30, then he will say, "The train leaves at 6:30." If he were to say, "I think (believe) that the train leaves at 6:30," he would be implying that he does not want definitely to commit himself about the time that the train leaves. Thus "think" like "know" operates differently in the first-person form from the way it operates in the third-person (or past) form. In both cases, they reflect the commitment or non-commitment of the speaker, rather than of the subject of the statement. See J. L. Austin, "Other Minds," in *Logic and Language*, ed. A. G. N. Flew (Second Series; Oxford: Basil Blackwell, 1955).
25. Thus Anscombe writes (*op. cit.*, p. 25): "The question is not refused application because the answer to it says that there is *no* reason, any more than the question how much money I have in my pocket is refused application by the answer 'None.'"
26. *Op. cit.*, p. 105. Nowell-Smith goes on to say that all logically good reasons imply a pro-attitude of some kind or other (pp. 111–112). In general, I agree with Nowell-Smith's analysis on this particular point, but I think he fails to bring out sufficiently clearly that motives are reasons that justify. Hence he also fails to distinguish between motives and what I have called "desires" and lumps them together under the heading of "pro-attitudes."
27. In most cases we are likely to give up and simply say: "Well, it just appeals to me because of the kind of person that I am, my temperament, my upbringing, etc." When we say this we are no longer attempting to give a justifying explanation but have switched to giving a descriptive explanation. (This kind of answer, incidentally, is much more akin to giving excuses than to providing reasons. See note 23.)
28. *Op. cit.*, p. 90.
29. Another difference between Nowell-Smith's A-sentences and formal reasons is that A-sentences are "neutral unless the context shows which force they have" (*op. cit.*, p. 155), that is, they do not have a pro- or con- force. In the sense in which a reason always has either a pro- or a con- force, reasons are not neutral. But the non-neutrality involved here is clearly different from what Nowell-Smith has in mind.
30. *Op. cit.*, p. 151.
31. For some suggestions along this line, see my *The Structure of a Moral*

Code, especially Chaps. IV–VI. The task, I believe, is to find a neutral definition of "morality."

32. Several important books and articles that concern themselves with the present issues have appeared since this essay was written. In particular, I regret not to have been able to examine the views about motives, reasons, and wanting presented in R. S. Peters, *The Concept of Motivation* (London: Routledge and Kegan Paul, 1958); A. I. Melden, *Free Action* (London: Routledge and Kegan Paul, 1961); and S. Toulmin, "Concept-Formation in Philosophy and Psychology," in S. Hook, ed., *Dimensions of Mind* (New York: Collier Books, 1961).

9

THE RELEVANCE OF MORALS TO OUR DENIALS OF RESPONSIBILITY

Francis V. Raab *University of Minnesota*

When a man fails to do what was expected of him or violates rules of morality or law, his fellow men show their disapproval by means of scorn, personal assault, or such systematized penalties as fining, banishment, imprisonment, or execution. Not only do they engage in such displays of disapproval, but they try to justify them by claiming that the offender deserves such treatment or that this treatment is an effective means of inhibiting undesirable conduct. Yet the retributive, utilitarian, and unconscious impulses to censure an offender have been inhibited by moral disapproval of censure when certain facts about him or about the circumstances of his misconduct are believed to refute charges or assumptions of his responsibility. I shall be mainly concerned to show how the selection of these facts may be influenced by moral considerations. To do this it will be necessary to call attention to certain features of the concept of moral responsibility.

Instead of the philosopher's opaque questions "What is the meaning of 'responsibility'?" or "What is the nature of responsibility?" we should ask: (1) What are the functions, if any, of "He is (or is not) responsible for what he did (or for what happened)"? (Of course, for "he" we can substitute "I," "Germany," etc.). (2) What considerations do we appeal to in backing such claims? (3) Can we justify appealing to such considerations? (4) What are the conceptual links between such claims and the notions of fault, guilt, blame, cause, doing something, etc.? I would also want to examine "He is a morally responsible person," "He has a weak sense of responsibility," "The responsibility for their care fell to him," "He made a responsible decision," "Under the Constitution, the federal government has no responsibility to provide medical insurance for the American people," "I shall hold myself responsible for their safety," "I hold you partly responsible for losing their business," "You are responsible only to Mr. Jones." But since, for the purposes of this essay,[1] some limitation of the subject is necessary, I shall examine only "He is not responsible for what he did," although what I say about it would, if true, hold true for "He is not responsible for what happened." Studying the latter would take us into additional problems, although in some cases it would be difficult to decide whether to say: ". . . what he did" or ". . . what happened."

I

The primary function of "He is not responsible for what he did" is to provide a moral reason why a person who has done something undesirable should not be censured. There are, of course, other reasons, moral and prudential, which would usually, or on a given occasion, save an offender from the censure of persons responsive to those particular reasons. In our moral community, making the above statement and providing suitable reasons for it would save an offender from censure. If a person admitted that the reasons were suitable, agreed that the offender was not responsible, but calmly censured him, we would realize that a moral (and, possibly, conceptual) failure had occurred. We would want to know whether he thought that not being responsible was neither a partial nor a sufficient reason for not censuring an offender. Because of the primary function, the statement has a secondary one like: "Do not censure him." If offenders were never censured we would have no use for the notion of not being responsible for what one has done. Our concern over their responsibility is in part a moral concern over the harm we do them when we hold them responsible.

The second question was: "What considerations do we appeal to in backing up an assertion that a certain person is (or is not) responsible for what he did or for what happened?" Some of these considerations, or things we regard as suitable reasons for denying responsibility, are: the agent was mistaken or didn't know about certain things; he didn't do what he did intentionally; he was coerced or inwardly compelled; his action was involuntary; he had no choice or alternative; he couldn't have prevented it from happening; and, he couldn't have helped doing what he did (where this is so because of certain facts about trying, and not like: "I just couldn't have: 'eaten another bite,' 'done anything to hurt his feelings,' 'kept the money I won from him' "). Of course, when the harm done is considerable, compensation felt to be due, and the action of the sort that is apt to be repeated by others, mere mistake or ignorance may not defeat the assumption of responsibility. We will ask whether the mistake or ignorance was culpable: Could the mistake have been avoided by being reasonably careful? Was the agent aware that he might have been acting in ignorance, and could he have gotten the facts by reasonable effort? Again, the fact that a harm was unintentional may not excuse because we may have reason to believe that the agent could have been more watchful. Thus, our rock-bottom reason for denying responsibility in serious cases is that the agent couldn't have helped doing what he did or couldn't have avoided a certain outcome.

Our reasons for claiming that a person couldn't have helped doing what he did are that he tried, even tried desperately, to avoid it; that no matter how hard he or anyone else had tried to prevent it or avoid doing it, he would not have succeeded.

However, we do not always need to consider such matters because we have come to regard a number of types of circumstances as excuses, as refuting assumptions of responsibility (I do not wish to imply that an excuse is merely a circumstance that defeats the assumption of responsibility for a harm). Such circumstances are that the offender was severely tortured, brainwashed, threatened with his life, drugged, panic-stricken, amnesic, or psychotic. If we were challenged to give reasons why we consider severe torture as negating responsibility for, say, making a confession to one's captors, we would do so by appealing to such facts as: no matter how hard anyone were to try to avoid confessing, he would not succeed; or, most people under such torture would confess despite their initial unwillingness to do so. When a case arises that does not seem to fall under any of the standard excuses, we would consider whether the offender tried to avoid a certain outcome, whether he did it unwillingly or unintentionally, etc.

Although we can easily think up or point to paradigm cases of a person who couldn't help doing something, we can also think up or point to cases that would make us hesitate to say whether he could or couldn't have helped doing something. Even in possession of a great deal of knowledge about the mental state of an offender, say, a neurotic drug addict who stole money to buy narcotics, or an impulsive psychopath who committed battery, we remain uncertain whether he could or couldn't have helped doing it. Thus one of the principal considerations in deciding whether an offender is responsible is "open-textured" (Waismann).

Second, the "criteria" by virtue of which we decide whether one of the various responsibility-defeating considerations applies are also open-textured. For example, to ascertain whether a person did something unintentionally, it would be desirable to find out whether he was sorry for what he did, whether he had a motive for doing it, whether what he did was done in a manner that was likely to produce the harmful result that was produced, etc. For each of these "criteria" we can conceive of borderline cases.

A final reason why the concept of responsibility is open-textured is that we are unwilling to say that the basic considerations currently appealed to are the only ones that will ever be relevant to its application. For example, we might come to excuse out of pity those offenders who have suffered greatly through personal misfortune even though their self-control or rationality is unimpaired.

2

With this fragmentary account of some of the logical features of the concept of responsibility in mind, we come to the main topic of this essay: In what way are moral considerations relevant—and which ones—to our denials of responsibility?

There seem to be three principal ways in which moral considerations bear upon our judgments that certain persons are not responsible for what they have done. First, that we morally sanction appealing to certain facts in deciding that a person is not responsible. Think how we would react if someone were to suggest that although a person absolutely couldn't have helped doing something, he should nevertheless be thought of as responsible when this will insure his being severely censured. Why do we allow the fact that a person couldn't have helped doing something (couldn't have avoided it, couldn't have prevented it) to count as a reason for judging him non-responsible, thus preventing him from being censured? Now one cannot argue that it would be unfair to censure him, for what would be the unfairness if no one were to be excused on such grounds? Nor can one say that censure would be immoral, for it would not be immoral if another sort of reason could be given (for example, censuring those who couldn't help doing harm will help to deter others) for not counting such a fact as a sufficient reason for not being responsible. One might argue that the harmful action of a person who couldn't help doing it in no way shows that he is morally defective—the action is not an expression of his character, nor is it due to negligence or to a failure to make an effort—hence censuring him would be hurting him without reforming him, and hurting another without reason is violating a very basic moral injunction. But what if a practice of censuring such persons helped to deter others and thus to protect the community? To overcome this objection we could point out that people would be terrified by a practice of being held responsible for what they couldn't help doing. Furthermore, once we no longer allow couldn't-have-helped-it to count as a sufficient reason for denying responsibility, then the way is open to hold people responsible who had nothing to do with some harm. But what if the terror of being the victim of such a practice was as probable as, and equal to, the terror of being a victim of someone's criminal tendencies, tendencies which might have been inhibited had certain persons who truly couldn't have done otherwise nevertheless been held responsible and censured? We might still say that a person who strictly couldn't have helped doing something must not be held responsible and thus censured, no matter how socially valuable it might be to hold him responsible. This would amount to having a categorical moral prohibition against censuring such a person.

This sketch of how one common "criterion" of non-responsibility might be sanctioned is in no way intended as the only rationale for supporting its use. I merely wish to show the moral considerations that might be appealed to. Plainly, a justification for not holding people responsible when they couldn't have helped doing something is one that we rarely feel called upon to give, even in critical cases of trying to decide whether a person is or is not responsible.

The second way in which moral considerations might influence verdicts that a person is not responsible for doing something harmful is that we might come to allow a certain kind of fact to count as an overriding consideration. For example, we might come to count an offender's past sufferings, ignoring the fact that his harmful action was intentional and could have been avoided. Now it might be objected that such a decision is just a decision not to censure him, and that it still leaves open the question whether or not he is morally responsible for his action. But it does so only because we are now morally and conceptually committed to basing responsibility judgments upon such considerations as whether he could help it and whether he did it intentionally. Suppose we all came to allow past suffering to save an offender from censure; we no longer blame him; we do not inquire further as to his responsibility based upon the customary considerations. Would we not have not merely a new excuse but an overriding consideration? To deny this is to claim that the present basic considerations are analytically connected to the concept of responsibility, and thus that it is not open-textured with respect to their addition or elimination. I see no reason why our current responsibility-holding practices might not change, in which case the type of acceptable reasons for ascribing or denying responsibility for harmful actions would change without disturbing the moral claim that if one is not responsible, he ought not to be censured.

If this point is sound, then the question arises whether there is any limit to the kind of fact that could be considered exculpatory or made into a criterion of non-responsibility. I think that there is because there are certain facts about all offenders which, if allowed as a ground of non-responsibility, would destroy the whole concept. For example, every offender might be excused on the grounds that he had no control over the formation of his character, or that his behavior had a cause or was predictable. Usually it is urged that such facts refute assumptions of responsibility because they imply that the offender couldn't have helped doing what he did. But what would we say of a culture in which no one was spared censure because one couldn't help doing something, but in which one was spared if one were the son of a chief, if one had been a brave warrior, or if one had suffered great misfortunes? Suppose also that members of this culture thought it wrong to censure the son of a chief, a brave warrior, and a Job, and that these moral attitudes were justified (as might easily be the case) by the moral framework and physical exigencies of the culture.

What I have just been saying seems to contradict my earlier statement that one of the "implications" of saying that someone is not responsible for something is that there is a certain type of reason why the offender ought not to be censured. Now it seems that I am admitting that radically different sorts of reasons might be acceptable. It seems that this implication does exist, but only within our moral and responsibility-holding practices and framework. I see no reason why our current responsibility-holding practices might not change, in which case we would rely on new criteria, wholly or partially; and thus the type of reasons acceptable for responsibility verdicts would change without impairing the "implication" that if one is not responsible he ought not be punished.

The third and very common type of situation where moral considerations become explicit is that in which the circumstances, physical or mental, in which a person did something wrong are not readily brought within the scope of a standard excuse, such as being insane or tortured, or under a basic consideration, such as the fact that he couldn't help it or that he didn't do it intentionally. When we cannot decide by appealing to the usual facts whether any of these standard excuses or considerations obtain, then our decision is probably going to involve reference to certain moral considerations. The empirical difficulties in deciding whether the compulsive psychopath or the neurotic drug addict who commits a crime could or couldn't have helped doing so, or did or did not do it intentionally, are notoriously considerable. Yet we wish to reach some decision, either in general policy or in some special case. In doing so, we will reflect on the moral considerations involved, such as the protection of society against such offenders, and the harm we do them and their families in censuring them. We have to balance at least these two moral considerations before we can say that a decision to hold or not to hold such people responsible is justifiable. Of course, some moralists might hold that whenever we are in doubt on empirical grounds that any of the standard excuses or "criteria" apply to an offender, then we ought not to censure him—and the severity of the censure increases the stringency of this obligation.

However, we shall more than likely arrive at a decision not to hold such offenders responsible by trying to extend, because they can be extended, the boundaries of our standard excuses or criteria. In forensic psychiatry some of those who believe that the psychopath should not be punished, at least capitally, are attempting to broaden the concept of insanity or to use persuasively the concepts of mental illness or disease. While the criminal act of a psychopath is far removed from the paradigms of a person who couldn't have helped doing what he did, one might argue that because he has no conscience and no responsibility for its absence, he couldn't have helped doing what he did —thus stretching this concept well beyond its paradigms. In this way moral attitudes can cause an extension of the range of application of a concept by allowing new facts to become relevant to its application.

We have considered the relevance to our denials of responsibility of such moral considerations as: When one is in doubt whether a standard criterion applies to an offender, one ought not to hold him responsible; or, One ought not to hold him responsible if censuring him would do no one any good; or, One ought to hold him responsible if doing so will prevent others from doing the same thing; or, possibly, One ought not hold him responsible if his action was predictable. Besides these considerations, there may be less conscious factors, such as repugnance to all punishment or vindictive impulses arising from unconscious hostility, which would tend to influence a person's responsibility verdicts in the borderline cases.

It is unlikely that the various conditions which we now regard as exculpatory will be the same as those conditions which in the more distant future we shall consider exculpatory. This is so because of likely changes in our conception of the value of the individual, in moral attitudes towards certain predisposing factors of behavior (neurosis, bad training, etc.), in our attitudes about the morality of legal punishment and social censure as fitting retribution and as a means for the protection of society, and in our conception of an individual's rights to have his person and property protected from criminal aggression. It is even conceivable that an influential number of people may come to think that the fact that a person had no control over the formation of the dispositions which produced the uninhibited desire to gain certain ends by criminal means is a reason for holding that he is not responsible.

The reason why moral attitudes are at least partial determinants of what excuses we do allow is that when we hold people responsible for harmful acts, we criticize, ostracize, or punish them. Because such behavior violates a very basic moral maxim, "Do not injure others," we scrutinize carefully the conditions under which people act as possible grounds for exculpation. On the other hand, failure to engage in behavior injurious to the offender would deprive the offender's victims of restitution, if needed, and might also deprive the community of protection against further harms perpetrated by this and other potential offenders.

3

A word or two on legal responsibility. When a judge says of an accused, "He is not responsible," he causes the accused to be released from criminal custody; for the court cannot inflict the stipulated punishment for an offense upon a man whom it recognizes as not responsible according to legal criteria. What the judge says does not imply that the accused is not morally responsible, or that he ought not to be criticized by his fellow men. Of course, it might be that the judge as moralist would go on to say that the accused is not morally responsible either, thus implying that he ought not to be punished or censured. Again, if the judge says that the accused is responsible—and I think he is unlikely to say this unless a denial of responsibility has been introduced and defeated—he is not implying that he thinks the accused ought to be punished. Judges have been known to sentence an offender to execution when the offender's type of mental disease did not come under a legal defense against criminal responsibility, even though the judge thought that on account of this disease the offender was not morally responsible for his act.

American courts are bound by precedent and statute to use certain criteria in judging an offender's responsibility. Some of these criteria coincide with those used in non-legal judgments of responsibility. Yet discrepancies are common. There was a time when the law did not recognize unintentional harm as a defense against criminal responsibility, but under the pressure of ecclesiastical thought it came to admit this as a defense against specific criminal charges. Today we find a considerable discrepancy between the criteria used by the law to decide an offender's responsibility when the issue of mental disease has been raised, and the criteria which psychiatrists and those who have been influenced by them think ought to be used to determine his responsibility. Their denials of the responsibility of certain kinds of offenders are intended to cause the law to stop punishing them. It is of great concern to moralists that the criteria of responsibility which the law uses be capable of being morally justified.

I have indicated some of the problems involved in giving a piece-meal moral justification for allowing each of many conditions to refute ascriptions of responsibility. If such justifications could be provided, we would be morally obliged to count such conditions as legal excuses. By way of contrast, Professor Hart in "Legal Responsibility and Excuses" [2] tries to provide a wholesale, though not exclusively moral, justification for having a legal system with excusing conditions. If his attractive reasons could not be rebutted, one would have doubly justified the incorporation of a particular set of excusing conditions into our law.

4

In an essay on responsibility one might be expected to say something about its relation to determinism, especially since I have maintained the common view that the fact that a person couldn't have helped doing what he did is one of the principal reasons for holding that he is not responsible. Perhaps something can be said to reduce the conceptual stress that is so often believed to be inherent in holding to determinism and the belief in moral responsibility.

It has been thought that a true causal statement of the form "X caused Y" implies that "Given X, Y (some action) couldn't have been helped." It is this putative implication that I wish to challenge. To see whether "Y couldn't have been helped" is so implied, we have to become clear about the criteria or reasons for claiming that a *person* couldn't have helped or avoided doing what he did, or that he couldn't have done what he should have done. We are all familiar with the sorts of cases that would be considered paradigms of these characterizations: a prisoner of war who has been thoroughly brain-washed or severely tortured signs a propaganda document; a person trapped beneath a car is unable to save his friend; a doctor becomes paralyzed or lacks the necessary skill to perform a certain operation. Why do we think of these as paradigm cases? Because we think that no matter how hard the person had tried to do what we wish he had done, he would not have succeeded—and perhaps an even stronger point, that no matter how hard anyone else had tried in those circumstances he would not have succeeded. Now I contend that these are the ultimately controlling reasons for saying that a person couldn't have done otherwise, and not the fact that what he did or what happened was caused. Certainly from the fact that an action was caused it does not follow that no matter how hard the person had tried to avoid doing it, he would not have succeeded. True causal sentences about a person's action are not reasons for holding that a person couldn't have done otherwise; nor is their falsity a necessary condition for the claim that a person could have helped doing what he did, and thus a necessary condition of moral responsibility.

But it will be objected that there is some sense in saying that if a particular event B is caused by A, then given A (and certain circumstances) no other event could have occurred. To this I agree provided that one is clear that the reason or criterion for saying that no other event could have occurred is that event B is uniquely deducible from some set of instantial statements. Now the fact that my behavior is thus deducible does not entail that had I tried to do something else I would not have succeeded, and thus is not a proper reason for claiming that I couldn't have helped doing what I did.

NOTES

1. This essay is an expansion of one read at the meeting of the American Philosophical Association in Cincinnati, Ohio, in 1958.
2. H. L. A. Hart, "Legal Responsibility and Excuses," in *Determinism and Freedom*, ed. Sydney Hook (New York: New York University Press, 1957), pp. 81–104.

INDEX

The manuscript was edited by Faith S. Schmidt. The book was designed by S. R. Tenenbaum using Linotype Janson cut in 1932 after the type face cut by Nicholas Kis in Amsterdam in 1690, but erroneously attributed to Anton Janson. The display face is Weiss Roman, designed by Professor E. R. Weiss and cut by Bauer in 1926.

Printed on Allied Paper Company's Paperback Offset Paper
Bound in Riegel Paper Corporation's Carolina Cover.

Manufactured in the United States of America.